1609: A Country That Was Never Lost

1609: A Country That Was Never Lost

The 400th Anniversary of Henry Hudson's Visit with North Americans of the Middle Atlantic Coast

American History Imprints / American History Press
Franklin, Tennessee
www.Americanhistoryimprints.com
www.Americanhistorypress.com
Book design by Chris Keegan

ISBN 13: 978-0-9842256-1-3
Library of Congress Control Number: 2009936060

First Edition September 2009

Printed in the United States of America on acid-free paper
This book meets all ANSI standards for archival quality.

Table of Contents

INTRODUCTION

Nitappi,

It would be easy to portray the seventeenth century as an age of ignorance and violence punctuated by exciting discoveries that broadened human horizons, but much the same might be said of our own time. Perhaps that is the attraction. So turn your calendar back to 1609 as we revisit the dawn of a great adventure, exploring not only unknown worlds, but also the dimly lit core of our own humanity. It has become (as we are wont to say) a small world, where collisions of cultures during the development of a global community echo into the present moment, and where monocultural hegemony threatens to overwhelm a broad diversity of lifestyle, language and inner life. Shock and awe mark the sudden confrontation of peoples unexpectedly thrown together. Each group has much to offer the other, but each holds its own mores superior. Only from a distance do we begin to appreciate how much we share in common.

History holds a mirror to human nature, its possibilities and imperfections. Too often, we see only what we want to see, merely exaggerating evidence that confirms our set beliefs. I refuse to be an accomplice; it is not my purpose to judge or to justify, to validate or devalue.

In preparation for the following contribution, I have tried to read everything of relevance over the years, relishing and absorbing firsthand accounts of the First Peoples in their original homelands. You can assess and evaluate the subjective nature and cultural biases of these accounts for yourself, while mining the wealth of descriptive material written about the Middle Atlantic Coast of North America and its native inhabitants from the sixteenth through the late eighteenth century. I have compiled and cross-referenced these early narratives for appraisal and interpretation, connecting as many dots as I think reasonable during the process. I am only able to do so because dedicated and gifted minds have ably translated and published this esoteric body of literature, and I am indebted to them for their scholarship. I am also grateful for the conversation and instruction of archeologists and historians, many of whom are considered "amateurs" in the finest sense of the word, who have shaped and corrected my thoughts on this subject matter. I still have a great deal to learn, and apologize in advance for any shortcomings. I am mainly indebted to my large circle of family and friends, especially my loving wife, Deborah, and my beautiful and talented children, Ivan, Ben and Anna. They continue to make my life a wonderful adventure of discovery.

This work has its genesis in a childhood curiosity. In his home near the summit of Foster Street in Newton, New Jersey, my grandfather, Ivan Wright, had a cellar display of Indian artifacts, which he and his father had collected throughout Sussex County. These worn stone tools and decorated shards of earthenware deeply connected me to the land, to the Great Appalachian Valley, its sheltering hills, its robust singing streams and slaty spine.

I have always loved history, with its inherent sense of exploration and adventure. I often accompanied Grandpa Wright into the woods and onto the river plains to search for fragments of a lost world. He pointed out the fact that European colonists associated indigenous sacred places with worship of the Devil, a pejorative association of the Great Spirit with the evil power of Christian belief. We visited Devil's Island, a limestone promontory on the margins of the great Paulinskill Meadows behind Newton, tracing a vein of flint along the ridge crest to an isolated vantage point, where I imagined the shimmering rhythm of turtle carapace rattles. My interest deepened when I learned that my great-grandfather, John Edward Brink, scion of the original settlers of Walpack Bend on the Delaware River, claimed descent from a full-blooded Minisink woman. I remember back to when I was about seven years old, learning to plant and tend a garden of Luther Hill corn, beans and milk pumpkins—the fabled Three Sisters—how Grandpa Brink would set four seeds of corn per hill, saying, "One for the moth, one for the crow, one for the droth and one to grow." The words that follow are the seeds I plant. I hope they will grow in the imagination and interest of others, respectfully and honestly perpetuating the memory of the ancient peoples of my homeland, both here and in their places of refuge.

I hope you enjoy this journey of self-discovery as much as I do.

Hiʊh, matzi,
Kevin W. Wright

ACKNOWLEDGMENTS

Over several decades of compiling research for this book, my associations with the Sussex County and Bergen County Historical Societies have proven invaluable, and I am especially indebted to such dear friends and mentors as Alex Everitt and Claire Tholl. My wife, Deborah Powell, deserves great credit for her unwavering confidence in me, and for her technical skills and eye for design in the preparation of images. I also gratefully acknowledge the editorial guidance and professional encouragement of David E. Kane, who worked diligently to transform my manuscript into a polished literary work.

Note: For easier reading, I have updated punctuation and spelling in most quotes except to preserve original variants of names, toponyms and other vocabulary, which may reflect interesting dialectal differences or contribute to a more accurate evaluation of their meaning. Many spellings are based upon interpretation of old handwriting. Likewise, distances on land and sea in these early accounts, given disparities among nations and the primitive methods of measure in the period this work covers, are likewise subject to interpretation. In describing Henry Hudson's trip along the North American Coast, for example, I have tried, whenever possible, to reconcile latitudinal observations with estimates of distance traveled, recognizing that other interpretations are valid.

1609: A Country That Was Never Lost

"And there are among them mysteries so hidden that only the old men, who can speak with authority about them, are believed."[1]
From *The Jesuit Relations and Allied Documents*

Seat yourself before the fire. It is Monday, October 16, 1679. Tantaqua, an eighty-year-old Hackensack sachem, is seated opposite missionary Jasper Danckærts.[2] In the Sanhican dialect, the old man's public name, *Tinteywe*, translates as "fire." He is the chief sachem's brother and next in line as clan leader and spokesperson. The missionary is curious, inquiring about humankind's creation. The old man's lined face pauses in mid-thought as if a deep memory has suddenly stirred within him. His wizened hand probes the edge of the crackling flames, picking out a charcoal brand. As shadows dance with ascending embers, he draws a small oval on the dirt floor, outlining four feet, a head and a tail. Gesturing with his hands, he speaks authoritatively, "This is a turtle, lying in the water around it. This was or is all water, and so at first was the world or the earth, when the turtle gradually raised its round back up high and the water ran off of it, and thus the earth became dry." After brief introspection, he plucks a reed from a kindling pile and plants it in the middle of the drawn figure. His voice again rises, "The earth was now dry and there grew a tree in the middle of the earth and the root of this tree sent forth a sprout beside it and there grew upon it a man, who was the first male. This man was then alone, and would have remained alone; but the tree bent over until its top touched the earth, and there shot therein another root, from which came forth another sprout and there grew upon it the woman, and from these two are all men produced."

In other words, we are all Turtle Clan.

THOSE WHO CAME FROM THE SALT SEA

Travel back seventy years to the year 1609. Tantaqua is but a boy, seated more distantly from the fire, listening to the elders converse.

Few had lived so long as to remember better days—by now, only stories of a warmer world were being passed down, merely hearsay, gathering the aura of fables. Of course, the climate had changed several times since the Ancient Ones first occupied this land, but so gradual were these changes over succeeding generations that no objective measurement was possible, even by the oldest and wisest. Still, global cooling was a growing topic around the fire, especially during the vast whiteness of the northern winter, when deep snows made movement difficult for man and beast. Winter lived year around in Lowaneu, the North, but its strength was growing, creeping southward and disrupting the habits of all creatures. Some said the moon shone brighter, its pull stronger as the nights deepened. Salmon appeared in the great tidal river, Sha-te-muc, where they were never before known.[3] Moreover, in some places, oysters were dying out. The old people said as much, and their thoughts were carefully remembered and passed on. But so far, their dreams had been silent, and no one knew the meaning of these things. Had humans somehow upset the equilibrium?

Before long the cold brought the Schwonack—"those who came from the salt sea"— fishing off the coast in great winged canoes. Soon they came ashore to repair their boats and dry their catch. They wore strange skins, spoke unfamiliar words and handled unknown tools and weapons. There was rivalry for their trade, but much anger at their treachery and kidnappings. Afterwards, there was dread for their strange sicknesses, which left few to bury the dead. These marvelous visitors were often at odds with one another, speaking conflicting tongues. They certainly were not dream-beings, as some had first supposed. Increasing in numbers, they turned trees into great huts and cleared forests for gardens. They brought unknown animals, which lived in meadows or rooted in woods, and dwelt in winter huts. They raised tamed birds for eggs and quadrupeds to eat, to skin, to ride and to work for them. They came to stay, cobbling together villages within sheltering bays or inland at the head of tides. Word of their arrival spread very far.

Figure 1. Tantaqua's mark on a deed dated January 6, 1676, for the sale of New Hackensack, extending from Old Hackensack north to French Creek at New Bridge, "adjoining to the Great Indian Field—called the Indian Castle" to Laurence Andriessen (Van Boskerk) & Company.

The newcomers were naturally surprised and curious about the land and its many indigenous inhabitants; some oddly called it a New World. Digging wells through the alluvium of ages, Swedish colonists on Delaware River and Bay were astonished to find rushes, reeds and clamshells buried twenty to thirty feet deep. It was just as the elders said, "This was once all water." Engineer Peter Lindeström, author of the first *American Geography* in 1691, reported the country thereabout appeared "as if it formerly had stood under water, for there is found everywhere on the ground an abundance of all kinds of mussels and shells, as well as other things that are found in the water."[4] Almost a century later, Swedish botanist Peter Kalm observed, "a great portion of the province of New Jersey, in ages unknown to posterity, was part of the bottom of the sea, and was afterwards formed by the slime and mud, and many other things which the river Delaware carries down along with it from the higher parts of the country."[5] However, colonists occasionally retrieved charcoal and firebrands from deep in the earth, inducing some to believe that humankind had inhabited America before Noah's Flood. Though natural phenomena other than human agency might produce charcoal, the recovery of deeply buried artifacts supported this claim. In 1750, Måns Keen and his neighbors about Raccoon and Penn's Neck reported well diggers finding "at a great depth in the ground such a trowel as the Indians use." Some found such artifacts "twenty feet under the surface of the earth."[6] Gauging the size of the overarching trees, these accidental archaeologists estimated the age of the forest covering the soil above these discoveries at several centuries. Though they correlated depth of burial with the passage of time, they could only speculate as to duration, lacking any reliable method of measurement. Keen thought the stone tool he removed from the earth resembled those he had seen the Indians in his neighborhood use, suggesting that ancestors of the extant native population had inhabited the land in remote time. So it appeared this New World was very old indeed, and had been peopled for uncounted ages. But only Nature kept the chronicle, piling leaf and loamy layer upon misplaced artifacts, for there was no other record made of persons and events before they vanished forever from living memory. North Americans recognized geologic evidence of a watery past and stumbled across archeological hints of their own origins, but they expressed themselves only in mythological terms, profound and enduring, as did most other peoples.

In 1656, Dutch commentator Adriæn van der Donck speculated upon the ancient peopling of the so-called New World, wondering whether "Columbus or Americus [Vespucci] can have found a country, which was never lost?"[7] In the seventeenth century, as today, a variety of opinions were tendered. Even then, some were vaguely aware of an ancient Nordic chronicle that described how "some persons well equipped and provided, sailed from part of Norway or Sweden in search of a better country, under the command of a certain chief named *Sachema*, and that they had never been heard from after they sailed; and as all the native chiefs of the New Netherland who reside along the rivers and sea-shore are called sachems, they conclude that the country was peopled by those adventurers."[8] Others thought the people and animals of North and South America constituted "a separate and entire new world, being entirely different in formation and condition from the old world…."[9] Still others believed —centuries in advance of the theory of plate tectonics—that only a narrow strait, easily crossed, had anciently separated Africa and South America. Geographical knowledge of the northwestern parts of North America was too lacking at the time to imagine other possible land bridges.

Seventeenth-century European commentators did not describe the North Americans they encountered with anthropological precision or methodical objectivity. In their eyes, the coastal North Americans shared an undifferentiated stone-age lifestyle. They failed to study the variations between stone projectile-points or pottery decorations among the various native communities. However, since the existence of this previously unknown population and landmass seemed to challenge the universality

Figure 2. "The Coming of the White Men" from the Mural by Howard Pyle, Hudson
County Court House, from the *History of Hudson County and the Old Village of
Bergen*, Issued by the Trust Company of New Jersey, Jersey City, NJ, 1921.

of their beliefs, some amateur theologians engaged the natives in religious
discussion. In the absence of organized worship and public rites in the style
to which they were accustomed, European observers generally concluded
that the natives had no knowledge of God (meaning "their God"). Unable to
comprehend the spiritualities that characterized native beliefs and behavior,
these observers spoke pejoratively of "sham-gods" and "devil-worship."
However uniform the material culture of North America appeared to
untrained eyes, Europeans quickly recognized, through commercial and
political interactions, diverse nations and languages among the Indigenes.
These so-called "nations" or "tribes" were often autonomous bands whose
sachem, or spokesman, was little more than headman, possessing little, if
any, coercive authority over his relatives. Family government was achieved
through consultation and consensus among males. Community was an
expression of kinship; the only larger bond among families or communities
was a common dialect and perhaps a shared world perception.

     Generations of school children are taught that a tribe called the
Lenni-Lenape inhabited the Atlantic coast of North America between the
Hudson River and the head of Chesapeake Bay at the time of European

contact. Does this assertion rest upon any foundation of fact? Who precisely were the Lenape? On June 17, 1654, Johan Classon Rijsingh, Director of New Sweden, defined the *Renapi* (Lenape) as "the natives who dwelled on the western bank of our [Delaware] river...."[10] At that time, twelve sachems, or heads of families, represented their interests.[11] The Swedes regarded them as the "most intelligent savages of several nations of savages," possibly because they resided in horticultural villages where sachems had greater authority over a larger population than was the norm.[12] Thus, in the historic record, the name *Lenape* referred to a dozen or so families of natives residing in the Schuylkill estuary. The name was never applied to the native inhabitants of the east bank of the Delaware River, no less to the entire Algonquian-speaking population of the Middle Atlantic Coast.

Strictly speaking, *Lenape* means "male." *Linnilenape* has been translated as "Indians of the same nation." But the word *nation* means something very different to modern ears than was intended by this usage. A related word, *Linaxu*, means "like unto." So the true sense of Linnilenape is "men of like identity" or perhaps "people with a common ancestry." In 1818, Reverend John Heckewelder, a Moravian missionary who worked among the dispossessed Delawares from 1762 to 1810, reported that "their name signifies *'original people,'* a race of human beings who are the same that they were in the beginning, *unchanged* and *unmixed*."[13] French sources assign *iriniou* as the Montagnais word for "a man." Keep in mind, Algonquian languages do not use sounds corresponding with our letters F, L, V, X and Z, and use a sound approximating R instead of L. To Western ears, they confounded the letters B and P, as well as C, G, and K.[14] Thus, the Montagnais word for "a male" (*iriniou*) could also be rendered *illiniou*. Westward, near the southern shores of Lake Superior, Father Jacques Marquette noted in 1673 that "when one speaks the word 'illinois' it is as if one said in their language, 'the men,' —As if the other Savages were looked upon by them merely as animals."[15] The Shawnee refer to indigenous peoples as *lenawe* and to males as *hileniiki*. Their word for life is *lenaweewiiwe*.[16] Thus *iriniou*, *illinois*, and *lenape* appear to be dialectal variations of the same Algonquian root word for "men."

Dispossessed remnants of those who had long inhabited the Atlantic slope took refuge in the northern Susquehanna Valley in the middle of the eighteenth century. Uniting against their pursuers, a fragile confederation of native communities evolved into the Delawares or Lenape. Placed in a precarious situation when war broke out between England and France in 1755, the Minisinks, then known as the Munseys, formed a league with two Delaware tribes, namely, the *Lenopi* and *Wanami*, choosing Teedyuscung for their chief sachem or king. For the common good, those who had been sachems before now willingly "resigned their dignity, contenting themselves with a place in the Council."[17] Teedyuscung appointed captains to regulate the military force of the combined nations. Stragglers who lived in their neighborhood without chiefs strengthened the new alliance. Some Mahicans, or River Indians, and Shawanese also joined, forming "a very considerable body" under unified command. New Jersey Governor Francis Bernard negotiated an end to hostilities at a conference held in Easton, Pennsylvania, in October 1758, where he met with King Teedyuscung, spokesman for the league of Chihohocki or Delawares, comprised of the Lenopi and Wanami, and the northern tribes of the Munseys, Mohiccons and Wapingers (or Pomptons).[18]

WHERE IS THE BEGINNING?

After inquiring about the origins of the Renappi in 1654, Swedish engineer Peter Lindeström concluded, "Those who are the sachems of the Indians do not know how to take such into observation…."[19] Two centuries later, Reverend Heckewelder recorded a quasi-historical tradition, which recalled an ancient migration to the eastern seaboard. Basing his writings upon what he had seen, heard and witnessed during his long residence among them, Heckewelder intended "to show, rather what the Indians of this country were previous to the white people's arrival, than what they now are; for now, the two great nations, the Iroquois and the Delawares, are no longer the same people that they formerly were."[20] Pushed from their own homelands, the Indians listened empathetically to scriptural stories of wandering tribes delivered from Pharaoh's oppression, in search of a Promised Land. Heckewelder's informants wove an intelligent contemporary response to their inhabitation of the Ohio Country, where burial mounds of an ancient Indian civilization begged explanation.

According to tradition, the Lenni-Lenape resided at some remote period in the western part of North America, when they decided for reasons long forgotten to migrate eastward. After a journey of many years, they arrived on the *Namæsi Sipu* (Mississippi), or River of Fish, where they encountered the Mengwe (Iroquois), who themselves had reached a more northerly station on this great river after a long migration. Scouts reconnoitering the country located east of the river discovered a very powerful nation called the *Talligeu* or *Talligewi*, inhabiting many large riverside towns. Some European listeners of this tradition identified the *Talligewi* with *Alligewi* (Allegany), the name of both a branch of the Ohio and its neighboring mountains. Perhaps attempting to explain the wondrous discovery of mastodon bones in the Illinois Country, the storytellers hypothesized that the *Talligewi* were once giants, or at least people of much larger size than the tallest of the Lenape. It was these extraordinary people who constructed the great burial mounds and ceremonial earthworks found throughout the Old Northwest Territory. The *Talligewi* refused to give permission for the Lenape and Mengwe to settle within their domain, but did allow them passage to seek a suitable homeland further to the east. However, seeing how great the numbers of these trespassers were, the *Talligewi* treacherously and furiously attacked the transiting Lenape, inflicting great losses. Stunned by this bloody betrayal, the Lenape were about to abandon their course when the Mengwe, previously satisfied with being spectators from a distance, offered an alliance on the condition that they too be permitted to settle the *Talligewi* country after its conquest. The Lenape and Mengwe then successfully attacked the now common enemy in their large towns and fortifications. Reportedly, the corpses of hundreds of warriors who fell in a battle were piled together in heaps and covered with earth, thus explaining the large burial mounds still to be found in that vicinity. While the Lenape lost many warriors in the heat of battle, their cunning allies, the Mengwe, always hung back, safely out of harm's way. After many years of warfare, the *Talligewi* fled down the Mississippi, leaving their former country to the conquerors. Consequently, the Mengwe settled in the vicinity of the Great Lakes and their tributary streams, while the Lenape took possession of the lands to the south. After centuries of peace and prosperity, hunters of both nations gradually crossed the mountains and discovered waterways flowing eastward toward the Atlantic Ocean. After a long period of exploration, these venturesome huntsmen returned home and informed their peoples of the advantages of these newly discovered and uninhabited lands bordering the Great Saltwater Lake (Atlantic Ocean). Concluding that the Great Spirit had destined this land for their occupation, they emigrated eastward in small groups, settling the four great rivers: Lenapewihittuck (Delaware River), Mahicannituck (Hudson River), Susquehanna and Potomac. Eventually, the largest body, reputedly comprising one-half of the whole population, settled the Atlantic seaboard, which they called *Scheyichbi*, that is, *Scheyiach-mbi*, meaning "at the water's edge." About one-quarter of the population—those who never learned of the *Talligewi's* defeat—removed to the interior of the country west of the Mississippi, while the other remaining quarter were thought to have remained in the *Talligewi* country east of that great river. Thus, the Lenape storytellers explained the dispersal of people who spoke dialects of a common Algonquian language ancestral to their own. What, if any, kernels of ancient memory reside within this oral tradition cannot be easily determined. This epic tale may be more illustrative of the Delawares' predicament in the Ohio Country at the start of the nineteenth century than of any prehistoric tribal wanderings—it provided the Delawares with an ancient claim to the Ohio territory by right of conquest.

Continuing the thread of the story, we learn that the wandering tribe who first settled *Scheyichbi* divided themselves into three bodies: the Turtle Tribe or *Unâmis*, who settled between the coast and the interior mountains; the Turkey Tribe or *Unalâchtgo*, who settled nearest the sea; and the Wolf Tribe or *Minsi*, being the most warlike, who settled among the mountains near the head of the great rivers, forming "a kind of bulwark for their protection, watching the motions of the Mengwe, and being at hand to afford their aid in case of a rupture with them."[21] The accounts written by Heckewelder confused clans with "tribal" identities. Moreover, these "tribal" names were not used until the various native communities withdrew from their coastal homelands into the interior of

Pennsylvania between 1740 and 1760. These designations are descriptive of general location, indicating whence different groups originated before their congregation in the Upper Susquehanna Valley. Unalâchtgo is taken from *W'schajahitcan,* meaning "seashore." Unâmis comes from *Nallahiwi,* meaning, "up the river." Minisink derives from *minnisais,* meaning, "at the small island," describing Minisink Island in the upper Delaware River. The Minisinks and their relations inhabited the ridges and valleys from the Highlands northwest to the Catskill-Pocono Plateau, between the Delaware Water Gap and uplands fronting the Hudson River from Jersey City northward to Kingston, New York. The Manhattans, Tappans, Machkentiwomi (Kakiat), Rumachenanck or Haverstraw Indians and Waoraneck or Esopus Indians were the easternmost tribes of this large and very loose alliance of kinship communities.[22] The territory of the Unalâchtgo and the Unâmis supposedly extended from the Hudson River southwest to the Potomac River and beyond. New groups sprang over the course of time from the supposed original subdivisions as families, for their own convenience, chose to settle distant locations and "increasing in numbers, gave themselves names or received them from others." These new groups usually chose names from "some simple natural objects, or after something striking or extraordinary...."[23] Thus the *Mahicanni* or Mahicans supposedly originated as a detached body who, through intermarriages and subsequent linguistic mixtures, acquired a dialect of their own. Similarly, the Nanticokes, who settled in Maryland and Virginia, became a detached and distinct polity.

According to legend, the Mengwe or Iroquois extended their settlements eastward from the Great Lakes district along the banks of the St. Lawrence River during the same interval that the Lenape first occupied Scheyichbi. Growing jealous of their southern neighbors, they sought to destroy their former allies through clandestine machinations and artful deceit. By planting a Lenape war-club beside the body of a murdered Cherokee, the Mengwe instigated a bloody war between those two nations. The Lenape, after having discovered the perpetrators of this deceitful crime, resolved upon the total extirpation of the Mengwe. It was the successful prosecution of this war that prodded the Mengwe into forming a mutually defensive league or covenant among their independent tribes, thus bringing the Five Nations into existence. The suggestion is that the Senecas, described as the most restless of the Iroquoian tribes, bore the brunt of Lenape revenge and sought the inauguration of a confederacy with their neighbors so that "by the commission of wanton hostilities, [they] would draw the more peaceable among them into wars and bloodshed..."

But what actually took place? Did a large, eastward moving group of Lenni-Lenape divide into three groups upon reaching the Atlantic coast? If so, why didn't seventeenth-century natives along the coast tell a similar version of this story? Did different Algonquian-speaking bands envelop the Iroquoian nations in a gradual, pincer movement over a long period of time? Or did the Iroquois migrate into their historic homeland surrounding the Lower Great Lakes and St. Lawrence Valley, displacing Algonquian-speaking inhabitants? What can we reliably say?

Any consideration of the possibilities must account for an unmistakable cultural divide running through the middle of what has recently (1984) been called "Lenapehoking," or the "Land of the Lenape." The Minisinks of the upper Delaware Valley were culturally and dialectally distinct from their southern and eastern Algonquian-speaking neighbors. Throughout the Late Woodland Period (circa 700 to 1700 CE), pottery vessels from central and southern New Jersey adhere to a ceramic tradition that extended from Virginia through the Delmarva Peninsula and southeastern Pennsylvania into New Jersey.[24] In sharp contrast, the pottery and stone tool culture of northern New Jersey, especially in the upper Delaware Valley, strongly resembles the proto-Iroquoian Owasco culture of the Mohawk Valley. So much so that the late and much respected Dr. Herbert Kraft recognized "some sort of socio-cultural dichotomy within the state [of New Jersey]."[25] Dr. Kraft concluded, "At times it is exceedingly difficult clearly to distinguish between the proto-Iroquoian Owasco culture, so well defined for New York State, and the pottery and other cultural specifications for the peoples living contemporaneously in the upper Delaware Valley."[26] While not impossible, it seems unlikely that one subdividing influx of peoples developed such distinct cultural markers, while speaking mutually intelligible dialects of the same language. So did this "socio-cultural dichotomy" evolve over an extended period or occur through sudden relocation?

Distinct Algonquian dialects spoken in the northern, central and southern portions of New Jersey in 1609 emphasize lines of cultural demarcation. The intercropping of corn, beans and squash in the Minisink country may coincide with the use of Owasco pottery. Tests of cooking residues imply the use of squash as early as 600 BCE in the northern Finger Lakes region and the use of maize by 100 CE.[27] According to the same study, beans were not cultivated in the northeast until 1300 CE. Three carbonized corn kernels excavated at the Medwin Knoll II and Medwin North sites at Walpack Bend and carbon-14 dated CE 1250±40, CE 1307±83 and CE 1350±90 provide documentation of the use of maize by the Owasco inhabitants of the Upper Delaware Valley between 1210 CE and 1290 CE[28] The Minisink Burial Ground, covering several acres atop a high bluff above the Delaware River between Great and Little Minisink Islands, provides another interesting correspondence: artifacts uncovered from the site span the entire Late Woodland Period, indicating a long occupation. Three radiocarbon dates associated with the burials are CE 1220, CE 1380 and CE 1490.[29]

A dramatic climatic shift impacted events in the northern temperate zone when a period of about 150 years of renewed glaciation occurred after 1300 CE. The shorter growing season and harsher winters may have pushed people southward in a series of displacements, resulting in conflicts over land and resources. After a century of mild weather, the Little Ice Age worsened around 1550 CE, and persisted with varying regional degrees of intensity until about 1850. The proto-historic Iroquoian culture developed out of the preceding Owasco Phase between 1450 and 1600 CE. The Little Ice Age also brought colder and wetter conditions, favoring an increase in oak, chestnut, hemlock and spruce trees. Hurons and their Algonquian allies pushed the Laurentian Iroquois south from the banks of the St. Lawrence River into northern New York sometime after 1535. The Iroquois League of Five Nations supposedly formed "one age (or the length of a man's life) before the white people (the Dutch) came into the country," or about 1550.[30]

Adding to this cultural mixture, European adventurers and colonizers aggressively settled the North Atlantic coast during the Little Ice Age, ultimately upsetting the natural equilibrium and balance of power.

In 1650, natives of the country who were "so old as to recollect when the Dutch ships first came here, declare that when they saw them, they did not know what to make of them, and could not comprehend whether they came down from Heaven, or were of the Devil. Some among them, when the first one arrived, even imagined it to be a fish, or some monster of the sea, and accordingly a strange report of it spread over the whole land," creating "great astonishment and surprise among the Indians." When the natives beheld men aboard these sea craft, "they supposed them to be more like devils than human beings." The natives "frequently say, that they knew nothing of any other part of the world, or any other people than their own, before the arrival of the Netherlanders."[31] In 1656, Adriæn van der Donck claimed there were Indians in New Netherland "who remember a hundred years," and if any other Europeans had visited the area before Henry Hudson's exploration in 1609, these elders "would have known something of them, and if they had not seen them themselves, they would have heard an account of them from others."[32]

The Dutch, who justified their inhabitation of the Middle Atlantic Coast by nature of first discovery, offered such statements as legal proof against competing national claims. Van der Donck, however, goes on to relate, "There are persons who believe that the Spaniards have been here many years ago, when they found the climate too cold to their liking, and again left the country; and that the maize or Turkish corn, and beans found among the Indians, were left with them by the Spaniards. This opinion or belief is improbable, as we can discover nothing of the kind from the Indians. They say that their corn and beans were received from the southern Indians, who received their seed from a people who resided still farther south, which may well be true, as the Castilians have long since resided in Florida. The maize may have been among the Indians in the warm climate long ago; however, our Indians say that they did eat roots and the bark of trees instead of bread, before the introduction of Indian corn or maize."[33]

Van der Donck was incorrect, however, in stating that "nothing of the kind" was to be learned from the Indians regarding the belief that Spaniards had introduced maize. In March 1680, Hans (aka, Piewecherenoes or Pierwim), a Hackensack Indian residing on Newark Bay near Constable's

Hook, informed missionary Jasper Danckærts that Spanish or Portuguese traders introduced Turkish wheat or maize, they being the first Europeans to visit their country, even before the Dutch appeared on the Hudson and Delaware Rivers.[34] Starting around 1500, English, Breton, Portuguese and Norman ships did frequent the Newfoundland fishing banks, and maintained an extensive trade with the coastal inhabitants. Spanish seamen first explored the Caribbean Basin, progressively probing Meso-America, South America and the littoral of the Gulf of Mexico. In these climes, the development of cultigens had profoundly influenced the lifestyle and social organization of hunter-gatherers, encouraging a demographic increase beyond the natural carrying capacity of the land. Communities dependent upon large-scale horticulture for nourishment evolved more complex, hierarchical social structures. Cultivation of maize, squash and pumpkins reached the southeastern United States from western sources about 1000 CE. Here, cultigens supplied a large portion of the diet, and larger, more centrally organized political units called *chiefdoms* arose, typified by ceremonial centers focused upon earthen temple mounds. Such a cultural transformation never occurred among northeastern Woodland Indian communities. In any case, it is not necessary to choose between Spaniards and southern Indians—some communities may have received cultigens from one source, while other communities may have received them from another. What is significant, however, is that these explanations for the advent of horticulture survived into the middle of the seventeenth century, implying that this important development had occurred comparatively recently among some peoples inhabiting the Middle Atlantic Coast.

Until the second quarter of the sixteenth century, the vast stretch of North American seaboard between New England and North Carolina remained uncharted. On a French-sponsored voyage along this stretch of coastline, Florentine pilot Giovanni da Verrazano sailed a Norman ship, *La Dauphine*, into Lower New York Bay, probably on or about April 11, 1524. He named the bay *Santa Margarita* in honor of Marguerite, older sister of King François I, who was born April 11, 1492 in the Château d'Angouléme.[35] He marveled at "its extent and attractiveness, for we believed that it was not without some resources of wealth as all the hills indicated the existence of minerals in them." [36] Before an "impetuous contrary wind" forced his return to sea, Verrazano admired "a very delightful place among some small hills, eminences, between which ran a very great river (*una grandissima riviera*) to the ocean, which was deep within to the mouth, and from the sea to the enlargement of the bay the rise of the tide was eight feet, and through it any heavy ship can pass." He found the shores "thickly inhabited" with people, "adorned with birds' feathers of different colors," who approached "with evident delight, uttering very loud cries of admiration." Passing the Narrows, the inquisitive explorer entered a sheltered harbor, which he described as "a most beautiful lake (*un bellissimo lago*), about three leagues in compass, upon which we saw boats, thirty in number, moving from one part to another with innumerable people, who passed from shore to shore to see us."[37] Verrazano gave the name *Angouléme* to New York Harbor, honoring the king's birthplace and original title as the Count d'Angouléme.

Consequentially, Verrazano and his brother, Girolamo, sighted and named the *Isthmus Verazanio* on March 25th, the Feast of the Annunciation, mistakenly identifying the 180-mile-long Delmarva Peninsula as a mile-wide isthmus, 200 miles long, dividing the Atlantic and Indian Oceans.

The Palisades; Hudson River.

Figure 3. 1915 Postcard View of the Palisades.

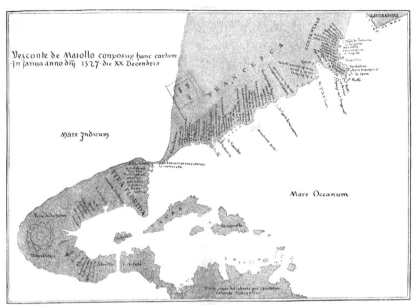

Figure 4. Italian cartographer Vesconte de Maiollo's Map, 1527, from
John Fiske, *The Dutch and Quaker Colonies in America*, Vol. I, New
York: Houghton Mifflin Company, 1899, Frontispiece.

Girolamo delineated this isthmus on a map in 1527. Most likely, vague
native descriptions of the Great Lakes and Hudson Bay misled credulous
European visitors into believing the "Oriental sea" was just over the western
horizon. It was only wishful thinking—the Verrazanos spied sounds or
bays beyond the seemingly endless chain of barrier islands, mistaking
these inland waterways for an open ocean washing the "blessed shores
of Cathay." Their speculation enticed eager adventurers. In 1584, English
geographer and promoter Richard Hakluyt popularized the notion that
only "a little neck of land in 40 degrees of latitude," divided the Atlantic
Ocean from the fabled "Sea of Verrazano," leading mariners to search for
the impossible.[38]

The Spanish and Portuguese were next on the scene. Esteban
Gómez sailed his 50-ton caravel, *Our Lady of the Annunciation*, along the
North Atlantic Coast between Maine and New Jersey in 1525, probing
the shoreline for a westward passage to the East Indies.[39] He named New

York Harbor for San Antonio, suggesting he entered it on the saint's feast day, June 13, 1525. Eventually it would come to be known as the Riviera de Gomez. Spanish seamen venturing into the region quickly recognized the suitability of New York Harbor as a watering and refitting station. Perhaps guided by Verrazano's description, French sloops navigated the Hudson River to the head of tides, commencing trade with the Mohawks near present-day Albany, New York. Floodwaters prevented completion of a fortified trading post on Castle Island, now Westerlo Island, at Albany, which French factors supposedly started building in or about 1540.[40] Jacques Le Moyne de Morgues, who had participated in an earlier failed attempt to plant a French Huguenot colony on the Florida coast in 1564, published a map of *Floridæ Americæ Provinciæ* in 1590. His map demonstrates a working knowledge of coastal Indians of the Delaware and Hudson estuaries, including the *Marracon,* later known as the *Narritacon,* residing on the west bank of the Delaware River. The *Sorrochos,* shown residing on both sides of the Delaware Capes, were part of the river tribes later known as Sawanoos, that is to say, "Southerners." Delaware Bay is marked *Funda Sorrochos,* or "South Bay". The *Honocoryous: cosagi,* shown to the east or northeast of the *Marracons,* probably indicates one of the "castles" of the Iroquois, possibly the Sonontouans (Senecas). Near the mouth of the Hudson River, however, his map reads: *Navigatione hic appulit* ("The ship landed here"). By this time, French colonists were wintering along the St. Lawrence River, meeting various indigenous peoples and learning about major geographic features of the hinterland. They were also trading up and down the Hudson River. In 1598, a small company of Dutch whalers of the Greenland Company was reported to have wintered on the shores of the Delaware and Hudson Rivers, erecting and occupying two small forts.[41]

VOYAGE OF THE HALF MOON

All this came at a time of increasingly harsh winters. The climatic fluctuation known as the Little Ice Age deepened between 1550 and 1750 CE. Expanding Arctic ice altered climatic zones southward, disturbing settled ways of life on both sides of the North Atlantic. Nevertheless, the search was on. A developing European palette for sugar and pungent spices to brighten an otherwise bland diet and to overcome the taste of poorly preserved meat lured merchants to far-off Malacca. Portuguese dominance of the Horn of Africa and sea routes to India, Indonesia and China encouraged Dutch and English merchants to explore the North American coast, and to venture upon northern polar seas for an alternative route to silk and spices. With the climate against them, sea ice repeatedly dashed hopes and claimed lives. Yet the lure of potential profit remained a fatal attraction. Commissioned by the directors of the Dutch East India Company of the Chamber of Amsterdam, Henry Hudson, a seasoned English pilot, sailed the *Halve Maen* (Half Moon) out of Amsterdam on April 4, 1609. Under specific orders to explore only a northeastern passage to India, they headed for the top of the world in their three-masted, fully rigged Dutch yacht, which had been designed for speed, and was prudently armed with two cannon and two swivel-guns. This 80-ton decked ship measured 58 feet, 6 inches long with a draft aft of 7 foot. Lacking the ship's missing log for reference, scholars disagree as to the complement of her crew, but eighteen English and Dutch sailors seems to be the generally accepted number. A small, open, single-masted, flat-bottomed scout boat, 12 feet long and 5 feet wide, was stowed on deck. Intended for coastal fishing and canal navigation, this *schuit* or *skuute* was handy for exploring shallow waterways.[42]

After a month's voyage, the *Halve Maen* reached Novaya Zemlya, a Russian island in the Arctic Ocean, where Dutch explorer Willem Barents had perished in 1597 after becoming trapped in frozen seas. Even as summer bloomed, sea ice continuously obstructed their progress. According to Emanuel Van Meteren's 1610 account, based directly on Hudson's log and journal, a "sea full of ice" and "the cold, which some of his men, who had been in the East Indies, could not bear, caused quarrels among the crew, they being partly English, partly Dutch, upon which Captain Hudson laid before them two propositions. The first of these was to go to the coast of America, to the latitude of 40°, moved thereto mostly by letters and maps, which a certain Captain [John] Smith had sent him from Virginia, and by which he indicated to him a sea leading into the western ocean, by the north of the southern English colony."[43] This was precisely the latitude where geographer Hakluyt noted Verrazano's isthmus and Western Ocean. Hudson's other option was to explore the frigid Davis Strait for a Northwest Passage. Fearful of a freezing voyage into the unknown and threatening mutiny, the Dutch and English crewmembers persuaded Hudson to steer for warmer waters. Disregarding his sponsors' narrow and deliberately confining instructions, Hudson turned and sailed south toward North America, stopping on May 30th at Strømø, largest of the Faroe Islands, located midway between the Shetland Islands and Iceland. Here he replenished his water casks and exercised the crews' sea legs. Tossed in a great storm on the North Atlantic on June 15th, their splintered foremast fell overboard. Four days later, on calmer seas, the ship's carpenter made needed repairs. A strong wind split their foresail on June 21st. Determining their position on a calm sea the next day, they steered west for "Newfoundland."

According to report of Johannes de Laet, a Director of the Dutch West India Company, Hudson and crew first arrived on the Georges Bank in the Gulf of Maine at the latitude of Cape Porpoise and Kennebunkport.[44] By July 1st, the *Halve Maen* was off Cape Sable, Nova Scotia. Two days later, they encountered a French fishing fleet on the Scotian Shelf. Hudson's crew netted 130 cod and marveled at the great schools of herring, but they were unable to preserve greater quantities of their catch due to their limited salt supply. On July 9th, Hudson conversed with a French fisherman off the Banc des Sables in island-studded Mahone Bay. Mists clouded their view for several days until clearing skies revealed white sand dunes and two sails on the horizon. The fog returned and Hudson's crew fished for cod on a quiet sea. On July 16th, they sighted five islands to the northwest, probably the Isle au Haut, Mount Desert, Vinalhaven and North Haven Islands in Penobscot Bay, Maine. On the following morning, it was too misty to approach shore safely. Instead, six Penobscot natives in two boats came out to them, one of whom spoke some French.[45] On July 18th, Hudson went ashore "at a place where there were certain natives with whom, as they understood, the French come every year to trade."[46] De Laet records the latitude as 44° 15', which runs through Great Cranberry Island, Seawall Point on Mount Desert Island and through Anns Point in Bass River Harbor on Blue Hill Bay, Maine. Further west on Blue Hill Bay, this is also the latitude of Eggemoggin Reach, bordering Deer Isle and Little Deer Isle. While the ship's carpenter cut a foremast on shore, the other crew members either searched for freshwater to replenish their casks or caught cod and lobsters.[47] They encountered more Eastern Abenakis in two French shallops, looking to trade beaver and other skins for red cassocks, knives, hatchets, copper kettles, trivets and beads. Hudson's crew finished work on the foremast and set its rigging on July 23rd, keeping a wary eye upon the native fleet. Finally, on July 25th, Hudson sent six men, armed with four muskets, in his *schuit* to capture one of the Indian shallops.[48] He then landed twelve men, armed with muskets and two small stone-shotted cannons, popularly known as "murderers." The raiders drove the Penobscot from their houses and "took the spoil of them, as they would have done of us."[49] The English and Dutch crewmen immediately quarreled over this "ill treatment of the natives." According to Meteren's interpretation, "The English, fearing that between the two they would be outnumbered and worsted, were therefore afraid to pursue the matter further." The *Halve Maen* quickly retreated to the harbor's mouth on July 26th.

The strong coastal current now swept the ship southward, and nine days later the crew sighted Cape Cod. Five men in the stolen shallop, sounding for depth, landed on Nauset Beach, near Pochet Island, and marveled at the grapes and "rose trees," possibly swamp honeysuckle or some other species of rhododendron.[50] On a very hot August 4th, the *Halve Maen* anchored near the northern end of the headland, probably at Nauset Harbor, where the crew heard "the voice of men call."[51] Hudson sent a boat to see if they were stranded Europeans, but instead found native Nausets. They took one on board and gave him several glass buttons. Returning to land, he leapt and danced and pointed to a river on the other side where they could fish. The crew observed Nausets smoking green tobacco in pipes with earthen bowls and red copper stems.

The *Halve Maen* continued south, swept by the coastal current. Riding in an "unknown sea," off Rehoboth Marsh in Delaware on August 9th, they cut the towed shallop loose after it ran against the ship's stern and split apart. The next afternoon, as rain clouds cleared, two curious dolphins swam alongside. A white, sandy shore appeared as a clear sunny day broke on August 17th. They were near Hog Island, Virginia, just south of Quinby

Inlet.[52] Hudson named this place Dry Cape. The next day they spotted three islands on Virginia's Eastern Shore, somewhere in the vicinity of the Great Machipongo Inlet, which divides Hog Island on the north from Cobb Island on the south. Hudson seemed unaware that the Delmarva Peninsula divides the ocean from Chesapeake Bay and instead believed he was at the outlet of the James River, where the new English colony of Jamestown was planted.[53] Carrying correspondence from his friend, Captain John Smith, of Jamestown, Hudson was in this latitude searching for a strait leading to the *Mare Indicum*, or Indian Ocean, which Verrazano had thought he glimpsed across a narrow peninsula. This would explain the *Halve Maen*'s southerly trajectory. Either due to unexpectedly strong currents or unfavorable winds, Hudson (like Verrazano) never actually entered Chesapeake Bay and the James River. Attempting to retrace Verrazano's watery tracks, Hudson sailed south. On August 21st, stormy seas again tore the foresail, which had to be taken down and mended. Meanwhile, superstitious crewmen grew nervous as the ship's cat ran crying from one side of the ship to the other.

On August 24th, they reached the latitude of Roanoke Island, sailing far off Oregon Inlet and the Outer Banks of North Carolina, in the vicinity of where Verrazano made landfall. The *Halve Maen* now swung north again, attempting to recreate the voyage of the Florentine pilot. Hudson anchored two days later off Cape Charles, near the southern tip of Wreck Island, on Virginia's Eastern Shore, once more having missed the entrance to Chesapeake Bay. At sunrise on the 27th they spied land, quickly recognizing the place they had put off from on August 18th. They continued their search north along the white sandy shore, which was full of bays and points of land. De Laet recorded that "they again discovered land in latitude 38° 9', where there was a white sandy shore and within it an abundance of green trees."[54] This would be at or near the Little Levels Camp Sites in today's Assateague Island National Seashore. It fit the description of the coast, which Verrazano "baptized Arcadia on account of the beauty of the trees."[55] At 6 o'clock, they came upon a harbor or estuary, with a sand bar blocking their entrance and many islands to the north—possibly what is now Ocean City Inlet on the Maryland shore.[56] Continuing north, Hudson arrived at Cape Henlopen, Delaware, on August 28th. Crossing the

Hens and Chickens Shoal, he sailed into Delaware Bay, noting the coast trending "Northwest with a Great Bay and Rivers."[57] The bay proved too shallow on the ebb tide for the *Halve Maen*, whose skipper was reluctant to explore further without a suitable shallow draft boat to sound the bottom in advance of his ship. Turning eastward at 5 o'clock in the morning, about an hour-and-a-half before sunrise, Hudson carefully navigated the Middle and the Prissy Wicks Shoals, scraping bottom at one point. Encountering occasional thunderstorms coming off the land on August 29th, the crew sighted the northern cape of Delaware Bay. Although Cape May appeared "all islands to our sight," it proved to be the tip of the mainland. On August 30th, the *Halve Maen* was off Seven Mile Beach on Cape May. The current once again carried them south into the ocean off Rehoboth Marsh on the following day, and they had to backtrack, reaching the ocean off Stone Harbor, New Jersey, on September 1st.

On September 2nd, they witnessed "a great fire" in the Pine Barrens, but could not see land at night.[58] At sunrise, "broken islands" appeared. Sailing along the shore, Hudson and his men "observed a white sandy beach and drowned land within, beyond which the land was full of trees...."[59] From when they first saw land, they sailed ten leagues along the coast until they came to "a great lake of water, as we could judge it to be, being drowned land, which made it rise like islands."[60] This was Barnegat Bay, where a great stream of water poured out of Barnegat Inlet. The land now rose to the north. Ship's journalist Robert Juet described the "high hills" of the ironstone-capped Navesink Highlands, rising 269 feet, as "a very good land to fall with, and a pleasant land to see."[61] Around 10 o'clock on September 3rd, the morning mist dissipated, bringing the Navesink Highlands again into focus. Juet recorded that "The land is very pleasant and high, and bold to fall withal."[62] At three o'clock, they came to "three great rivers," possibly, from south to north, the Metedeconk River, the Manasquan River and Shark River. They sailed for the northernmost, probably Shark River Inlet, but found it too shallow. Frustrated, they then sailed southward and anchored in six fathoms (30') of water.

On Friday, September 4th, the mariners saw "it was good riding further up," so they sent the boat to sound and discovered a good harbor, entering the Lower Bay, just beyond Sandy Hook. Some men took the boat

THE DISCOVERY OF THE HUDSON

Figure 6. James Grant Wilson (Editor), *The Memorial History of the City of New York From Its First Settlement to the Year 1892*, **Vol. I, New York: New-York History Company, 1892.**

and went on land to net fish, catching ten large mullets, each a foot-and-a-half long, and a ray so large it took four men to haul it into the ship. According to De Laet, the coast "was higher land than they had yet seen, along to a lofty promontory, behind which was situated a bay, where they ran up into a roadstead behind a low sandy point, in latitude 40° 18'."[63] Since this would be the latitude of Long Branch, Hudson apparently explored the Shrewsbury River between the Atlantic Highlands and Sandy Hook. Dispatching a boat to sound and finding between four (24') and seven (35') fathoms of water, they sailed in and rode in five fathoms (25'), oozy ground, and "saw many salmons and mullets and rays, very great."[64] Juet described a country full of blue plums and tall oaks, poplars and other woods useful in shipbuilding.[65] According to De Laet's relation of Hudson's account, "they were visited by two savages clothed in elk-skins, who showed them every sign of friendship."[66] These emissaries were Aquamachuques, part of a larger tribe of Sanhicans, who inhabited the shores of Sandy Hook and Raritan Bay, extending westward into the interior of the country.[67] That night, the wind drove the ship aground, but without harm, for it cradled in soft sand. The floodtide at daylight on September 5th re-floated the *Halve Maen*. Hudson sent his *schuit* to sound the bay, finding three fathoms (15‘) by the southern shore of Sandy Hook Bay, possibly between Conaskonk Point and Matawan Point.[68] While it is difficult to say with any certainty, a version of the 1616 *Figurative Map* shows the Aquamachuques' villages along the Rapatacok, or Luppatatong, Creek, which empties into Keyport Harbor.[69]

According to shipmate Juet, the skipper ventured on land and "saw a great store of men, women, and children, who gave them tobacco at their coming on land."[70] "When I came on shore," Hudson noted, "the swarthy natives all stood and sang in their fashion. Their clothing consists of the skins of foxes and other animals, which they dress and make garments from skins of various sorts. Their food is Turkish wheat [Indian corn or maize], which they cook by baking, and it is excellent eating. They soon came on board, one after another, in their canoes, which are made of a single piece of wood. Their weapons are bows and arrows, pointed with sharp stones, which they fasten with hard resin. They have no houses, but slept under the blue heavens, some on mats of bulrushes interwoven, and some on the leaves of trees. They always carry with them all their goods, as well as their food and green tobacco, which is strong and good for use. They appear to be a friendly people, but are much inclined to steal, and are adroit in carrying away whatever they take a fancy to."[71] Besides attire of loose-fitting deerskins and furs, the crew beheld some natives elaborately dressed "in mantles of feathers" as Verrazano had reported eighty-five years earlier.[72] They carried red copper tobacco pipes and wore ornaments of yellow copper around their necks. They traded green tobacco for beads, knives and woven clothing. Some native women brought hemp.[73] Their gardens yielded a "great store of Maize or Indian wheat, whereof they make good bread." Venturing up into the woods, the mariners beheld a great oak forest. One of the natives brought dried currants aboard the *Halve Maen*, which the crew found "sweet and good."[74] Resenting what they considered a penchant for petty thievery, the Europeans otherwise

MANHATTAN ISLAND IN THE SIXTEENTH CENTURY.

Figure 6. James Grant Wilson (Editor), *The Memorial History of the City of New York From Its First Settlement to the Year 1892*, Vol. I, New York: New-York History Company, 1892.

found the Sanhicans "very civil."[75] At night, the natives returned to shore, while the *Halve Maen* rode quietly at anchor in Sandy Hook Bay. The crew slept uneasily, being wary of their visitors. They had good reason to be anxious, for it is likely the ship attracted other eyes—the day's proceedings had been watched enviously, for the Sanhicans had deadly enemies across the bay, namely, the "strong and warlike" Manhattans, whose principal village, Werpoes, stood on the banks of Collect Pond near the southern tip of Manhattan Island.[76] Since this was hardly the first European vessel to enter the bay, there may have been past wrongs to avenge.

On September 6th, Hudson sent John Coleman and four others in the *schuit* over to the north side to sound the "other river," which was four leagues away. They found deep water, 18-20 fathoms, in the Narrows and a narrow river to the westward, which would be the Kill von Kull. They described the lands "as pleasant with grass and flowers and goodly trees as ever they had seen and very sweet smells came from them."[77] They went in two leagues, and "saw an open sea and returned."[78] This was most likely Newark Bay. On their way back, "they were set upon by two canoes, the one having twelve, the other fourteen men."[79] The night came on and it began to rain, so that their match went out and they had one man slain in the fight, which was their second mate, an Englishman named John Coleman, killed "with an arrow shot into his throat and two more hurt."[80] They couldn't relocate the *Halve Maen* in the darkness. So great was the ebb tide, their grapnel (small anchor) failed to hold, so they labored back and forth on their oars all night to prevent being swept out to sea.

Day dawned fair on September 7th. The boat crew could not reach the mother ship until 10 o'clock, bringing the dead man, whom they carried onto a point of land and buried, calling the spot "after his name, Coleman's Point."[81] They then hoisted their *schuit* and raised her sides with waste boards for defense. Keeping close watch, they slept with one eye open. The natives came aboard the next day, exchanging tobacco and corn for knives and beads. The Aquamachuques showed no signs of knowing about Coleman's death, even when the crew deliberately outfitted their boat, still stained with Coleman's blood, to test their reaction. It now became clear that various tribes "often engaged in wars among themselves" and hardly formed one government or society.[82] On the morning of September 9th, "two great canoes came aboard full of men; the one with their bows and arrows and the other in show of buying of knives to betray us; but we perceived their intent. We took two of them to have kept them, and put red coats on them, and would not suffer the other to come near us. So they went on land, and two others came aboard in a canoe; we took the one and let the other go, but he which we had taken got up and leapt overboard."[83] The *Halve Maen* then weighed anchor and went off into the channel of the river, anchoring there for the night. The following morning they found that the middle of the sand-banked river was shallow for the distance of a league. They finally located a depth of 7 fathoms (35'), perhaps in the Arthur Kill, before anchoring again for the night "in soft oozy ground." September 11th was a very hot day. Setting sail at 1 o'clock, Hudson entered the Upper Bay, described as "a very good harbor for all winds."[84] According to De Laet's report of Hudson's journal, the *Halve Maen* anchored in the river near what is today the south end of Riverside Park (40 ° 48') at 103rd Street, opposite Edgewater.[85] The commerce-minded Hudson described the location "as pleasant a land as one can tread upon, very abundant in all kinds of timber suitable for shipbuilding and for making large casks. The people have copper tobacco pipes, from which I inferred that copper must exist there; and iron likewise according to testimony of the natives, who, however, do not understand preparing it for use."[86] The natives came aboard with gifts of corn and tobacco, displaying friendship.

Robert Juet reported September 12th as a warm, clear day. Twenty-eight canoes full of men, women and children came "to betray us; but we saw their intent and suffered none of them to come aboard of us."[87] They brought oysters and beans, which the crew bought. They had "great tobacco pipes of yellow copper and pots of earth to dress their meat in."[88] The people departed at noon. Two hours later, Hudson weighed anchor and turned into the river two leagues, halting again near the Spuyten Duyvil, below today's Henry Hudson Park, on Palisade Avenue in the Bronx, where a monument to Henry Hudson would later be dedicated in 1938.[89]

Lifting anchor at 7 A. M. on September 13th, the *Halve Maen* rode the floodtide four miles upriver. When the tide turned, the ship

Figure 7. Begun in 1912 and dedicated January 6, 1938, the Henry Hudson Monument stands in Henry Hudson Park on Palisade Avenue, Kappock Street and Independence Avenue in the Bronx, New York. [*Photo by Deborah Powell*]

anchored at Yonkers, opposite the Alpine Boat Basin. Four native canoes sailed out, but Hudson would not let the people aboard, although the crew bought a "great store of very good oysters" for trifles.[90] Hudson weighed anchor in the afternoon, riding the floodtide two-and-a-half leagues farther before anchoring for the night in the Tappan Zee near Dobbs Ferry. They saw a high point of land, five leagues to the north and east, which may have been Hook Mountain or the bluffs of Mt. Airy above Croton Point. Approaching the Highlands on September 14th, Juet observed, "The land grew very high and mountainous. The river is full of fish."[91] Hudson sailed twelve leagues further to Peekskill Bay and the strait between Jones

Point on Dunderberg Mountain and Roa Hook. Here the river was a mile wide, with very high land on either sides. They continued a league and a half northwest through deep water to the present location of the Bear Mountain Bridge, then northeast five miles to Gees Point at West Point, then northwest two leagues to Pollepel Island, beyond Breakneck Point, opposite Storm King Mountain, where they anchored.

HENRY HUDSON IN THE HIGHLANDS.

Figure 8. James Grant Wilson (Editor), *The Memorial History of the City of New York From Its First Settlement to the Year 1892*, Vol. I, New York: New-York History Company, 1892.

A 1616 map shows the Pachami residing opposite Klinkersberg, the original name for Storm King Mountain, near Fishkill in Dutchess County.[92] The sky cleared soon after sunrise on September 15th and the ship ran upstream twenty leagues to the outlet of Esopus Creek at Saugerties. The crew marveled at the great store of salmon in the river. Hudson's two captives climbed through a porthole and escaped, calling to the crew in scorn after they were under sail. The 1616 map shows a tribe called the Waoranecks residing on the Roundout Creek. The Waranawankoughs (Waronawanka) lived on the opposite side, near Rhinebeck. Nearing the Catskill Mountains that night, Hudson first encountered the inhabitants, who were described as "very loving people and very old men: where we were well used."[93] Their boat caught a great store of fish. September 16th was very hot and clear. They tried again to catch fish, but got few "by reason their canoes had been there all night."[94] In the morning, the people brought ears of Indian corn, pumpkins and tobacco, which the crew bought for trifles. That evening they weighed anchor and sailed two leagues higher, staying near Cementon until daybreak.[95]

Robert Juet recorded fair weather and a very hot day on September 17th. Setting sail at sunrise, the mariners ran six leagues higher, reaching shallow water with small islands and seven fathoms (35') of water on both sides. Toward nighttime, they ran aground, possibly on the Middle Ground Flats, but heaved off, ran aground again in the channel, and had to await the flood tide to free themselves. On the fair morning of September 18th, Hudson dropped anchor at latitude 42 ° 18', which would correspond with the Hudson Anchorage, either near Four Mile Point on the west bank or Stockport Flats, above Stottville, on the east bank. According to Robert Juet, "the master's mate" went ashore in the afternoon with "an old savage, a governor of the country; who carried him to his house, and made him good cheer."[96] According to De Laet, Hudson was the one who went ashore to meet with friendly Mahicans. Hudson wrote: "I sailed to the shore in one of their canoes, with an old man, who was the chief of the tribe, consisting of forty men and seventeen women; these I saw there in a house well constructed of oak bark and circular in shape, with the appearance of having a vaulted ceiling. It contained a great quantity of maize and beans of last year's growth and there lay near the house for the purpose of drying enough to load three ships, besides what was growing in the fields. On our coming near the house, two mats were spread out to sit upon and immediately some food was served in well-made red wooden bowls; two men were also dispatched at once with bows and arrows in quest of game, who soon after brought in a pair of pigeons, which they had just shot. They likewise killed at once a fat dog and skinned it in great haste with shells, which they got out of the water. They supposed that I would remain with them for the night, but I returned after a short time on board the ship. The land is the finest for cultivation that I ever in my life set foot upon and it also abounds in trees of every description. The natives are a very good people; for, when they saw that I would not remain, they supposed that I was afraid of their bows, and taking the arrows, they broke them in pieces and threw them into the fire, etc."[97]

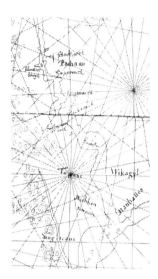

Figure 9. Detail, *Carte Figurative*, showing discoveries of Captain Cornelius Hendricks, dated August 18, 1614 and copied July 27, 1841 by P. H. Loffelt.

On September 19th, floodtide came at 11 o'clock, propelling the ship two leagues above the shoals, where they anchored in eight fathoms (40') of water near Coxsackie, between Rattlesnake Island and Kinder Hoeck, which later became the town of Stuyvesant. Once again, "The people of the country came flocking aboard, and brought us grapes and pompions, which we bought for trifles. And many brought us beavers' skins and otter skins, which we bought for beads, knives and hatchets."[98] They remained all night. On the following morning, the master's mate took the boat with four men upriver and found two fathoms of water and a narrow channel along Houghtaling and Lower Schodack Islands, about two leagues beyond the anchored ship. They continued northward, measuring seven to eight fathoms, but returned by nightfall. Despite their wish to explore further, too many people came aboard on September 21st for them to do so. Making good use of his time, the ship's carpenter went on land to construct a foreyard. The master and his mate decided to try some of the chief men of the country, to see "whether they had any treachery in them. So they took them down into the cabin and gave them so much wine and *aqua vitae* that they were all merry: and one of them had his wife with them, who sat so modestly, as any of our country women would do in a strange place. In the end one of them was drunk, which had been aboard our ship all the time that we had been there: and that was strange to them; for they could not tell how to take it. The canoes and the folk went all on shore: but some of them came again and brought strips of beads, some had six, seven, eight, nine, ten, and gave him. So he slept all night quietly."[99]

On the morning of September 22nd, the master's mate and four crewmen took the boat to sound the river higher up. The people did not come on board the *Halve Maen* until noon. When they saw that the

formerly drunken chief was well, "they were glad," so they came aboard at
3 o'clock.[100] Presenting gifts of tobacco and beads, a chief made an oration
and, gesturing, showed Hudson all the country round about. They then
sent someone on land to bring back "a great platter of venison dressed by
themselves; and they caused him to eat with them. They made him reverence
and departed, all save the old man who lay aboard."[101] The exploratory
group got eight or nine leagues upstream, but upon measuring only seven
feet of water, they realized they could proceed no further, and returned
that night during a rain shower. According to Meteren, "they sailed up
the river as far as 42° 40'."[102] This would place the northernmost point
of exploration just beyond the Patroon Island Bridge in Albany, which
now carries Interstate 90 over the Hudson River. Having sailed nearly 150
miles inland, Hudson had reached a dead end. Disappointed, he weighed
anchor at 12 o'clock on September 23rd and sailed two leagues down to the
Middle Ground Flats, but the tide was out and they were aground for an
hour before floodtide came and the ship floated into deeper water. They
continued downstream seven or eight leagues on September 24th, running
aground on a bank of ooze in the middle of the river at half ebb tide
(possibly on the Hog's Back above Barry Town) and so were compelled to
wait for floodtide. They whiled away the hours on land, gathering chestnuts.
At ten o'clock they slipped into deep water and anchored. Enjoying fair
weather, the crew walked on the west side of the river on September 25th,
near Kingston, noting "good ground for corn and other garden herbs, with
great store of goodly oaks and walnut trees and chestnut trees, ewe trees,
and trees of sweet wood in great abundance, and great store of slate for
houses and other good stones."[103] On the following morning, September
26th, the ship's carpenter accompanied four crewmen to cut wood. Two
canoes came upriver from the place where they first found "loving people
and in one of them was the old man that had laid aboard of us at the other
place."[104] He brought another old man with him, who presented strips of
shell beads to Hudson "and showed him all the country there about as
though it were at his command."[105] Hudson dined with the two old men
and one of their wives, "for they brought two old women and two young
maidens of the age of sixteen or seventeen years with them, who behaved
themselves very modestly."[106] Hudson presented one old man with a knife

and they gave him tobacco. Departing downstream at one o'clock, they made signs that the ship should follow them, for they were within two leagues of the place where they dwelt at present-day Kingston.

The morning of September 27th was fair, but with a wind coming from the north. The ship again ran aground at half ebb. Unable to heave her off, they waited until half floodtide and sailed downstream six leagues to the vicinity of Crum Elbow at the northern entrance to the Long Reach. The old man came aboard and tried to get them to anchor, so they could dine with him, but with the benefit of a fair wind, Hudson declined his invitation. The elderly sachem left, "being very sorrowful for our departure."[107] At five o'clock, they anchored in fourteen fathoms (70') and the boat went on shore opposite the ship to fish. The master's mate, boatswain and three others went on land to fish, but were unable to find a good place. Nevertheless, they landed a mixture of twenty-five mullets, breams, basses and barbels in an hour's time. At daybreak on September 28th, the *Halve Maen* weighed anchor at half ebb, sailed two leagues and anchored again, probably near Poughkeepsie, awaiting the return of high water. At 3 o'clock, they weighed anchor and continued downstream three leagues, settling at nightfall near Danskammer Point.

On September 29th, the air was dry. They set sail early in the morning, running down three leagues to a low water and anchored near Storm King Mountain. Indians appeared in a canoe, but refused to board. They brought maize, which the crew bought for trifles. At 3 o'clock, when the ebb came, they weighed anchor and turned down to the edge of the northernmost of the mountains, where they anchored, "because the high land hath many points, and a narrow channel, and hath many eddy winds."[108]

Despite fair weather on September 30th, a stiff gale howled through the mountains. The people of the country came aboard with small animal skins, which the crew purchased. Describing what may be the site of West Point, Juet thought, "This is a very pleasant place to build a town on. The road [that is to say, the river] is very near and very good for all winds, save an east north-east wind."[109] The mountain appeared to contain some metal or mineral, for the trees were blasted, and some mountains were barren with few or no trees. The people brought a stone on board "like to an emery (a stone used to cut glass), it would cut iron or steel: yet being bruised small and water put to it, it made a color like black lead glistening: it is also good for painters' colors."[110] They departed at 3 o'clock.

The narrow passage through the Highlands is about seventeen miles long, with bellowing winds that often obliged vessels to lower or shorten their sails. The *Halve Maen* weighed anchor on October 1st at 7 o'clock with the ebb tide, and sailed below the mountains, traveling seven leagues to Croton Point and anchoring in Haverstraw Bay on the floodtide at noon. "The people of the mountains came aboard us, wondering at our ship and weapons."[111] The crew bought some small skins. That afternoon, one canoe kept hanging under the stern with one man in it, which they could not keep from thence, who climbed up by the rudder to the cabin window and stole Juet's pillow, two shirts and two bandoleers. The master's mate shot him in the breast, killing him, whereupon the rest fled—some in their canoes, while some leapt out of them into the water. The crew manned their boat and retrieved the stolen items. One Indian that swam got hold of the boat, trying to turn it over. The cook cut off his hand with a sword and he drowned. By this time, ebb tide came and they weighed anchor. Sailing two leagues downstream into the broad Tappan Zee, near Upper Nyack and Philipse Manor, they anchored at dusk.

They started off at daybreak on October 2nd and ventured seven leagues downstream. When floodtide came, they anchored again, this time near Manhattanville at 125th Street. The Indian who swam away from them when they were going upriver now reappeared, bringing many others, "thinking to betray us."[112] Hudson's crew perceived their intentions, and forbade them to board the ship. Two canoes, full of men with bows and arrows, shot at the ship's stern. In response, Hudson's crew discharged six muskets, killing two or three of the bowmen. Then about a hundred Manhattans came to a point of land to shoot at the ship. Juet fired a Falcon, instantly killing two of them, whereupon the rest fled into the woods. They persisted, sending out another canoe with nine or ten men to meet the ship. Juet shot it through with the Falcon, killing one of its occupants. The crew once again fired their muskets, killing three or four more. The natives finally retreated, and the ship got down two leagues beyond that place and anchored in a bay, free from all danger from their attackers on the other side of the river. Here they admired a good piece of ground, which lay beside a white-green cliff that looked as though it were made of copper or silver. The trees growing on it were "all burned" while the other places were as green as grass: "it is on that side of the river that is Manna-hata. There we saw no people to trouble us…"[113] They were likely seeing the serpentine cliff of Castle Point in Hoboken. Rain and wind on the morning of October 3rd drove the ship aground, but the shifting wind drove them off again. Because of the inclement weather, they anchored all night.

The *Halve Maen* navigated out of the river on October 4th. Relying upon their original soundings, they shadowed the northern side of the Lower Bay as they departed. Clearing the inlet by noon, they hauled in their *schuit* and steered toward the ocean. The great pilot was frustrated. Reflecting Hudson's mindset, Emanuel van Meteren thought, "More could have been done if there had been good will among the crew and if the want of some necessary provisions had not prevented it."[114] Once at sea, dissension continued to ripen, and the debate took an ugly turn. The Dutch mate argued for wintering in Newfoundland and resuming their search for the Northwest Passage through Davis Strait the next spring. Hudson, fearful "of his mutinous crew, who had sometimes savagely threatened him," decided against this course of action.[115] He cited the lack of proper provisions with which to endure the cold. No one, it seems, wanted to return to Holland, which made Hudson suspicious, so he instead agreed to winter in Ireland, a decision that met with general approval. As it turned out, the *Halve Maen* docked at the Range of Dartmouth, Devonshire, England, on Saturday, November 7, 1609. Hudson contacted his employers and proposed to search again for the Northwest Passage, if the directors would forward sufficient funds to outfit a new expedition. The skipper proposed replacing six or seven crewmembers, and increasing their number to twenty. In January 1610, the English government prevented Hudson's return to Holland and Emanuel Van Meteren, Dutch consul in London, "thought probable that the English themselves would send ships" to explore Hudson's river.[116]

The North Americans

North American history materializes in the logs and journals of Western European explorers who gingerly probed the many bays and inlets of the Atlantic coastline. Johannes De Laet, Director of the Dutch West India Company, wrote his *History of the New World*, which was published in Dutch as *Nieuwe Wereldt, ofte Beschrijvinghe van West-Indien* between 1621 and 1624, piecing together accounts of early navigators such as Henry Hudson, Adriæn Block, Hendrick Christiænssz and Cornelis May.[117] Nicolæs Janszoon van Wassenaer, an Amsterdam physician, published current historical accounts in periodical pamphlets, beginning in 1621.[118] He incorporated accounts of the West India Company's adventures in New Netherland covering 1623-1630 in his *Historisch Verhael*. Of course, the literary output could be no better than the quality of information supplied. The most violent method of obtaining this consisted of kidnapping natives, who were then presented as court curiosities, trained as interpreters, and culled for geographic intelligence. Their ultimate fate could be worse. At least fifty-seven Newfoundland natives were brought to Portugal in 1501 and sold into slavery.[119]

There was a significant communication gap between the natives and early explorers. Many pioneer settlers of New Netherland, and elsewhere, mistakenly believed that the natives possessed only "an easy language, which is soon learned."[120] They usually failed magnificently to pronounce "difficult aspirates and many guttural letters, which are formed more in the throat than by the mouth, teeth and lips, to which, our people not being accustomed, make a bold stroke at the thing and imagine that they have accomplished something wonderful."[121] Consequently, most Europeans were only capable of speaking broken fragments of the language, "sufficient for the purposes of trading, but this is done almost as much by signs with the thumb and fingers as by speaking...."[122] To be understood under such circumstances, natives commonly spoke "only half sentences, shortened words, and frequently call out a dozen things and even more; and all things, which have only a rude resemblance to each other, they frequently call by the same name," perhaps to compensate for their hearer's limited command of vocabulary and grammar.[123] Comprehending the richness of North American aboriginal languages, Dominie Jonas Michælius of the Dutch Reformed Church described the pidgin jargon of commerce in 1628 as "a made-up, childish language" since most Europeans who mastered this simplified form of speech were usually "bewildered when they hear savages talking among themselves."[124]

Numerous autonomous bands or familial communities inhabited the northeastern woodlands. Contemporary descriptions and maps of New Netherland name the Aquamachuques, Ermomex, Kichtawanghs, Machkentiwomi, Mahikanders (Mahicans), Manhattans, Matouwax, Matovancons, Minnessincks (Minisinks), Naraticons, Sanhicans, Sawanoos, Sintsings, Tappaens, Waoranecks, Wappinges, Waranawankongs and Wiquaeskecks.[125] Acknowledging no integrated, cohesive polity, each group had its own governing elders and inhabited its own territory. The various bands were generally limited to a single-family connection and reportedly "often engaged in wars among themselves...."[126] Recognizing some degree of consanguinity and cultural identity, they occasionally formed alliances. Even in these instances a single sachem rarely enjoyed unquestioned command, acting instead as a spokesman for all interested parties.

The various Algonquian-speaking communities of the Middle Atlantic region were probably *matridemes*, wherein "residence is principally matrilocal and in which most of the marriages are locally exogamous."[127] A "deme" is a territorial and political kinship unit composed of a small village or band, whose members are not segmented by lineages or sibs based upon a belief in descent from a common mythological ancestor, and who are generally aware of their bilateral genetic relationship to all or most other members of the band. In contrast, the Iroquois traced their descent through three matriclans, whose mythological ancestors were: the Tortoise (*Anaware*), supposedly the greatest and most prominent clan, boasting descent from the Creatress who scraped together the Earth by groping through the waters collecting handfuls of mud while seated upon the back of a Tortoise; the Bear (*Ochkari*); and the Wolf (*Oknaho*), who claimed to be "a progeny" of the Bear. These clans carried "the beast after which they are named (as the arms in their banner) when they go to war against their enemies, as for a sign of their own bravery."[128]

De Laet stated the general perception when, summarizing eyewitness accounts, he reported how the indigenous population inhabiting a vast territory between the head of tides on the Hudson River and the head of Chesapeake Bay, "divided into many nations and peoples, differ much from one another in language though very little in manners."[129] Wassenaer commented upon "so great a diversity of language," which varied every fifteen to twenty miles among "so many tribes," who "if they meet they can hardly understand one another."[130] Firsthand observers quickly realized neighboring tribes often spoke dialects of the same language, "not very different and the tribes can usually understand their dialects."[131] In 1647, the *Journal of New Netherland* told how native peoples "dwell together in tribes, mostly of one consanguinity, over which commands a chief who is a general and is generally called *Sackema*, possessing not much authority and little advantage, unless in their dances and other ceremonies."[132] Each so-called tribe or nation composed "one separate society, and usually keep together; every tribe or nation has its own chief, and is a separate government, subject to its own laws and regulations."[133] While North Americans clearly "descended from one parent-stock, …they seldom marry out of their own tribes," perpetuating the remarkable diversity of language, dialect and culture.[134] In 1656, Adriæn van der Donck concluded, "The nations, tribes, and languages are as different in America as they are in Europe."[135]

Van der Donck reported four distinct Indian languages spoken in New Netherland, but he was not quite precise in his use of labels.[136] In fact, he lists only two distinct language families: Algonquian and Iroquoian. He divided the Iroquoian Family (which he called *Minquas*) into subfamilies such as Mohawk, Seneca and other inland tribes, including Huron and Susquehannock. He identified three Algonquian dialects, namely: *Manatthan*, *Sawanoos* (Southerners) and *Wappanoos* (Easterners). The compass orientation of his labels is obviously centered upon the view from Fort Amsterdam on Manhattan Island. The Manhattan dialect has subsequently become known as the *Minsi* dialect, but for symmetry should probably be called *Lowanne,* or Northern. It was spoken in 1656 by North Americans living along the Hudson River, at Neversink Highlands along Sandy Hook Bay, and upon Long Island. The Lowanne Subfamily also comprised tribes inhabiting the Ridge-and-Valley province extending between the Lehigh River and the Berkshire Mountains. Viewing contemporary maps of New Netherland, it appears the Wappanoos Subfamily referred to Algonquian tribes living east of the Connecticut River along the southern New England coast. The Sawanoos Subfamily included the South River Indians (Lenape or Delawares) residing upon the Delaware Capes northward to Trenton. Since another group, the *Sanhicans,* had been pushed inland from the western shores of Newark Bay by the time Van der Donck made his linguistic observations, we might add the possibility of an intermediate dialect, the *Sanhican* ("those who make fire with wooden drills"). These Algonquian dialects were mutually intelligible, as might be expected. Differences in pronunciation and vocabulary became pronounced with increasing distance between communities.

The former existence of three Algonquian dialects within a relatively narrow compass of territory speaks to the autonomy of diverse Algonquian communities. Since this writing only deals peripherally with the so-called Wappanoos of southern New England, we will divide Algonquian-speaking tribes residing between the Hudson and Susquehanna Rivers into three dialectal groupings: (1) *Lowanne,* or Northerners, including Minisinks and Manhattans; (2) Sanhicans; and (3) Sawanoos, or Southerners. The clustering of families into these three dialectal groupings was not made by any conscious decision—as legend might have it—but rather through gradual adaptation to three different resource-areas: (1) those inhabiting the Highlands and Appalachian Ridge-and-Valley; (2) those inhabiting the Piedmont; and (3) those inhabiting the Inner and Outer Coastal Plains. Dialectal groupings may also correspond with loose family alliances. We can only speculate whether or not three reported distinctions among gathering bands of Delawares and Minisinks after their westward migration from ancestral homelands, namely, *Unalâchtgo, Unâmis* and *Minsi*, recall these earlier dialectal family-alliances.

LOWANNE LENAPE, OR NORTHERNERS

Algonquian-speaking communities fronting the west bank of the Hudson River above Upper New York Bay comprised a dialectal subgroup, the Lowanne or Northern Lenape. Referring to this dialect in 1656, Adriæn van der Donck noted, "With the Manhattans, we include those who live in the neighboring places along the North River, on Long Island, and at the Neversink."[137] While this geographic distribution of Lowanne speakers was true at the time Van der Donck wrote, it had not been so prior to 1635. According to the 1625 edition of De Laet's *Nieuwe Wereldt*, the Manhattans occupied the east side of New York Bay.[138] The testimony of Hudson and his crew led De Laet to conclude the Manhattans were "a bad race of savages, who have always been very obstinate and unfriendly towards our countrymen."[139] In his *Historisch Verhæl*, published semi-annually between 1621 and 1631, Nicolaes Van Wassenaer simply said, "the Manhates are situate at the mouth" of the Hudson River.[140] In 1626, Peter Minuit, Director General of New Netherland, famously purchased Manhattan Island and established Fort Amsterdam at its tip. The first settlers found "land fit for use, deserted by the savages, who formerly had fields there."[141] After the sale of their home island, the original inhabitants of Manhattan took up residence across the river on Bergen Neck. In 1628, Isaack De Rasieres reported that Bergen Neck, being "the northwest land opposite to Manhatas," was "inhabited by the old Manhatesen; they are about 200 to 300 strong, men and women, under different chiefs, whom they call Sackimas."[142] Robert Juet, of Hudson's crew, also used the name *Manna-hata*, or "island," to describe Castle Point in Hoboken, on the west side of New York Harbor. Though Bergen Neck is actually a narrow peninsula, it was mistakenly thought to be an island. Here the Palisades rose, making the western bank of the river "more mountainous" than the opposite shore, earning it the Dutch appellation of *Bergen*, meaning, "scarp."[143] While no record has been preserved of the sachems who sold Manhattan, Arromeauw and Tekwappo were Manhattan elders and joint owners who conveyed Hobocan Hackingh, extending south to Ahasimus, bounded east by the Hudson River and west by lowlands, to Michiel Paauw on July 12, 1630. Aiarouw, Ackitoauw, Camoins, Matskath, and

Winym are listed as inhabitants and co-owners of Ahasimus and the little island called Aressick in a deed to Michiel Paauw for Ahasimus, lying south of Hobokan Hackingh, dated November 22, 1630. Given phonetic inconsistencies in the rendering of Indian names, it is probable that Aiarouw and Arromeauw refer to the same individual. After selling the southern half of Bergen Neck as far north as Wiehawken in 1630, the Manhattans moved westward.

Wickquaesgeck was the name given to the country stretching beyond the outlet of the Harlem River, "where there is maize-land, but all stony and sandy, and where many pine trees grow," situated directly across the Hudson River from Tappan.[144] Wickquaesgeck derives from *wiquajeck*, meaning, "the head of a creek," and refers to the head of the Saw Mill River, northeast of present Tarrytown, Westchester County, New York. In 1628, Isaac De Rasieres described this area above Manhattan as "high, full of trees, and in some places there is a little good land, where formerly many people have dwelt, but who for the most part have died or have been driven away by the *Wappenos*."[145] The Wappanoos or Wappinges (literally, "the Easterners,") comprised bands, speaking a distinct dialect, who resided at Alipkonck, Sinsing, Kestoubniuk, Keskisckonck, Pesquaskeck and Noch Peem. The original inhabitants of Wickquaesgeck, or at least a band residing east of the Bronx River, were soon driven southwest across Staten Island, onto the western shores of Raritan Bay.

In 1640, Captain David De Vries complained that the Hudson River above Manhattan "has nothing but mountains on both sides, little capable of sustaining a population, as there are only cliffs and stones along the [west bank of the] river ... There is here and there some maize-land, from which the savages remove the stones and cultivate it."[146] North of the habitations of the old Manhattans upon Bergen Neck, we find two distinct native communities. In February 1624, Van Wassenaer's *Historisch Verhæl* placed, "the Mechkentowoon, Tapants, on the west side" of the Hudson River.[147] De Laet also reports "a nation of savages, named Tappaans," on the west side of the first reach of the Hudson River, "where the land is low."[148] In 1640, this stretch of lowland was described as a large flat of about two or three hundred morgen [Dutch unit of land measurement] of clay soil [that] lies under the [Palisades] mountains, three or four feet above the water. There was "also much maize-land ... too stony to be ploughed" and a creek later named Sparkill, which drained through the Palisades onto the river flats.[149] In April 1640, Captain David De Vries purchased this lowland as an addition to his plantation at Vriessendæl, now Edgewater, New Jersey.[150] *Tappan* is said to derive from the Algonquian, *thuphanne*, translated as "cold stream."

The Tappans had close neighbors, for Van Wassenaer mentions the Mechkentowoon in the same breath. According to the 1633 version of De Laet's *Nieuw Wereldt*, the Machkentiwomi lived opposite the Manhattans. This tribe's name derives from *machkachtawunge*, meaning "red bank of a river." Mention of a tribe by this designation fades from sources at an early date, so we are left to wonder about their ultimate fate. Where was Machkachtawunge? Some sixty-three years after De Laet's original reference, Daniel Honan and Michael Hawdon received a deed, dated June 5, 1696, for a vacant tract of land in Orange, (now Rockland) County, New York, commonly called Kackyacktaweke. Presenting another version of this place-name, the Return of a Survey for 7,470 acres, dated April 25, 1710, issued to Elias Boudinot, John Auboyneau, John Barberrie and Peter Fauconnier, mentions "an Indian field called Maygahgtayako," situated on the southwest side of Pascack Brook in present-day Spring Valley, New York. This Indian plantation, variously known as Kackyacktaweke, Hackyackawack or Maygahgtayako, is probably the origin of the historic toponym (place name) *Kakiat*. These various variations of the name may all be approximations of Machkachtawunge.

If indeed the Machkentiwomi resided on a tributary of the Hackensack River, then they would have been close neighbors and relations of the Tappans.[151] Deed evidence suggests the Tappans and Machkentiwomi occupied the northern valley of the Hackensack River and its major affluents, south to French Creek at New Bridge, and the present boundary between Teaneck and New Milford. Their territory also extended south upon the tableland atop the Palisades to Espating, now Union Hill, and Wiehawken. On the west side of the Hackensack River, their territory passed along the Kinderkamack Ridge, southward across Cole's Brook at River Edge and continued along the Red Hills above the

Figure 10. Detail, *Carte Figurative*, showing discoveries of Captain Cornelius Hendricks, dated August 18, 1614 and copied July 27, 1841 by P. H. Loffelt.

City of Hackensack through Hasbrouck Heights southwest on the upland to the Passaic River.

The *Rumachenanck*, or Haverstraw Indians, occupied territory upon the west bank of the Hudson River, northeast of the Tappans, with whom they were closely affiliated.[152] A stream noisily cascaded down the Palisades at Haverstraw.[153] The Esopus Creek borrows its name from the Algonquian word, *sipo*, meaning, "creek." On its banks, the Indians cultivated "much maize-land, but all somewhat stony."[154] Recounting tales of the earliest Dutch seafarers to visit the region, Nicholas Van Wassenaer stated, "In one place, Esopes, are two or three tribes."[155] He locates the Pachany, Warenecker and Warrawannanckx along this stretch of the Hudson River, placing the Pachany on the east bank. The Waoranecks inhabited "a place called Esopus," situated at a narrow pass of the Hudson River about present-day Saugerties, New York, where "a sharp point of land … juts out, covered with sand, and opposite a bend in the river...'[156] The name may be an approximation of *Wewoatangiks*, meaning, "wise men."[157] Subsequent events showed the Waoraneck, or Esopus tribe, to be relations of the Minisinks. In 1625, De Laet's *Nieuw Wereldt* placed the Waranawankoughs "a little beyond" Esopus, on the opposite side of the river, near Rhinebeck. a little to the north of the Waoraneck, "where there is a creek, and the river becomes more shallow … here are several small islands."[158]

The Mahicans or Mahikanders resided at the head of tides on the Hudson River, taking their name from the root word, *hikan*, literally meaning "at the head of the tides." In 1818, Reverend John Heckewelder stated that the real name for this people was *Mahicanni*, but they were variously known as Mahinkanders, Mourigans, Mahingans, Mohiccons, Mohegans and Muhheekanew. Heckewelder claimed this Algonquian-

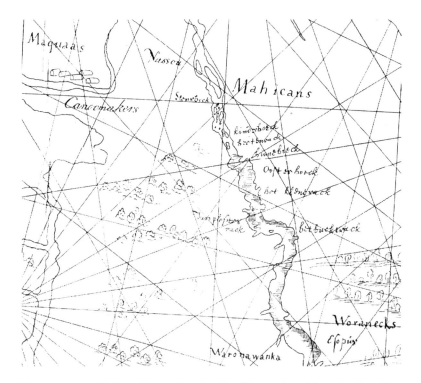

Figure 11. Detail, *Carte Figurative*, showing discoveries of Captain Cornelius Hendricks, dated August 18, 1614 and copied July 27, 1841 by P. H. Loffelt.

speaking tribe originated as a detached body of the Lenape who, through intermarriage and the mixing of their two languages, acquired a dialect of their own.[159] According to Van Wassenaer's *Historie Van Europa* (1621-1632), the *Maikans* were "a nation lying 25 leagues [approximately 67 miles] on both sides of the [Hudson] River, upwards."[160] De Laet, who relied heavily upon the testimony of Captain Adriæn Block, reported the Mahicans occupied the east side of the Hudson River, above Fort Orange (Albany) and opposite Sturgeon's Hook and Fisher's Hook, near Shad Island.[161] Evidence suggests the Mahicans allied with their Algonquian-speaking neighbors residing on the east bank of the Hudson River to the south. Wassenaer identified these communities: "*Wiekagjock, Wyeck* [Nyack], on the East side [of the Hudson River]."[162]

Captain Cornelis Jacobsen May established a colony of about eighteen families, protected by Fort Orange, among the Mahicans in the spring of 1624. Internecine warfare soon broke out over access to the new European trading post. The Mahicans drove the Maquaas (Mohawks) from their easternmost "castle," situated on the Mohawk River near present-day Amsterdam, New York, in 1626. In the spring of 1628, the Mohawks and Mahicans renewed their war, resulting in a Mahican defeat, when many of their number were killed or captured. The Mahican sachem Kanaomack sold the land along the Hudson River near Fort Orange to Director Peter Minuit and the Council of New Netherland, who purchased it on behalf of Killiaen van Rensselaer on August 13, 1630.[163] At a peace treaty concluded with Director-General William Kieft on August 30, 1645, Aepjen, Sachem of the Mahikanders (Mahicans), also spoke for the Wappink, Wiquaeskecks, Sintsings and Kichtawanghs. In 1646, Isaac Jogues stated the Mahicans, called Wolves (*Loups* in French), "are nearest to the settlement of Renselærswick and to Fort Orange."[164] Their enemies, the Mackwaes, or Iroquoian Mohawks, lived on the west side. In October 1659, the Mohawks used a Mahican sachem as their messenger to the warring Esopus Indians. By 1659, the Mahicans blended with the *Catskill* or *Highland* Indians, who, by their own report, numbered about 110.

MINISINK OR BACHOM'S COUNTRY

The first hand accounts of seafarers, trading factors and pioneer planters were generally limited to description of North Americans fronting the coast and ocean-flowing streams. However, early on, a misadventure occurred which shone a dim light upon the hinterland. In 1614, the Ogehages—an Iroquoian people also known as the Minquas or Susquehannocks—captured three Dutchmen who were assisting their enemies, the Mohawks. In the spring of 1616, Captain Cornelis Hendrickssen, skipper of the *Onrest* (*Restless*), was dispatched from Holland on a voyage of discovery. According to his report, filed on August 18, 1616, he entered the Delaware River, where he "traded for and bought from the inhabitants, the Minquaes, three persons, being people belonging to the [New Netherland]

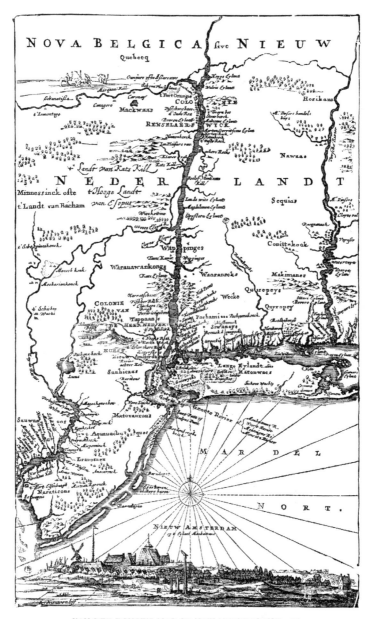

VAN DER DONCK'S MAP OF NEW NETHERLAND, 1656

Figure 12. Van Der Donck's *Map of New Netherland*, 1656, from John Fiske, *The Dutch and Quaker Colonies in America, Vol. I*, New York: Houghton Mifflin Company, 1899, 230.

company [an association of Amsterdam merchants formed in 1614], which three persons were employed in the service of the Mohawks and Mahicans, giving for them kettles, beads and merchandise."[165] Captain Hendrickssen's *Figurative Map*, included in the 1616 report to the States General, relied upon information from "Kleynties and his Companions ... respecting the locality of the Rivers and the position of the tribes which they found in their expedition from the Maquaas [or Mohawks] into the interior and along the New River [that is, the Susquehanna River] downwards to the Ohchage (i.e., the Enemies of the aforesaid northern tribes)." Expanding on this information with the aid of subsequent records, it is possible to piece together a picture of the interrelationship of various native groups who seem to have otherwise eluded the Dutch during their government of New Netherland. Deed conveyances and other documents, mostly written after the Dutch capitulation of their colony in 1664, suggest that the Manhattans, Tappans, Machkentiwomi (Kakiat), Haverstraw and Esopus were the easternmost bands of a larger alliance of families, dispersed in concentric rings radiating outward from Minisink Island in the Upper Delaware Valley. These various affiliated bands inhabited the ridges and valleys from Shawnee-on-the-Delaware to the fonts of the Delaware River upon the Catskill-Pocono Plateau, extending east to the Hudson River.

Inland of the first range of Highlands, at least three related groups are identifiable: the Minisinks, the Pequannock and the Tohockonetcong. The Minisinks inhabited the country of that name in the Upper Delaware Valley. The Pequannock resided east of Lake Hopatcong near the headwaters of the stream that carries their name.[166] Their territory extended southeast to the Watchung Ranges. Eastward, between the Ramapo Mountains and Saddle River, their territory blended into the domain of their relations and allies, the Machkentiwomi (or Kakiat) and Tappans. On June 16, 1695, Onageponck and Hielawith, of Pequannnock, and Tajapogh, Sachem of Minising (Minisink), sold a large tract of lowlands comprising the upper part of Pompton Plains to Captain Arent Schuyler. Tajapogh was the same Minisink sachem who sold 5,500 acres near Pequannock and Pompton, beyond the Passaic River, to Arent Schuyler on June 6, 1695.[167]

The Tohockonetcong band of Minisinks dwelt near the headwaters of the Paulinskill. Tradition places their principal settlement on the southern

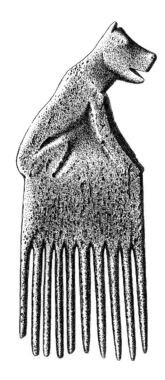

Figure 13. Minisink Bone Comb, from George G. Heye and George H. Pepper, Exploration of a Munsee Cemetery near Montague, New Jersey, New York: The Museum of the American Indian, 1915.

margins of the Paulinskill Meadows, in and around present-day Newton, and on the shores of Swartswood Lake, both situated in Sussex County, New Jersey. Our only knowledge of this band comes from West Jersey surveyor John Reading's *Journal* of 1715.[168] On May 26, 1715, an Indian guide from Allamuchahocking (Allamuchy), named Nomalughalon, accompanied Reading along the path towards the Tohokkenetcong River (Paulinskill), crossing Paquassing or Pequest Creek.[169] Upon reaching the watershed of the Paulinskill, "the Indian seemed very unwilling to go any further that way, saying that Tohokkenetkong Indians would be angry with him for showing their land. He went home again."[170] The natural boundary between the neighboring Tohokkenetkong and Allamuchahocking bands was the slate ridge forming the watershed between two tributaries of the Delaware River—the Paulinskill and Pequest Creek. This also formed part of the boundary between the neighboring Minisink/Lowanne and Sanhican alliances.[171] Prehistoric cemeteries existed on the drift terraces bordering the Paulinskill Meadows at Germany Flats and Hampton Township within the territory of the Tohockonetcong.[172]

The Minisinks, later known as Minsi or Munsee under various spellings, formed a loose alliance of autonomous communities, culturally distinct from their Algonquian-speaking neighbors southeast of the Pequest Valley and south of the Passaic Range of Highlands. Precariously positioned amongst warring Iroquoian nations, their strategic location necessarily involved them in alliances and confrontations with powerful neighbors. While archaeologists have disputed the use of fortifications in the Minisink country, it is notable that in 1663, the Minisink chiefs requested a small cannon to be used in their fort to protect their corn against the Senecas.[173]

The Algonquian-speaking Minisinks were an Owasco Phase culture, virtually indistinguishable from the protohistoric Iroquois in many respects, yet possibly with unique features as well. They occupied the Upper Delaware Valley in horticultural villages situated on friable alluvial flats, complimented by a scattering of seasonal resource stations, mainly fall/winter hunting camps and spring fishing areas. Minisink derives from *minnisais*, meaning, "at the small island." A large burial ground and an "old land fort," on the sandy bluff of the Jersey shore, opposite Minisink Island, marks their ceremonial heartland.

Dutch cartographers gleaned important information regarding the Upper Delaware Valley from "Claes de Ruyter, an old and experienced inhabitant of that country."[174] According to a letter which the Directors of the Dutch West India Company addressed to Jacob Alrichs, their Vice-Director stationed at Fort New Amstel, in April 1659, Claes Jansen De Ruyter had "kept house some time with the Indians living high up the [Delaware] river and about Bachom's country."[175] De Ruyter was a carpenter by trade, who also kept a popular tavern called the *Blue Dove* on Pearl Street in New Amsterdam.[176] As early as 1645, he was listed as an Algonquian interpreter.[177] D. Gualthero de Ræt's map of *Belgii Novi*, published in 1647, designates the territory between the headwaters of the Delaware and Susquehanna Rivers as *Minnessinck ofte t'Landt van Bacham* [Minisink or the Land of Bacham]. Who was Bacham? The minutes of a meeting held in the Council Chamber at Fort Amsterdam on May 15, 1664, offer an explanation: On that occasion, Seweckenamo "arose and said in behalf of the Esopus savages substantially, that he had asked his God (whom he called *Bachtamo*, and to whom he appealed several times as a witness to grant), that he might negotiate something good with the Dutch in the presence of all the chiefs now here and that the treaty made might be as solid as a stick, which he took hold of, one end was attached and firmly united to the other." *Bachtamo* may be a Dutch interpretation of the word *Machtando*, which, according to an 1888 *Lenâpé-English Dictionary*, is a shortened form of *machti-manitto*, meaning "Great Spirit."

The Minisinks and affiliated families apparently possessed a distinct religious tradition, perhaps associated with Late Woodland burial grounds near Port Jervis, Minisink and Germany Flats in Sparta, New Jersey. The Germany Flats burial ground featured flexed burials incorporating personal possessions or grave goods. William Gunderman accidentally unearthed this cemetery while plowing in a field near his house along Houses Corner Road in Sparta Township, on April 25, 1842. He struck "some hard substance, which proved to be a human skull."[178] Four or five other skeletons, nearly entire, each "contracted in a narrow space, as if drawn up together and not deposited at length," were found nearby, all buried in the light, dry sandy soil, not more than two feet below the surface. Grave goods included "a number of small pieces of pottery, figured and rudely ornamented, bucks-horn, arrowheads, shells, &c." Once the remains were determined to belong to "the aborigines of our country, which were here inhumed after the Indian fashion," the excavations were respectfully discontinued.

Based upon Clæs de Ruyter's information, the 1647 *De Ræt* map identifies four places in the Upper Delaware Valley by approximations of their aboriginal names: (1) *t'Schepinaikonk*, (2) *Meoech konck*, on what may be the Neversink Branch; (3) *Mecharienkonck*, situated at or near present-day Matamoras, Pennsylvania, opposite the confluence of the Neversink and Delaware Rivers; and (4) *t'Schichte Wacki*, apparently located near Minisink Island.[179] Adding information gleaned from later sources, it is possible to piece together a general picture of the locations and interrelationships of various native communities in this region. By 1715, the Minisinks lived in villages located above the confluence of the Neversink and Delaware Rivers, the most northerly being along the Delaware River at Cochecton, New York. [180] In June 1719, John Reading, a West Jersey boundary commissioner, listed four Minisink towns along the Neversink River between Huguenot and Carpenters Point, namely, (1) *Peanpeck*, now Huguenot, New York; (2) *Sandiunquin*[181]; (3) *Totinquet*, along Roundout Creek, near Napanoch, New York[182] and (4) *Oquekumsey* on the south side of the river, now Deposit, New York.[183] *Machippacong* was located about six miles below the confluence of the Delaware and Neversink Rivers. Continuing south, Indian trader Solomon Davis resided along the river at *Wendianmong*, near Millville in Montague Township, opposite Milford, Pennsylvania.[184] Here, a natural depression in the hills and river bluffs between Brick House and Milford opened the great route to the west, where roads diverged to the Susquehanna and to the Lake Country of central and western New York. John Reading described *Mennisinke*, situated three miles south of *Wendianmong*, as "a place where there is a considerable deal of good lowland and two very large islands, both of which I suppose belong to Jersey. Here are the ruins of an old land fort built as reported by the Shawwenocs [Shawnee] when they first inhabited this country and a very great number of Indian's graves."[185] The "old land fort" was perhaps a small earthen mound, which the Shawnee erected when they relocated from the Upper Mississippi Valley to a settlement above the Delaware Water Gap in 1692.[186] Reading also noted, "There is in the above town [*Mennisinke?*] 26 married couples, 61 male persons unmarried, 58 females ditto."

Documents show that allied native families, who otherwise resided at some distance apart, utilized resource stations in the Upper Delaware Valley. An old sachem residing near Trenton Falls in 1633 told Captain Thomas Young, "there was a mountainous country, where there were great store of elks and that before the war with the Minquaos [Susquehannocks], they were wont to go thither to hunt them, but he said that neither he himself nor any of his people had ever been further than those mountains."[187] According to a deed, dated August 1713, a tract called Mattaloning at Walpack Bend had recently belonged to Raweeneka, who was proprietor and seller of lands upon the Passaic River and its branches.[188] At this same date, the upper part of the Minisinks belonged to Taphow (also spelled Taepan) and his relations. Taepan was involved in selling land near Pekquanack and Pompton. The Minisink Patent of March 1702 included "great Menisink Island and the land about it called Tashoghkaken." Tashoghkaken may be an approximation of *Tachquoakcheen*, referring to the "fall hunt."

Several resource stations were sited near the outlet of tributary streams, suggesting that watersheds defined hunting territories. While we know little specifically about this area, among the Montagnais people of Canada, a family of about twenty persons would erect a bark lodge, continuing their residence so long as game could be found within a circuit of ten or twelve miles. Beaver and porcupine were hunted in early winter, while moose and caribou became prey when deep snow hindered their movements and revealed their tracks. Unlike the Minisinks, these northern hunter-gatherers had no caches of corn to supplement their diet of game.[189]

A deadly epidemic ravaged the Minisink country in the spring of 1660. On June 1, 1660, seven canoes full of men, women and children came down the Delaware River en route to the lower Susquehanna Valley. Reportedly these refugees lived near the Minisink Indians and fled "for fear of a certain *Manito*."[190] For some time thereafter, Minisink hunters traveled great distances to hunt peltries and to trade. In 1680, a large Minisink hunting party traveled "as far as the *Spanish* Indians."[191] After a brief battle, with losses on both sides, the Minisinks journeyed westward toward the Illinois Country, where they encountered several other bands of refugees from Rhode Island, New York and Virginia. These included Abenakis and Mahicans, who had fled warfare and disease in their own lands and were wintering around Fort St. Louis.[192] In the end, the Minisinks had little to show for their exertions. On September 12, 1681, Rathquack, a Minisink sachem, in New York City said his people spent their beaver pelts, which they intended to exchange for winter clothing, on drinking rum.[193] Even worse, about sixty drunken men had been killed in knife fights over the past three years. Depleted in numbers by disease, alcoholism and warfare, the Minisinks adopted a clever defensive strategy, planting refugees in the natural corridors leading into their homeland. After living among the Shawnee and traveling with them for nine years, Matasit, a Minisink sachem, visited Fort St. Louis in 1690 and persuaded a Shawnee sachem named Kakwatcheky (Weswatewchy) to settle his people in the Minisink country.[194] An advance contingent of one hundred Shawnees reached the Delaware River in August 1692. On August 12, Captain Arent Schuyler was dispatched to lead a Shawnee delegation to Albany in order to make peace between the newcomers and their long-standing enemies, the Senecas. On August 18, Matasit, as head of a Minisink delegation, informed New York Governor Benjamin Fletcher, "they had long been absent from their native country, and did desire to be kindly received, as they in former days received the Christians, when they first came to America. They pray the same likewise in behalf of the Strange Indians they have brought along with them."[195] By July 1693, the Senecas reached an accommodation with the Shawnee, approving their settlement above the Delaware Water Gap. The Shawnee consequently established a village named *Pechoquealin* (Pahaquarry) upon the west bank of the Delaware River near the mouth of Shawnee Run, at Shawnee, Lower Smithfield Township, Monroe County, Pennsylvania. They also established several plantations across the river on the Pahaquarry Flats in Warren County, New Jersey.[196]

At about the time the Shawnee settled above the Delaware Water Gap, the Minisinks invited the Oping (Wapping) or Pompton Indians to settle at Pompton, New Jersey, astride the main overland trail that entered the Highlands en route to the Minisink country. The *Oping, Wappings, Wappingers* or *Highland Indians* (*Wappanoos* literally means "Easterners") comprised several tribes with a distinct dialect, who originally resided on the east side of the Hudson River at *Alipkonck, Sinsing, Kestoubniuk, Keskisckonck, Pesquaskeck* and *Noch Peem*.[197] Although their kinfolk, the Minisinks, refused to war against the Dutch, the Esopus Indians did find willing allies in the neighboring Wappingers, who joined them in attacking Dutch farmsteads at Wiltwyck in June 1663. These Indians settled at Pompton sometime after the end of the Esopus War in 1664.

Governor Fletcher dispatched Captain Arent Schuyler to the Minisink country in February 1695, seeking intelligence of French activity in the neighborhood. Traveling from New York City, Schuyler reached "Maggaghkamieck [Port Jervis] and from thence to within a day's journey of the Mennissinck" on February 6, 1695.[198] At eleven o'clock the following morning, he met at Minisink "with two of their sachems and several other Indians," who reported that no French or their Indian allies had been in their country. He was informed that Arnout Cornelius Viele, an Albany trader and interpreter who had traveled into the Shawnee's country about fifteen months ago, "intended to be there [at Minisink] with seven hundred of ye said Shanwans Indians, loaded with beaver and peltries, at ye time ye Indian corn is about one foot high (which may be in the month of June)."[199] Viele reached the Minisinks at the appointed time, for on August 28, 1695, he and a company of Mahicans met Governor Fletcher at Esopus, seeking protection for the Shawnee. He reported that 300 Shawnee were expected "quickly to follow."[200] On May 20, 1697, Arent Schuyler received a grant of "a certain tract of land in Minisink country, in the province of New York, called by the native Indians *Warensashskennick*, otherwise called *Maghawaemus*; also a certain parcel of meadow, or vly, called by the Indians *Warensaghskennick*, situate, lying, and being upon a certain run, called by the Indians, and known by the name of *Minisink*, before a certain Island called *Menayack*, which is adjacent to or near to a certain tract of land called by the Indians *Maghakeneck*, containing the quantity of 1,000 acres and no more."[201] *Maghakeneck*, later called Mackhackamack, is now Port Jervis, New York.[202] The small creek, called Minisink by the native inhabitants, is probably the Bena Kill.

A series of land grabs marked the first years of the eighteenth century in the Minisink country. On March 14, 1702, nine Manhattan real estate speculators purchased a vast tract of land, extending from the Sand Bergh to the west side of a cedar swamp lying west of the land called *Shackoenka*, south to the Division Line of New Jersey and east to the land called *Shawenkonk* (Shawangunk), meeting the bounds of land purchased by Doctor John Bridges & Company and by Captain John Evans.[203] This tract included the "great Menisink Island and the land about it called *Tashoghkaken* and the cedar swamp aforesaid."[204] Kisekaw, Orackquehowas, Jan Conelle, Orapequine, Wawassowaw, Rumbout and Cornelawaid were the native owners and grantors. Seven of the same New York investors joined Doctor John Bridges and four others in acquiring the so-called Wawayanda Patent on March 5, 1703.[205] This tract extended east from the Shawangunk Mountains to the Highlands, being bounded south by the undefined Division Line of New Jersey. *Wawayanda* is the Minisink word for "egg-shaped," although it is uncertain precisely which natural feature is described. At least three native sachems or elders involved in the Wawayanda Patent, namely, Wawastawaw, Cornelaww and Rumbout, participated in the previous sale of 1702.[206] Two other grantors may also have participated:[207] Since the letters "w" and "m" are frequently interchangeable in European spellings of Algonquian names, it is possible that the individual mentioned as either Wawassowan or Wawastawaw in these transactions may be the Minisink sachem elsewhere called Wemessamy or Memmesame in 1663-64. He is probably the same sachem listed as Mowessawach in the sale of lands at *Pemrachquinming* on the second river or creek, lying west from the Remopock River (Ramapo River), to Peter Fisher and Philip Koning, of Japock (now Yapough in Oakland, Bergen County) on April 21, 1727.[208]

On June 11, 1703, Copockron, Samawan, Keskentems, Cookham, Asshewantuck, Necomacapock, Guntawamuck, Tendemunge, Abraham Mametukquim and Packiskham, the native proprietors of various tracts of land in the Minisink country, conveyed *Magockamack* and *Magascoot* to five New York merchants, including Philip French, the Mayor of New York, for £400.[209] The boundary survey of the Minisink Patent began "at a certain place called by the Christians Old Bashes Land," probably located upon the Basherkill, a tributary of the Neversink River, and ran thence by a northwest and by a north line to a certain river or kill commonly known by the Christians and Indians by the name of the Fish Kill, which is the main stem of the Delaware River above its confluence with the Neversink River. The survey line continued across the Delaware River to the top of the mountains and so southerly along the said mountains until it comes to the Great Minisink Island and from thence easterly to the limits and bounds of the purchases made by Doctor John Bridges & Company and Captain John Evans.[210] Lucas Kiersted, the Indian trader at Ramapough (Ramapo), and Samuel Hitting, witnessed the transaction.

The Minisink Patent remained vacant for some time. On March 20, 1765, Alexander Colden, Surveyor-General of New York, officially objected when the proprietors of this patent filed a map and partition of the tract in his office, stating, "the said Proprietors have greatly intruded on the King's Lands." In 1765, the Surveyor-General noted the Evans Patent had been voided. In its absence, the proprietors of the Minisink Patent simply extended their boundary as much as twenty-five miles east of the Shawangunk Mountains, adding about 150,000 acres to the estimated 250,000 acres encompassed by their original grant. New Jersey authorities properly regarded these lands as their territory. On May 30, 1709, the Provincial Council of New Jersey ordered Arent Schuyler to send for Matasit, Kakowatcheky, Ohwsilopp, Meshuhow and Feetee, "sachems of the Manisincks (Minisinks) and Shawhena (Shawnee)," seeking their participation in an expedition against French Canada.[211] Matasit was one of four Minisink sachems—the others being Ambehoes, Yamatabenties and Echkamare—who inhabited the Minisink country about 1715, according to Johannes Decker's affidavit of 1785.[212]

SANHICANS

Speaking a distinct dialect, the Sanhicans occupied the rich crescent of tidal lowlands fronting Raritan Bay, Staten Island and Newark Bay as far north as the head of tides on the Hackensack and Passaic Rivers. Their territory was shaped like an arrowhead, its broad base formed by the wetlands bordering Newark and Raritan Bays and its point at the head of tides on the Delaware River at Trenton.[213] The Aquamachuques, an affiliated community, occupied the south shore of Raritan Bay from the Neversink Highlands west to the South River. Captain John Smith included the "Atquanachuke" (Aquamachuques) among "several nations of sundry languages that environ Powhatan's territories," locating them on his 1612 map along an oceanic bay to the northeast of Virginia. The *Dutch Figurative Map* (1616) shows Sanhicans occupying the littoral of Newark Bay. The 1630 sale of Staten Island identifies its proprietors not with the Manhattans, but with the Sanhicans, Aquamachuques and their relations, the Mateuwax, of Long Island, who obtained their livelihood by fishing in Jamaica Bay. Although the northern part of Long Island was more fertile than its southern shore, Peter Kalm reported in 1749, "the Indians formerly chose the southern part of the island to live in, because they subsisted on oysters and other products of the sea... The island is strewed with oyster shells and other shells, which the Indians have left there..."[214] Matouwax is likely a transliteration of *meteauhock*, meaning "periwinkle." Long Island was a major source of the shore-dwelling mollusks, whose shells were fashioned into beads.

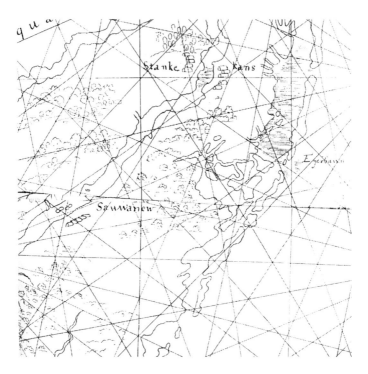

Figure 14. Detail, *Carte Figurative*, showing discoveries of Captain Cornelius Hendricks, dated August 18, 1614 and copied July 27, 1841 by P. H. Loffelt.

In 1628, De Rasieres described the tidal waters of the Hackensack and Passaic Rivers, commingling in Newark Bay, as a "little river, which we call 'Achter Col'," meaning "behind the neck of land."[215] Thereabout he observed, "there is a great deal of waste reedy land; the rest is full of trees, and in some places there is good soil, where the savages plant their maize, upon which they live, as well as by hunting." The Hackensacks, whose village stood near Kips Bend on the Hackensack River in Teaneck, were affiliated with the Sanhicans, but also claimed the land whereon the city of Newark now stands. The toponym *Hackensack* derives from *Achkinckeshacky*, also spelled *Ackinsack*, which may be a transliteration of *Achsinnigeu-haki*, meaning, "stony land." The Hackensacks conducted their winter hunt on Long Island.

According to De Laet's *Nieuw Wereldt* (1630 edition), the Delaware River ran "some distance northwest, in the same direction as its bay, makes a bend to the northeast, and comes very near to the estuary of the North [Hudson] River, in the region where dwell the Sankikans (Sanhicans) and Matovancons."[216] The westward range of the Sanhicans can be delimited. Sankikan Kill is probably Assanpink Creek, near the Falls of the Delaware River. Lindeström identifies *Sanckhickan* as a neck of land in Falls Township on the west side of the Delaware River, between two islands called Menahanonck, now Bile's Island, and Kentkateck, now Moon Island. Thus the Sanhicans were listed as a nation of Indians inhabiting the Delaware River. The Matovancons do not appear in lists of the Delaware River tribes, possibly because they lived inland. The Millstone River was originally known as the Matawang, and it seems likely that the name of the inhabitants who inhabited this tributary of the Raritan River was corrupted to the Matovancons.

According to De Laet's *Nieuw Wereldt*, the Sanhicans were "deadly enemies of the Manhattans, and a much better people."[217] In an account written by Isaack De Rasieres in 1628, the paths leading from Raritan Bay toward the Delaware River "in the neighborhood of the Sanhicans" were then little used, since natives residing along New York and Raritan Bays "live in a state of constant enmity with those tribes."[218] There was also trouble on the Delaware River: the Susquehannocks killed about ninety Sanhicans in February 1633. The Sanhicans were driven from the west shore of Raritan Bay by the Roaton or Raritanghe, who the Wappenos expelled from Wickquaesgeck, a territory on the east side of the Hudson River, above the East River.[219] The Raritans invaded Staten Island and forcibly occupied the lower Raritan Valley. The Dutch concluded a peace treaty with them in 1634, after which they continued to trade with them by sending a sloop there every spring. By July 1640, the Raritans were described as "a nation of savages who live where a little stream [the Raritan River] runs up about five leagues behind Staten Island."[220] At a peace conference with the Dutch in 1649, Pennekeck, sachem of Achter Col, "said the tribe called Raritanoos, formerly living at Wisquaskeck (Wickquaesgeck) had no chief, therefore he spoke for them, who would also like to be our friends...."[221]

It is unknown whether the Sanhicans blended with their conquerors, or moved elsewhere. They probably joined remnants of the Sawanoos Lenape, eventually forming the *Unalimi*, or Unâmis, who took their name from their location *Nallahiwi*, or "up the river." Their displacement early on, however, should sound a note of caution in discussions of cultural boundaries between native communities based upon later representations, including the oft-cited deeds relating to the 1758 Treaty of Easton.[222]

SAWANOOS, OR SOUTHERNERS

Sawanoos was one of several Algonquian dialects spoken in New Netherland in 1656.[223] According to Johannes de Laet's *Nieuwe Wereldt* and subsequent descriptions, the Sawanoos were—as their name literally states—"the southern nations" who inhabited the shores and inland creeks of the Delaware River and Bay.[224] He noted "divers nations of savages, namely, the Sawanoos, Naraticons (Narritacon), Ermomex, or Armeomecks, [and] Sanhicans" inhabited the Delaware River and Bay.[225]

The Sawanoos occupied the Atlantic coastal plains. In the last century, large shell-mounds and Indian artifacts were found along Hill's Creek, at Chelsea, near Atlantic City. Another great shell-heap occupied part of the ground where Atlantic City was built. In 1890, twenty-one Indian skeletons, found three feet underground, were exhumed at Pleasantville in Atlantic County, together with several flints, many arrows, a stone knife, two flakes and a stone mortar. Two Indian skeletons were also discovered beneath a large cedar tree at Chestnut Neck, the head of one encased in a turtle-shell. One of the largest shell heaps was found on the marsh skirting what is known as the Great Bay, about a mile from the mainland. In historic times, Sawanoos Lenape communities were established at Leeds Point, and to the north, on Willis and Osborne Islands.[226]

Cornelis Hendrickssen's *Figurative Map*, dating to August 1616, located the *Sauwenew* (Sawanoos) on the east side of the Delaware River, opposite the mouth of the Schuylkill, between present-day Woodbury and Gloucester City. Scattered remains of native artifacts have been found all along Woodbury Creek.[227] The Sanhicans dwelt "on the upper part of the South River" (or Delaware River), that is to say, near Trenton.[228] Hendrickssen placed *Stankekans* on both sides of the Delaware River near Trenton.

To promote Sir Edmund Plowden's efforts to colonize the Delaware River in 1644, shipmaster Robert Evelyn, of Maryland, addressed a letter to Madam Plowden, Sir Edmund's wife, who had underwritten the New Albion Patent.[229] His knowledge of the land between the Delaware and Hudson Rivers in Sir Edmund's patent, called "New Albion," was firsthand, for Evelyn claimed he "with my uncle [Thomas] Young" had resided on the Delaware River for four years.[230] Considering later accounts, indicating Captain Young and Robert Evelyn attempted to learn the Indian language, Evelyn's description might be considered a valuable contemporary description of native inhabitants. Yet, written about five years after his departure from the Delaware River, his account seems inexplicably confused. Master Evelyn reported eight tribes inhabiting the northeast side of Delaware Bay and River between the mouth of the Maurice River and Trenton Falls, and he makes incidental mention of another tribe on the west side of the river. Listing "the king of Kechemeches, having as I suppose about 50 men," who resided near the Maurice River Cove, Evelyn may refer to Keshuwicon, a sachem who participated in the June 9, 1693 sale of a tract of land "betwixt Cohannsick (Cohansey) & Prince Morris [Maurice] River," to Jeremiah Basse, agent for the West Jersey Society.[231] The Mantes River (Mantua Creek) lay about thirty-six miles northwest of the king of Kechemeches, a little above the Bay and a sand bar, where the king of Manteses (Mantes) with about 100 bowmen occupied "a flat level of rich and fat black marsh mould," extending about twenty miles along the shore of the Delaware River and about thirty miles "up a fair navigable deep river."[232] It was here that Edmund Plowden intended to plant his colony. All indicators suggest a location along the coast between Cohansey Creek, which is about thirty miles in length, and the Salem River, also about thirty miles long. However, most Swedish and Dutch sources identify the Mantes Indians with the Mantes Kill, later called Mantua Creek. According to Lindeström's *Geographia Americæ* (1654-55), the east side of the Delaware River from the Delaware Falls at Trenton northward was "mostly inhabited by the Mantesser (Mantes), which nation is the rightful owner of the east side of the [Delaware] river, bondmen and servants in this river, and the river was formerly mostly occupied by these savages, yet this nation is now much died off and diminished through war and also through diseases."[233] Lindeström said that the land at Trenton Falls "along the river edge is generally rich and occupied by a large number of plantations ... but overgrown with an unspeakable multitude of grapevines...."[234] The Mantesser were skilled hunters and fishermen who sold their surplus fish and game to the Swedes and to Indians living on the west side of the Delaware River. Like most other native communities, they subsisted solely on fish and game "when their grain gives out."[235]

Following Master Evelyn's description and continuing another eighteen miles, say, from Cohansey Cove, brings us to "a fair deep river, 12 miles navigable, where is freestone, and there over against [that is, on the opposite side of the Delaware River] is the king of Sikonesses."[236] Here he may be describing Salem Creek, which is navigable for almost fifteen miles with sandstone near its banks. Evelyn also refers to Sickinesyns, also known as Sinquees, a sachem who confirmed the sale of land on the southwest side of Delaware Bay, extending about forty-five miles between Cape Henlopen to the mouth of the Delaware River to Samuel Godyn on July 30, 1630. Sinquees (if the same individual) was chief over land on the Schuylkill, called Armenveruis, who sold the site of the Dutch Fort Beversrede to Arent Corssen, commander at Fort Nassau, in 1648. He was also one of four sachems who sold land called Tamecongh, or Sand Hook, on the west side of the Delaware River between the Minquas Kill and Boompjes Hook to Peter Stuyvesant on July 9, 1651.[237]

Next Evelyn lists the "Asomoches River and king with an hundred men."[238] Lindeström's map of *Nova Suecia* places *AsamoHackingh* between the headwaters of Alloways Creek and Salem River, near present-day Pittsgrove. Consequently, the Salem River was sometimes called the *Asamo Hacking*. The next creek above Salem River, which Evelyn seems to call the Asomoches, would be Oldmans Creek, which Lindeström calls *Kagkikanizackiens Sippus*. Missionary John Campanius recorded the name of Kagkikanizackiens Sippus (sipo, *creek*) as *Tangilenohacking*, meaning *Little Man's Land*.

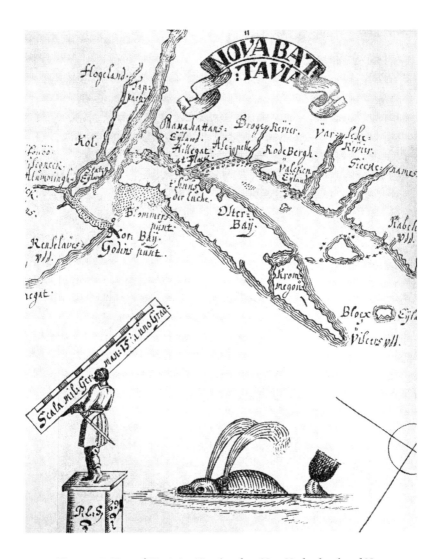

Figure 15. *Map of Virginia, New Sweden, New Netherland and New England, 1654-56, from Peter Lindeström,* Geographia Americæ.

"Next," according to Robert Evelyn, "is Eriwoneck (Ermomex) a king of forty men where we sat down."[239] Erwoneck is Arwawames Kill, now known as Little Timber Creek, where Evelyn settled (or "sat down") on the site of Fort Nassau. "The king of Ramcock (Rancocus) with a hundred men" resided five miles to the north.[240] Ramcock is identifiable as *Rancocus*, although Rancocus Creek is about fifteen miles north of Little Timber Creek. The king of Axion (Atsion) with two hundred men was to be found "four miles higher."[241] Lindeström's map of *Nova Suecia* places Assajüngh (Atsion) on the shore of the Delaware River, north of the outlet of Wirantapeck Kill, later known as Assiscunk Creek, at Burlington.[242] On another map, Lindeström uses the more recognizable form of Atsayans, which is presently Atsion. "Next" to the king of Axion, that is to say, "ten leagues [about thirty miles] over land an inland king of Calcefar with an hundred and fifty men" resided, perhaps upon the Mullica River between Atsion and Batsto.[243] Eighteen miles above the Atsayans, Evelyn told of "a creek called Mosilian, the king having two hundred men."[244] This creek was located south of the Falls of the Delaware River at present-day Trenton. The name of Mosilian Creek is otherwise unknown, unless it may be a far-fetched approximation of Matawang River, later known as the Millstone River.[245]

In summary, Robert Evelyn accounted "all the Indians to be eight hundred, and are in several factions…."[246] He enumerated about 790 warriors residing along the eastern shores of the Delaware, adding another 150 men under the inland king of Calcefar, for a total of 940 warriors. If the average family included five persons, then the entire native population of the area under consideration comprised roughly 4,700 people. During his residence upon the Delaware River, the various Algonquian river tribes were at "war against the Susquehannocks, and are all extreme fearful of a gun, naked and unarmed against our shot, swords, and pikes."[247]

THE IROQUOIAN CRESCENT

Iroquoian tribes occupied a vast crescent of territory extending between the head of tide on the Hudson River, the shores of the Great Lakes and the outlet of the Susquehanna River on Chesapeake Bay. During the second quarter of the eighteenth century, Cadwallader Colden composed *The History of the Five Indian Nations Depending on the Province of New-York in America*, painting a portrait of the Iroquois, which would shape perceptions of these people for subsequent generations. He began by telling a Cain-and-Abel type story of how the Algonquian-speaking Adirondacks, hunters by occupation, came into conflict with the corn-planting Iroquois after a period of peaceful commerce and friendship. At a time when game was scarce, a party of six Iroquois, hoping thereby to "acquire skill in hunting," joined a hunting party of Adirondacks.[248] Their hosts, who considered hunting a more noble pursuit than horticulture, became jealous of the success of the Iroquoian hunters and consequently killed them in their sleep. Angered by these murders, but fearful of the power of the Adirondacks, these Iroquois removed from their town near the present site of Montreal to the territory south of the St. Lawrence River. In 1660, Father Jerome Lalemant extracted from "the memory of their old men," that "toward the end of the last century, the Agnierronnons [Mohawks] were reduced so low by the Algonkins that there seemed to be scarcely any more of them left on earth."[249] This remnant, however, "like a noble germ, so increased in a few years as to reduce the Algonkins in turn."[250]

Such stories contrast the horticultural base of Iroquoian society with neighboring Algonquian hunters-and-gatherers. Gardening had been sufficiently long-standing and successful among the Iroquois to result in cultural traits and a social organization readily distinguishable from those who only harvested Nature's wild bounty. By the seventeenth century, the Iroquois may have practiced horticulture for as long as seven centuries. Yet, as a reminder of earlier ways, the Huron moon calendar still measured "the seasons of the year by the wild beasts, the fish, the birds, and the vegetation."[251]

Horticulture flowed from Meso-America along the Mississippi and its tributaries, and onto the shores of the Great Lakes. Domesticated plant foods sustained larger populations, which were better organized and often hierarchically directed, not only for efficient cultivation of their gardens, but also as protection against marauders. As in other times and places, headmen became hereditary chiefs and ceremonies marked the passage of the celestial bodies through the horticultural calendar. People congregated in fortified hilltop towns, hoarding great stores of crops. With a more adequate and reliable food base, rudimentary castes of craftsmen, warriors, priests and nobles developed. Coordinated task work not only fed a greater number of people, but it created a means and the time for building public works such as mounds, temples, fortifications and irrigation canals. The expansion of population and of land cleared for gardens depleted natural resources in the immediate vicinity of settlement, but it also created a surplus to trade for scarce commodities. The winter hunt remained a highly organized expedition into the snowy depths of the northern forest, capable of harvesting fifty or more deer in one communal drive. The aggression of the hunt was sometimes ritually channeled into warfare, wherein human prey were by some accounts captured, excruciatingly tortured and sacrificially consumed.

Societal evolution attained the formative stage of *statism*, as allied chiefdoms routinely met in consultative councils. In the long run, the success of the Iroquois may be attributed not to their ferocity but to their organizational skills. In 1635, Father Jean de Brebeuf reported, "some twelve other nations, all settled and numerous," besides the Hurons, spoke Iroquoian languages.[252] These included the Sonontoerrhonons, or Senecas, the Onontaerrhonons, also known as the Onondagas or "mountain people," the Ouioenrhonons, or Ohioans, the Onoiochrhonons, or Oneidas, the Agnierrhonons, also known as the Maquaas, Mengwe or Mohawks, and the Susquehannocks, also known as Minquas.[253]

Maquaas, or Mohawks, called themselves *Kajingahaga*. In 1625, they inhabited the Mohawk River above Albany. Their enemies, the Mahicans, drove them away from their fortified town near present-day Amsterdam, New York in 1626. The Mahicans considered the Maquaas a "deceitful race." For killing and devouring prisoners, they "were not considered by the Lenape as a pure race or as rational beings; but as a mixture of the human and brutal kinds."[254]

In December 1634, Jeronimus de la Croix, Willem Tomassen and Harmen Meyndertsz van den Bogaert, surgeon of Fort Orange, undertook an arduous westward journey along the Mohawk River toward the Oneidas' lands, located south of Oneida Lake. According to their journal, the Mohawks resided in four, fortified-hilltop, matriclan communities, called "castles," and in smaller villages situated along the Mohawk River. The first castle, or palisaded village, consisting of three-dozen bark-covered lodges arranged in rows similar to streets, was Onekagoncka.[255] It was situated on a high hill, a mile west of Schoharie Creek. Only women were then resident at the place, the men being absent on the winter hunt for deer, bear and turkeys. The longhouses were "full of corn," some storing as much as 300 bushels.[256] Great quantities of pumpkins were also baked and eaten. Continuing southwest along the Mohawk River toward the second castle, the Dutchmen passed two villages, namely, Conowarode, with its six longhouses, and Schatsyerosy with twelve longhouses. The second castle, called Canagere, was "built on a hill, without any palisades or any defense."[257] Sixteen longhouses stood here, together with "a good many graves."[258] Only old women and children were at home during the winter hunt. A tamed bear was being fattened at one of the lodges. The third castle, called Schanadisse, was situated on a very high hill surrounded by flatland. It enclosed thirty-two longhouses, each containing from four to six hearths.[259] Continuing westward, the nearly frozen travelers passed the riverside village of Osquage, with its nine longhouses, and the village of Cawaoge, with its fourteen longhouses, also situated on a very high hill, stood about three miles beyond Cawaoge.[260] Three rows of palisades, fallen into disrepair or removed for other purposes, once enclosed fifty-five longhouses, all stocked with corn and beans. Bear meat, beans and dried strawberries were offered in trade. Bread was baked with nuts, cherries, dried blueberries and sunflower seeds. In mock combat, opposing teams, outfitted with helmets and armor fashioned of braided reeds, jousted with clubs, sticks and axes. On their return trip through this locale on January 16, 1635, the Dutch emissaries followed "a very even footpath that had been made through the snow by the savages who had passed this way with much venison, because they had come home to their castle after hunting…."[261] Consequently, in some of the longhouses they saw "more than forty or fifty deer cut in quarters and dried…."[262]

Onneyuttehage, the Oneida town, was situated near Oneida Creek. On the outskirts, the Dutch travelers saw three graves, each surrounded by a palisade fence painted red, white and black. A chief's grave had an entrance surmounted by a large wooden bird and was painted all around with images of dogs, deer, snakes and other animals.[263] The Oneida castle, situated on a high hill, was circumscribed by two rows of palisades punctuated by gates facing east and west; the west gate being surmounted with "three big wooden images, carved like men," from which three scalps fluttered.[264] To the Dutch observers, the sixty-six longhouses within the walls were "much better, higher, and more finished" than they had seen at other Iroquoian settlements, and "a good many houses had wooden fronts that are painted with all sorts of beasts."[265] The people within slept on elevated boards. The visitors saw as many as six-dozen dried salmon, caught in the adjacent river, hanging from the rafters in some houses. The residents of Oneida castle mentioned two additional castles beyond their own, namely, Onondaga and Koyocke.

HURONS

According to Father Gabriel Sagard, a French Jesuit, the name of the Hurons was an approximation of *Ahouandâte*.[266] The Hurons' country, situated upon the eastern shores of Lake Huron, was "tolerably level, with many prairies, many lakes, many villages."[267] Here, from 1626 through 1639, about 30,000 people inhabited approximately twenty Huron villages with at least one village containing eighty longhouses and another, forty longhouses. The residences of the Hurons were "made of large sheets of bark in the shape of an arbor, long wise, and high in proportion; some of them are 70 feet long."[268] Their corn was reportedly "of the small sort, which ripens sooner than the other." Its kernels were small, but produced "more and better flour in proportion" and it began to ripen about the middle of August.[269] Hurons regulated "the seasons of the year by the wild beasts, the fish, the birds, and the vegetation; they count the year, days, and months by the moon."[270] The Attignaouantan, or Bear Nation, was considered the oldest and largest Huron matriclan, "having received into their country and adopted the others." They held the most southerly position; their principal village was called Teanaustaye.[271] Another important village was called Ihonatiria, located near the center of the Huron nation. The Arendarhonons were the easternmost Huron clan.[272]

In the spring of 1634, about 1,500 Senecas defeated an attacking party of nearly 500 Hurons, killing 200 and capturing more than 100.[273] On March 16, 1649, Mohawk and Seneca warriors destroyed one of the largest Huron villages. The Hurons then dispersed, some to Detroit, some among the Illinois, some to Three Rivers, and others to Quebec.[274] Huron survivors were known as *Ahouandâte*, or Wyandots.

THE SUSQUEHANNOCKS

According to John Smith's *Description of Virginia and Proceedings of the Colonie*, published in 1612, the Susquehannocks were a tribe of "great and well proportioned men ... like giants to the English," numbering "near 600 able and mighty men," who were "palisaded in their towns to defend them from the Massawomekes, their mortal enemies."[275] By Smith's account, the Massawomekes were a populous tribe who dwelt "beyond the mountains from whence is the head of the river Patawomeke [Potomac]... upon a great salt water, which by all likelihood is either some part of Commada [Canada], some great lake, or some inlet of some sea that falls into the South Sea [Gulf of Mexico]."[276] Smith's party of discoverers encountered seven bark canoes "full of these Massawomekes" at the head of Chesapeake Bay and found their material goods to be of superior manufacture to those of local tribes.[277] The name that Smith's native guide gave these boatmen was literally descriptive of the scene: *Massawomeke* or *mushwe-homwock* means, "those who come by canoe."[278] Several writers have previously assumed these Massawomekes to be a Mohawk raiding party, but more likely they were *Mannahoacks*, the collective name given to eight mountain tribes, five of whom were settled between the Potomac and Rappahannock Rivers and the other three between the Rappahannock and York Rivers.[279] As early as 1565, Indians conveyed bison skins down the Potomac River and along the shore in canoes to trade with the French.[280]

The French knew the Susquehannocks as *Andastogueronnons*, from the name of their chief town, *Andastes*, which was situated about two days' journey beyond the head of navigation at Smith's Falls on the Susquehanna River. However, it is uncertain just how long they resided there before Captain Smith's encounter in 1608. Some scholars claim that the Susquehannocks were driven from settlements on the North Branch of the Susquehanna, building their fortified village near Washington Boro, Pennsylvania, about 1580. Indeed, there is some circumstantial evidence to indicate a more northerly homeland at some time previous to 1608. First, they engaged in inveterate warfare against the Mohawks. Secondly, in October 1658, several Esopus sachems informed Director-General Stuyvesant, "the *Minquaes* [Susquehannocks] had told them, you are our subjects and have to submit to us or hide yourselves, as we also have to submit to the *Dutch* or hide."[281] Thirdly, Captain Smith noticed French trade goods among them. Lastly, the arrival of the English in the Chesapeake and the Swedes on the Delaware River provoked the Susquehannocks into regional wars to establish their dominion in the lower Susquehanna and Delaware Valleys. Peter Lindeström, Swedish engineer and cartographer, reported Susquehannocks "of two kinds, Black and White Minquas."[282] The Black Minquas lived further in the interior, or at least more distant to New Sweden than did the White Minquas. However, they must have resided fairly near the borders of Virginia or Maryland, because Lindeström, describing events in 1654-55, noted, "the English of Virginia carried on war against these Minquas."[283] Fifteen Englishmen were captured and cruelly tortured after an unsuccessful assault upon a palisaded village of Black Minquas. Their sachem wore a necklace strung with the severed fingers of these captives, and their severed toes were suspended from a string and worn around the knees. After the flesh rotted away, the bones were scraped clean and worn as ornaments "to show his great courage,—the greater skeleton bones these Minqua sachems carry, the braver warriors they are supposed to be."[284] The Minquas were also entirely covered with tattoos. In 1653, Adriæn van der Donck noted the Black Minquas were so called "because they wear a black badge on their breast."[285] This was possibly a polished slate pendant. In contrast, the White Minquas, or Susquehannocks, may have worn a shell pendant. In August 1749, Peter Kalm reported some Hurons wore "a large shell on the breast, of a fine white color, which they value very highly...."[286] In any event, the Black Minquas were one of the inland tribes, distant from tidewater European settlements, who, together with the Senecas, Mohawks, Adirondacks and Hurons, were principal suppliers of beaver peltries.[287] On July 10, 1643, inhabitants of Fort Christina testified that Black Minquas and other Indians appeared at the Swedish fort with hostile intentions but "ran into the woods with clamors" after a cannon was pointed at them.[288]

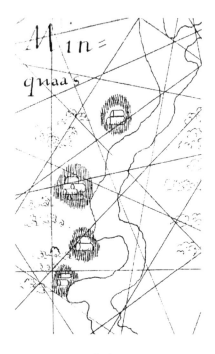

Figure 16. Detail, showing Minquaas' fortified villages on Susquehanna River, from the *Carte Figurative*, showing discoveries of Captain Cornelis Hendrickssen, dated August 18, 1614 and copied July 27, 1841 by P. H. Loffelt.

In 1614, the Susquehannocks, known to the Dutch as *Minquas*, were at war with the Mohawks. In that year— as previously noted—they captured three Dutchmen who assisted their enemies. In the spring of 1616, Captain Cornelis Hendrickssen, skipper of the *Onrest*, ransomed these three company agents.[289] In an attempt to reconcile his own coastal chart with the rescued prisoners' knowledge of the hinterland, Captain Hendrickssen noted, "that the places of the tribes of the Senecas, Gacheos, Capitanasses, and Jottecas ought to be marked down considerably farther west into the country." The tribes settled along the Susquehanna River were subsequently listed as the Minquaas, Capitanasses, Gacheos, Senecas, Canoe-makers (Caughnawaga), Konetotays and Matanackouses.[290] Susquehannocks occupied "only three villages, which are in the midst of more than twenty others, on which they make war without assistance from their friends; for they are obliged to pass through the thickly settled country of the Chouontouaroün [Ontarios, a name used by Champlain for the Seneca, Cayuga and Onondaga], or else they would have to make a very long circuit."[291]

In August 1615, the Hurons received word that 500 warriors of an allied nation planned to join them in an attack upon a palisaded Oneida village, situated south of Lake Oneida. Champlain sent one of his interpreters, Etienne Brûlé, to the strongly-palisaded town called Carantoüan, "which was provided with more than eight hundred warriors."[292] Some claim this town stood upon Spanish Hill, near the confluence of the Chemung River and the North Branch of the Susquehanna.[293] Some identify this "allied nation" as the Susquehannocks. Others contend they were Eries, also known as the Cat Nation, who resided southeast of Lake Erie. Unfortunately, this army was "very long in getting ready" and, although only three days' journey from their destination, arrived two days late for the battle.[294] Returning to Carantoüan, Brûlé spent the winter "exploring the country and visiting the tribes and territories adjacent to that place, and in making a tour along a river that debouches in the direction of Florida, where are many powerful and warlike nations, carrying on wars against each other." He eventually reached Chesapeake Bay.[295]

After their success against the Huron in 1649, the Mohawks and Seneca were again reduced, for the Susquehannocks and their allies "waged such energetic warfare against them during ten years that they were overthrown for the second time, and so humiliated that the mere name Algonkin made them tremble."[296] By this time, the Dutch began to furnish firearms "with which it was easy to conquer their conquerors" and "it has also put into their heads that idea of sovereign sway to which they aspire..."[297] Although the Mohawks did "not exceed five hundred men able to bear arms, who occupy three or four wretched villages," they were able, by 1660, to "hold dominion for five hundred leagues around."[298]

First Impressions

Most perceptive Europeans did not dismiss Indians as less human or less capable than themselves. On the contrary, those first upon the scene regarded North Americans "in their actions high-minded enough, vigorous and quick to comprehend or learn, be it right or wrong, whenever they are so inclined."[299] Peter Lindeström recognized "these Indians are people of various qualities," describing them as "quick, skillful in working with their hands, willing, clever and ready to learn and grasp a thing … a brave people, daringly revengeful; are eager for war, fearless, heroic ... have a good memory, are intimate in conversation, industrious and diligent, clever, charitable, wide awake, bold, inquisitive, patient and hardened to stand much hardship."[300] He also found them "a trustworthy and good-hearted folk, when they are not angered, and even brave-hearted [enough] to risk death for their good friends..."[301] As in every society, some were "very mischievous, haughty, … eager for praise, wanton, bestial, mistrustful, untruthful and thievish, dishonorable, coarse in their affections, shameless and unchaste."[302] But most possessed a great store of "reasonable understanding resulting from practical experience, which they certainly possess without any desire for further instruction; they are naturally civil and well disposed, and quick enough to distinguish between good and evil…."[303] Despite hardships, they consistently displayed a healthy sense of humor and "generally delight much in mirth."[304]

When interacting with strangers, Indians tended towards "taciturn, steady, and pensive dispositions and tempers, [using] few words, which are well considered, uttered slowly, and long remembered; they say no more than is necessary to the subject in hand."[305] By nearly all accounts,

Figure 17. Woodcut of couple and longhouse from David Pietersz deVries, *Korte Historiael, ende Journaels Aenteyckeninge van Verscheyden Voyagiens in de vier deelen des wereldts-ronde,* **Hoorn: Symon Cornelisz Brekegeest, 1655.**

they avoided "unnecessary chatter," being "serious and of few words..."[306] Astonishingly, they "never interrupt or contradict one another, 'till two of them have made an end of their discourse; for if ever so many be in company only two must discourse at a time, and the rest must keep silence."[307] They were described as so transparent and direct "that they cannot simulate, nor do they know of any deceit, but do not imagine that anything could pass from a man's tongue without coming from the heart."[308] Clarity, courtesy and exactitude marked their dealings with outsiders, since spokesmen represented the consensus of their community, reached privately through debate. Lacking a written language, they were careful to commit the terms of any agreement to memory.

Physically, Europeans regarded North Americans as "well proportioned ... varying little from the common size" with "broad shoulders and slender waists." They naturally varied in stature, some being "tall, some of them, medium, and some, short; a well proportioned people, slender and straight as a candle."[309] Their musculature was developed in conformity with their lifestyle and they were fast, enduring runners. Competing in races, Roger Williams claimed many Indians developed the ability to run eighty to a hundred miles on a summer's day. Consequently, they were "light and nimble of foot, subtle of mind," and generally "well adapted to travel on foot and to carry heavy burdens."[310] Most could also swim.[311] Lindeström thought them "strong in their arms, but very weak across their back, very agile and limber, running like horses...." He observed native hunters "so arm strong" that they could shoot a bow and arrow farther than any gun could reach. Embarrassingly, no European could defeat a native wrestler.

Physical fitness apparently contributed to superior health and long life. In 1750, descendants of the first Swedish planters along the Delaware River informed Peter Kalm that, at the time of the Europeans' arrival, Indians often lived to a very great age and "according to common accounts, it was not then unusual to find people among the Indians who were over a hundred years old."[312] They attributed this longevity to frugal living and drinking pure water. Birth deformities and infirmities from crippling diseases were rarely evident, perhaps because those so afflicted did not survive. Lunacy and mental retardation were absent, perhaps for the same reason. Until whitened with age, their hair was "jet black, sleek and uncurled, and nearly as coarse as a horse's tail." The native population boasted "fine brown eyes and snow-white teeth." Many admired how they kept "their teeth in a fine, white condition as long as they live."[313]

In March 1525, Verrazano described the natives of Wilmington Beach on Pleasure Island, near Cape Fear, North Carolina, saying, "They go nearly naked, wearing only about the loins some skins of small animals similar to the martens. A girdle of woven grass encircles the body, to which they fasten the tails of animals, which hang down as far as the knees. All the rest of the body is nude, as is also the head. Some of them wear drapery in like manner made of the feathers of birds."[314] A century later, Lindeström observed, "while the savages grow up they go quite naked, the very way they are born to this world, with the exception of the money they carry on themselves, knowing no shame...."[315] Despite their comparative lack of clothing, Indians were able to "withstand the cold, in fashion, and fear it little." Adriæn van der Donck marveled how they were "never overcome with the cold or injured by it." When the cold became especially bitter, they did "not pursue their customary pleasures, particularly the women and children; for the men do not care so much for the cold days in winter as they do for the hot days in summer."[316]

Verrazano described the sun burnt natives of the Outer Banks as "black, not very different from that of the Ethiopians. Their hair is black and thick, but not very long; it is worn tied back upon the head in the form of a little tail. In person they are of good proportion, of middle-stature, a little above our own, broad across the breast, strong in the arms, and well-formed in the legs and other parts of the body; the only exception to their good looks is that they have broad faces, but not all of them, for we saw many who had sharp ones, with large black eyes and a fixed expression. They are not very strong in body, but acute in mind, active and swift of foot as far as we could perceive by observation."[317] Proceeding up the coast to the Delmarva Peninsula, Verrazano found people "lighter colored than those past, dressed in certain grasses which grow, pendent from the branches of trees, which they weave with various ends of wild hemp. The head bared in the same form as the others."[318] He described a man who came down to the beach as "handsome, nude, with hair fastened back in a knot, of olive color." Later commentators thought their skin was nearly white, but tended to "yellowness ... caused by the heat of the scorching sun." Others described them as "bordering on an olive color."[319] Lindeström thought the Indians of Delaware Bay "of brownish color."[320]

Such differences of opinion and description are attributable not only to the normal range of human skin tones and to the seasonal effects of the sun, but also to the their custom of smearing "different kinds of grease" on skin and hair for protection against the elements.[321] Quaker Francis Pastorius intimated that natives "besmear their children with grease, and let them creep about in the heat of the sun, so that they become the color of a nut, although they were at first white enough by Nature."[322] This partly explains Gabriel Thomas's description of the Indians, published in 1698, as being "of complexion black, but by design, Gypsy-like, greasing themselves with bears'-fat clarified, and using no defense against the injuries of the sun and weather, their skins fail not to be swarthy."[323] In 1656, Van der Donck thought men greased their bodies with bear and raccoon fat "to defend themselves against the cold..."[324] When Indians from Staten Island first greeted Jasper Danckærts in 1679, he noted, "their hair hangs down from their heads in strings, well smeared with fat, and sometimes with quantities of little beads twisted in out of pride."[325] Reverend Johannes

Megapolensis claimed the Mohawks used bear's grease "to make their hair grow better and to prevent lice."[326] In July 1749, Peter Kalm noted how Indians near Crown Point prepared an oil from bear's fat, "with which in summer they daub their faces, hands, and all naked parts of their body, to secure them from the bite of gnats. With this oil they likewise frequently smear the body, when they are excessively cold, tired with labor, hurt, and in other cases. They believe it softens the skin and makes the body pliant and promotes longevity."[327] Naturally, to the European onlooker, they might appear "slovenly, careless, and dirty of persons, and are troubled with the evils which attend filthiness."[328]

Different pigments made from mineral and plant substances were "seen daily on the Indians, who understand their nature and use them to paint themselves in different colors." Because "the glossy metallic appearance" of mineral pigments possessed "the most brilliancy," these were held "in higher estimation than colors derived from herbs and plants."[329] Metallic pigments were "mostly made of stone, which they know how to prepare by pounding, rubbing and grinding."[330] The natives also used various plants to prepare "fine, lovely and bright colors." Juice from selected berries was sun-dried on flat slabs of bark about six feet long and three feet wide. Occasionally, smooth stones were heated and placed into the slabs of juice "to dry out the moisture speedily." They then scraped the dried pigment from the bark and placed it into small carrying bags. Colors such as red, blue, green, brown and yellow were stored separately in "small bags of paint." Animal fat was mixed in as an adhesive.[331] Such "beautiful colors of all kinds" were used in "their neat and artistically painted work of bird feathers, tobacco pipes and more such [things].[332]

Body paint was widely used by North Americans as an outward signification of the wearer's mood. Natives intentionally painted their faces "strangely with red or black lead, so that they look like fiends."[333] As late as 1749, Peter Kalm saw Hurons using red body paint, although some daubed their faces with black.[334] Most observers thought black represented grief and red represented joy, but European cultural bias may have been a factor in their interpretation.[335] Many natives ornamented themselves with tattoos by "cutting their bodies or painting them with various colors, sometimes even all black, if they are in mourning, yet generally in the face."[336] On the other hand, young men and women of courting age identified their availability by painting "a few black stripes on their faces," which can hardly be construed as signs of grief.[337] In 1626, Father Charles L'Alemant described the practice of the Montagnais and related tribes of eastern Canada, saying, "There were some whose noses were painted blue, the eyes, eyebrows, and cheeks painted black, and the rest of the face red; and these colors are bright and shining like those of our masks; others had black, red and blue stripes drawn from the ears to the mouth. Still others were entirely black; except the upper part of the brow and around the ears, and the end of the chin, so that it might have been truly said of them that they were masquerading. There were some who had only one black stripe, like a wide ribbon, drawn from one ear to the other, across the eyes, and three little stripes on the cheeks."[338]

Peter Lindeström considered tattooing a form of ritual bloodletting. On the first evening of a long march, upon striking camp, an Indian made fire. Taking "a piece of flint as long as a finger, which he has prepared and fitted for this purpose, sharp as a razor, with this he cuts himself all over his body into the deepest flesh, on his arms, thighs and legs, the depth of a finger, according to the depth of the flesh, deeper or less, standing before the fire to shake off the blood, which runs off him, as if one had butchered an ox. When he has allowed as much blood to run off as he thinks proper, then he takes a kind of ointment, which he smears over his body, wherever he has cut himself. Before morning, it is healed and run together and blue streaks remain after it just as when one burns oneself with powder, wherefore the savages appear entirely striped and streaky and especially the Minquas ... When now the savage has thus removed some blood, he may march and run as fast and as far as he wants to, he will not tire."[339] Many Hurons had "figures on the face and on the whole body, which are stained into the skin, so as to be indelible ... These figures are commonly black; some have a snail [that is, a spiral figure] painted on each cheek, some have several crosses, some an arrow, others the sun, or anything else their imagination leads them to. They have such figures likewise on the breast, thighs and other parts of the body; but some have no figures at all."[340]

Kalm's *En Resa til Norra America* (*Journey to North America*) includes a description of how Indians painted "various designs on their bodies and that these are put on in such a way that they remain as long as the natives live." Kalm did not recall seeing any other color than black used in tattoos, but men who accompanied him said they also used a red dye, made from cinnabar or vermilion, a toxic mercury sulfide collected from hot paint springs. Black dye was made from the cooled charcoal of an alder tree, which they pulverized by rubbing it between their hands. The artist mixed this powder with water, allowing it to become saturated. The design for the tattoo was first sketched on the body with a piece of charcoal. They then dipped a needle into the prepared dye and pricked the skin, carefully following the lines of the charcoal outline. They wet the tip of the needle in the dye between every puncture, thereby embedding the color under the skin. When the wound healed, the colored design was permanent. Men found the puncturing process "rather painful, but the smart gradually diminishes and at the expiration of a day the smart and pain has almost ceased."[341]

In 1642, David De Vries reported, "their clothing is a coat of beaver-skins over the body, with the fur inside in winter and outside in summer; they have, also, sometimes a bear's hide, or a coat of the skins of wildcats, or *hesspanen* [raccoon]."[342] Bear hides were made into "doublets; while others have coats made of the skins of raccoons, wildcats, wolves, dogs, otters, squirrels, beavers and the like, and also of turkey's feathers."[343] Swedish colonists reported, "that the Indians formerly dyed all sorts of leather with the bark of the chestnut oak."[344] In 1656, Adriæn van der Donck saw "clothing made of weasel, bear, deer, and buffalo skins, &c."[345] In warm weather, they went "almost naked, except a lap which hangs before their private parts, and on the shoulders a deer skin or a mantle, a fathom square, of woven turkey feathers or peltries sewn together."[346] De Vries also observed "coats of turkey's feathers, which they know how to plait together."[347] Most observers described a winter covering of "dressed deer skin; some have a bear's skin about the body; some a coat of scales; some a covering made of turkey feathers which they understand how to knit together very oddly, with small strings."[348] To produce such beautiful mantles, old men tied painted feathers to a net of very fine mesh, so neatly and strongly that the feathers would sooner break off than come loose.[349] The feathers were attached to basswood strips and "so arranged that the brilliant surface formed the outside of the dress."[350]

Father Charles L'Alemant, Superior of the Missions of Canada, met with Montagnais and other Algonquians of the Maritime Provinces in Tadoussac, at the outlet of the Saguenay River, in 1626. He observed men in warm weather wearing only "a piece of skin which falls from just below the navel to the thighs." In winter, they covered themselves with furs "of the beaver, bear, fox, and other animals of the same kind, but so awkwardly, that it does not prevent the greater part of their bodies from being seen." Some wore a bear fur, with the hair on the outside, draped "under one arm, and over the other, hanging down to the knees. They were girdled around the body with a cord made of dried intestine. Some are entirely dressed." Women were "decently covered; they wear skins fastened together on their shoulders with cords; these hang down from the neck to the knees." They also girdled themselves with a cord.[351]

Duffel, a heavy woolen fabric used for overcoats, quickly replaced animal skins after European contact, serving as blanket by night and dress by day. Woven cloth was considered "better for the rain."[352] Once available, men and women started wearing "a plaid [a rectangular blanket worn as a cloak] of duffels cloth of full breadth, and three ells long [about ten feet] ... over the right shoulder, drawn in the form of a knot about the body, with the ends extending down below the knees."[353]

Shoes and stockings were prepared from deerskins, made soft by continually being worked in their hands, or occasionally, for winter wear, from buffalo skins traded from distant tribes. Sometimes they curiously ornamented their moccasins with wampum.[354] Lindeström mentions "sippackor or laced shoes of deer skin, bordered and decorated with their money." The Sawanoos, or Southern Lenape, used a shortened form, sippack or shi pak, when referring to shoes. Northern Algonquian speakers, including the Minisinks, apparently used machtsin, a contraction of matchschipak, from which the word moccasin is derived. The Mohawks made cornhusks into lightweight shoes and sacks, but these were not very durable.[355]

Coastal artisans worked "great cockles" or periwinkles into white and black sewan beads for personal jewelry and for use as currency.[356] They either harvested conch shells from the sea or gathered them twice yearly when they washed ashore "in very great numbers." Sewan, also called wampum, was made by striking off the thin part of the shell, preserving "the pillars or standards, which they grind smooth and even and reduce the same according to their thickness, and drill a hole through every piece and string the same on strings."[357] Each oblong bead was "about the length of a wheat kernel and somewhat thicker; but the largest, as thick as a thick straw, and the length in proportion to their thickness; larger or smaller, they are not used."[358] The beads were ground or polished very smooth, even on the ends, and had a copper-colored streak, "which the kernel by nature contains...."[359] Beads were valued not only for their individual color, but also for their workmanship. Indians would not accept beads with worn or broken edges that did not "fall close together on the cord" and tested strings of wampum by stroking the whole cord of beads over the nose to see if it glided smoothly, without imperfections.[360]

According to Roger Williams, white mollusk-shell beads, which the natives made from the stems of the *meteauhock*, were called *wampum*, which signifies "white," while "black, inclining to blue" or purple beads, made from the shell of the *poquauhock*, an Atlantic surf or hen clam (*Spisula solidissima*), were known as *Suckauhock*, from the root word, *sacki*, meaning "black." The Dutch preferred the Algonquian word, *sewan*, for wampum, which derived from the word for "loose," referring to unstrung beads counted out by hand. In 1700, Pastorius described sewan as "oblong corals, ground out of sea-mussels, sometimes white and sometimes light brown, and fastened on strings."[361] Seashells used to make sewan were chiefly white, except for a pointed end of violet color; this dark purple part of the shell produced the so-called "black" sewan. Hurons wore necklaces of violet wampum, interspersed with the white variety, "made of the shells which the English call clams (*Venus mercenaria* L.)."[362] The Renappi also manufactured blue-black and white beads. The Black and White Minquas, otherwise known as Susquehannocks, were said to have made a red sewan.[363]

Peter Lindeström described sewan as "oblong stones, with holes drilled through them, and threaded on strings, that they can be measured by fathoms according to their value and use."[364] It served for "native money."

Thousands of wampum strings "were exchanged every year for peltries near the seashores where the wampum is only made."[365] The valuation of sewan was measured "by the hand or by the fathom."[366] In December 1648, each fathom of wampum consisted of three ells, some one-sixteenth less.[367] Lindeström stated that a *styver's* worth, or exactly six beads of white wampum, was counted "by a certain measure from the end of the thumb nail to the first joint of the thumb."[368] Six beads of red or black-blue sewan were worth two *styvers*, exactly double the value of white beads. In New Netherland in 1656, black sewan was reportedly "worth more by one half than the white."[369] In New Sweden, the red and black-blue sewan were "valued in the place of gold; three of these stones are worth one *styver* or one *öre* silver money."[370] In 1700, twelve brown sewan were "worth as much as twenty-four of the white pieces..."[371] Special craftsmen were designated to turn and grind the shell money, one person producing not more than about six to eight *styvers* worth a day.[372]

Strung "in a very artistic way," Indians wore shell beads "in the place of gold chains," in head bands, as earrings, necklaces or bracelets, "wherewith after their manner they appear very fine."[373] Sachems would wear "a crown or hood of it."[374]

Also in the way of personal decoration, long, coarse and stiff strands of deer hair were tied into bundles with small bands and fashioned into "rings for the head, and other fine hair of the same color" was hung from the neck "like tresses."[375] Indians dyed deer hair "a beautiful scarlet." One European observer thought these braided headdresses of "soft shining red hair" made them "appear like the delineations and paintings of the Catholic saints."[376] Males also wore such elaborate headgear, but only when "they have a young female in view."[377]

Both men and women used tobacco "with pleasure."[378] They smoked it at home, while playing "a game with pieces of reeds, resembling our card playing."[379] Commonly, the coarse skin of the skunk, with its long hair, was made into tobacco pouches, "which they carry before them."[380] Lindeström described the use of "tobacco pipes an ell in length, which are screwed together with leather, to lean on, and in these pipe-heads will go a handful of tobacco." He reported, "Very neat tobacco pipes with all kinds of birds and animals on the pipe head, very beautifully painted and glazed."[381] One of these pipes was placed in the mouth of a corpse at the time of burial, which had a "head of green or black stone."

Unfamiliar with tobacco pipes and their use in welcoming strangers, Verrazano and a landing party of twenty crewmen attempted to approach a young man, who fearfully backed away, "showing a burning stick as if to offer us fire."[382] When the European sailors "made fire with powder and flint-and-steel … he trembled all over with terror." When Verrazano shot off a gun, the young man "stopped as if astonished and prayed, worshipping like a monk, lifting his finger toward the sky, and pointing to the ship and the sea he appeared to bless us." His gesture suggests he regarded the gunshot as thunder.

THE CIRCUIT OF SEASONS

While a colonial farmer might support his family with the produce of twenty improved acres of land, each Indian counterpart required six hundred acres to provide sufficient animal and plant food for his sustenance.[383] Peter Kalm, investigating Indian manners from the accounts of the oldest Swedish settlers of the Delaware Valley, concluded, "The corn, some varieties of beans, and melons, comprised almost the whole of the Indian agriculture and gardening; and dogs were the only domestic animals in North America. But as their agriculture and their gardening were very trifling, and they could hardly live two months in a year upon their produce, they were forced to resort to hunting and fishing, which at that time, and even at present [1749], furnish their chief subsistence; and they also in part had to rely on the products of plants and trees."[384] Kalm later confirmed the Indians "lived chiefly by hunting and fishing, and had hardly any agriculture. They planted corn and some species of beans and pumpkins; and at the same time it is certain that a plantation of such vegetables as serve an Indian family during one year take up no more ground than a farmer in our country [i.e., Sweden] takes to plant cabbage for his family. At least a farmer's cabbage and turnip ground, taken together, is always as extensive, if not more so, than all the cornfields and kitchen gardens of an Indian family. Therefore, the Indians could hardly subsist for one month upon the produce of their gardens and fields. Commonly, the little villages of the Indians are about twelve or eighteen miles distant from each other." Given the small extent of their horticulture, "fish and meat constitute a very large part of their food."[385]

Community was purely an expression of kinship, and very few people married out of their own tribes.[386] Subsistence tasks were assigned according to age and gender. The diet of hunters-and-gatherers was "meat, and fish of every kind, according to the seasons, and the advantages of the places where they reside." They depended upon the flora and fauna "that is fit for food, which the country and the places of their settlements afford, and that they can obtain."[387] As Verrazano first observed in March 1525, "There were also many signs, which led us to suppose that the inhabitants often sleep in the open air without any covering but the sky."[388] Of the original inhabitants of Narragansett Bay, he further said, "They change their habitations from place to place, as circumstances of situation and season may require. This is easily done, for they have only to take with them their mats, and they have other houses immediately prepared. There live in each a father and family to a very large number, so that in some we saw 25 and 30 souls."[389] Likewise, in September 1609, Henry Hudson observed Aquamachuques along the shore of Raritan Bay "had no houses, but slept under the blue heavens, some on mats of bulrushes interwoven, and some on the leaves of trees." These people "always carry with them all their goods, as well as their food and green tobacco, which is strong and good for use."[390] Johannes De Laet summarized the observations of early mariners, noting some natives led "a wandering life in the open air with no settled habitations; lying stretched upon the ground or on mats made of bulrushes, they take both their sleep and food, especially in summer, when they go nearer to the sea for the sake of fishing." Van der Donck also saw natives lying "under the open sky or little better" during hunting and fishing seasons. By his observation, they did "not live long in one place, but move about several times in a year, at such times and to such places as it appears best and easiest for them to obtain subsistence."[391] Peter Lindeström recorded the Renappi habit of winter domesticity and summer nomadism, writing, "During the summer they have no certain dwellings, but move about here and there around the country. However, in

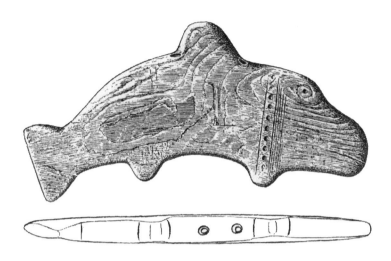

Figure 18. Shell Pååhra or fish totem, from George G. Heye and
George H. Pepper, *Exploration of a Munsee Cemetery near Montague,
New Jersey*, New York: The Museum of the American Indian, 1915.

the fall each and every sachem has a house built for himself, which he and
his subjects can live in during the winter, and during the summer they
sing with the rabbit [and make a house] in every bush."[392] On extended
stays at resource stations, Indians erected "temporary huts or shanties"
rather than their more permanent dwellings.[393] For those inclined to
live in fortified villages, notably the Iroquois, the Dutch observed how
they "seldom leave altogether" their "castles" and large towns, but moved
frequently "from other situations," locating near ponds, lakes and rivers
in summer and in fishing season, but retiring to the woods and hunting
grounds in fall and winter.

The first moon after the end of February marked the start of a
New Year and its arrival was occasion for a great festival. In spring and
for part of the summer, families erected temporary huts at their fishing
and hunting camps, where women tended their crops in small clearings
and gathered wild plant foods.[394] Surrounding brushwood provided a
communal hunting ground. Using nothing more than a small, sharp stone

or deer scapula for tillage, women began to break up the earth in small clearings at the end of March.[395] They scraped the soil into square mounds resembling molehills, set about two-and-a- half feet apart, so that a person could easily walk and weed between them.[396] About six grains of corn were planted in each mound in April, when the earth had warmed. After the maize grew to the length of a finger or more by the middle of May, the women planted three or four Turkish beans in each mound, which then grew up the growing cornstalks like a beanpole. Pulled weeds were "drawn round the corn hills" to provide mulch and to suppress weeds. Since the stalks and husks matched the colors of the "white, red, blue, flesh-colored, brown, yellow and spotted ears," mature corn patches were quite a splendid sight.[397]

From March through June, fishermen harvested smelt, shad, striped bass, white salmon, herring and sturgeon. The best fishing places were located at the first falls marking the head of tides, where natives closed the creek with a *kassanoor* or fish weir.[398] These were constructed when the water was low by either planting a brush fence, woven of intertwining twigs, in the sand bottom, or by securely attaching a net to posts, forming a V, pointing downstream. They then piled stones in a low wall on both sides of the net or brush fence so that fish swimming along the bottom encountered this obstacle and were guided into a central purse or wickerwork trap. Above the purse, a wooden figure resembling the *Manito* was fixed as a bob to signal a catch.[399]

Fish were trapped behind the weir in low water at ebb tide, allowing fishermen to either catch them with their hands or pierce them with spears or arrows.[400] Some accounts describe fishermen making a downstream sweep from a point about a mile above the weir, using a rope woven of wild vines, which stretched across the stream, whereon boughs about six feet in length were attached. Moving slowly with the current, with some guiding the ends of the rope and others supporting it in the middle with wooden forks, they frightened the fish into the purse in the middle of the weir. Other fishermen stood along the two angles of the weir, driving fish into the opening "with poles and a hideous noise."[401] Weirs could catch one or two hundred eels in a single tide.

Wild hemp, a perennial species of Dogbane found on sandy riverbanks, fields and thickets, was spun into netting.[402] Nets, some measuring up to 40 feet long, were set in rivers on brush or sticks, 6 to 9 feet deep. Stone sinkers weighed the net down, and sticks, about a yard long, round and sharp at the end, were attached for floats.

Harpoon fishing was done from canoes at night. An oarsman sat at the stern, while the harpoonist stood at the prow with a bark or split pine torch, searching for his prey. Eels were pierced by harpoon and thrown into the boat.[403] These long fish were then split up the back for cleaning, the heads and tails removed, and the remainder cut with numerous slits "so that the smoke may thoroughly penetrate them." They were hung from poles in the houses.[404] Otherwise, fishermen shot fish in deep water with a bow and arrow, or caught them on hooks made of bone or bird's claws.[405] Sun drying or smoking was used to preserve great quantities of striped bass and other fish.

Large oyster beds lined the estuaries of the Hudson and Delaware Rivers, and coastal communities used oysters and other shellfish for their chief food source. The soft meat was removed from the shell and hung to dry in the sun. European colonists in the Hudson Valley remarked upon the immense piles of oyster and mussel shells "made formerly by the savages, who subsist in part by that fishery," which readily identified "the places where it is certain that the Indians formerly built their huts."[406] On occasion, small mountains of discarded shells were even found several miles from the sea, left by natives who consumed their contents in great numbers. As late as 1750, the descendants of these former coastal communities returned to the oyster banks to catch this favored food, in order to sell it to inland tribes.[407]

Contrary to popular imagination, the primeval forest was not dark and dense, but rather open woodland with a great deal of high grass underfoot.[408] This was not entirely a natural condition, but rather the outcome of human interference. By the middle of July, high bushes covered much of the land, making passage impracticable. The natives made it a yearly custom to burn "the woods, plains and meadows in the fall of the year, when the leaves have fallen, and when the grass and vegetable substances are dry."[409] Such brush burning served several purposes: it cleared vegetation from the hunters' path, making walking easier and allowing them to stalk prey quietly without "the crackling of dry substances" underfoot to alert and frighten animals.[410] Furthermore, brush burning improved and rejuvenated vegetative growth during the ensuing spring. This early form of woodland management favored deer, which fed upon the regrowth. Women observed how the strong young shoots of high-bush blueberry, which spring up after a fire, bore large sweet berries.[411] Lastly, fire was used "to circumscribe and enclose the game within the lines of the fire, when [the game animal] is more easily taken, and also, because the game is more easily tracked over the burned parts of the woods."[412] The fire did not usually kill green trees, but rather scorched only the outside bark to a height of three or four feet above ground. In thick pinewoods, however, the blaze often ascended to the treetops, creating a firestorm fueled by wind, dry needles and resin. Places unaffected by the autumn brush burning were "fired in the spring in April."[413]

The spring hunt began as soon as the grass was dry. A sachem arranged his kinfolk in a huge circle. Each person rooted up the grass around him to create a fire-break, then the dry grass was ignited "so that the fire travels away, in towards the center of the circle, which the Indians follow with a great noise, and all the animals which are found within the circle, flee from the fire and the cries of the Indians, traveling away, whereby the circle through its decreasing is more and more contracted towards the center." The enclosing ring of hunters opened fire on the penned animals with their bows and arrows while they were still at a safe distance from each other "and thus they get a great multitude of all kinds of animals which are found there."[414] Another stratagem used in hunting deer was to drive herds into water where men in boats easily dispatched the swimming animals.[415] Sachems organized the "general hunt" for deer with "a hundred more or less joining in the hunt." Much like communal fire drives, those selected to be drivers stood about a hundred paces apart, beating flat thigh bones with a stick, driving deer before them into the river. Drivers steadily closed ranks as they approached the river "and whatever is between any two of them, is at the mercy of their bows and arrows, or must take to the river."[416] Hunters in canoes tossed a lasso around an animal's neck, tightening it until the animal suffocated.[417] Despite the loss

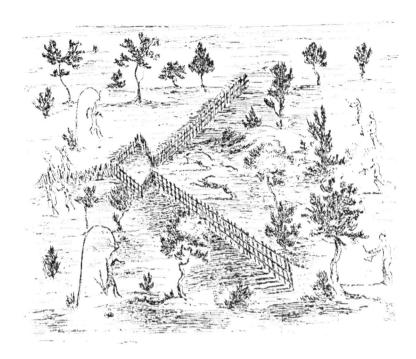

Figure 19. Hunting drive with fyke and snares from David Pietersz deVries, *Korte Historiael, ende Journaels Aenteyckeninge van Verscheyden Voyagiens in de vier deelen des wereldts-ronde*, Hoorn: Symon Cornelisz Brekegeest, 1655.

of many thousands annually to predation by wolves and hunters, deer remained incredibly numerous.[418]

Other species were also used as game. Native hunters esteemed the flesh of black bear, especially the forequarters, plucks (various internal organs) and thick layer of fat "as a great dainty."[419] Left to their wilderness ways, black bears subsisted on grass, herbs, wild grapes and berries, fattening in fall upon acorns and chestnuts. They retired into the mountains for their winter hibernation, seeking shelter in a burrow under projecting rocks or in a thick, brushy wood where large trees had fallen. In springtime, bears were caught in traps, but the greatest numbers were killed in winter when they were groggy and defenseless.[420] According to Van der Donck, bear hunters "dress themselves as Esau did, in clothes which have the flavor of the woods…that they may not be discovered by their smell."[421]

With careful study of their habits and habitats, grey foxes, raccoons, ground hogs, skunks, squirrels, rabbits, otters, beavers, muskrats and minks were hunted with nets, snares, arrows or darts.[422] With the exception of mink, all were eaten.[423] Night-rambling raccoons sheltered in hollow trees, stealing fruit, corn and eggs under cover of darkness.[424] Before being hunted to near extinction for their peltry, native hunters used traps, dogs or clubs to kill beavers for their meat and skin.[425] Muskrats, with shining blackish-brown fur, nested in twig beds in dens on the banks of lakes, brooks and rivers, the entrances littered with mussel shells.[426] Minks spent their days in hollow trees along riverbanks, feeding at night upon fish, birds and small rodents.[427] Porcupines made dens beneath large rock outcrops, and were caught by dogs or in traps, especially when snow hindered their movement.[428] Skunks were carefully skinned, to remove the scent glands, before the meat was cooked. Prepared with the hair on it, skunk skin was used to make tobacco pouches.[429] Humans were not the only hunters. Wolves were numerous, preying upon small animals, especially fawns. They hunted individually and in packs of eight to ten members, especially in winter.[430] Mountain lions, short-tailed American wildcats and the tree-climbing lynx were also skilled predators.[431]

Every spring and fall, migratory waterfowl alighted in great flocks upon coastal marshes, in woodlands, upon river meadows and inland lakes. Early commentators mention geese, herons, cranes, teal, ducks, widgeons, whistlers, bitterns, swans, cormorants, divers, coots and pelicans.[432] Innumerable birds also filled the woods with their whistling, fluttering and chattering.[433] The most important games species were turkeys, quail, grouse, woodcock, whip-poor-will, pigeons and blackbirds. Native hunters shot or knocked down ravens, eagles, buzzards and hawks and hunted small birds such as finches, chirping birds, wrens, sparrows, orioles, hummingbirds and blue jays.[434] Arrows, darts and snares were used for bird hunting.[435]

Wild turkeys, weighing from twenty to forty pounds each, roamed the countryside in large woodland flocks.[436] Turkeys could only fly "one or two thousand paces, and then fall down, tired of flying, when they are taken by the savages with their hands, who also shoot them with bows and arrows."[437] Commonly hunted in winter, after they fattened upon the autumn mast of the forest floor, large, long-legged turkey cocks proved "extraordinarily fast" runners. Even though deprived of the power of sustained flight, they could not be caught "unless their legs are hit also."[438] Consequently, upon the approach of winter, Indians set snares along brooks and small runs of water, using the bulbous roots favored by turkeys as bait. Some turkeys were "caught by dogs in the snow."[439] Habitually roosting in trees, many were shot at night. Some natives kept tamed turkeys near their huts.[440]

Great coveys of Northern Bobwhites fed upon grass seeds at the forest edge, roosting in trees and nesting in spring under bushes or openly on hilltops. When startled, they rose from their concealment in thickets, swamps or woods.[441] They were hunted with rods and sticks, or shot from their roosts. Ruffed Grouse were once prolific in the Highlands of New York and New Jersey, living in pairs or small coveys, and favoring wooded uplands where pine, hemlock and other evergreens predominated. In early May, females lay eight to fourteen eggs in a leaf-lined nest at the base of a tree, stump or decaying log.[442] Ruffed Grouse feed upon the seeds of wild grapes, chestnuts and woodland berries. Since these small partridges produce a roaring noise when fanning their wings as they rise, early writers called them *drummers*.[443]

The mud snipe or woodcock is a migratory woodland bird of nocturnal habit. Arriving here in earliest spring, sometimes in February, they nest on the ground in secluded woodland, emerging from the protective cloak of the forest only after twilight to feed at springs and streams. Flocks descend upon riverside marshes and open meadows in July, probing the soil with their long bills in search of worms and grubs. Great autumn migrations of woodcock cross the Delaware Bay from Cape May to Green Creek in late October and early November.[444]

Named for their unusual nightly whistle-calls, a covey of Whip-poor-will could raise "a great noise in the woods" at twilight and at dawn. A nocturnal hunter, the Whip-poor-will flies near the ground among low bushes. At night, it pecks insects from the bark of fallen timber, but is expert in darting after winged insects, supposedly hunting along steep, brushy stream banks. In daylight, it retires to well-wooded high ground.[445] The female lays a pair of eggs in an open field on a woodland edge, nesting in dead leaves. Migratory, Whip-poor-wills arrive in April and depart for the tropics in early September. Certain New Jersey Indians claimed "that these birds, which are restless and utter their plaintive note at night, are the souls of their ancestors who died in battle."[446]

Pigeons were so astonishingly numerous during spring and fall migrations "that they resemble the clouds in the heavens and obstruct the rays of the sun."[447] Prodigious flocks roosted in the forest from the middle of April to the end of May, feasting successively upon the ripened seeds of red maple, elm and the edible kernels of beechnut.[448] At this time, groups of several hundred natives would gather at these breeding places, "where they live a month or more on the young pigeons, which they take, after pushing them from their nests with poles and sticks."[449] Pigeons were either shot on the wing, on the ground and from their roosts in trees.

Large flocks of blackbirds made their "appearance at harvest when the corn is ripe."[450] Swedish naturalist Peter Kalm distinguished two very different species of "corn thieves" that were commonly confused because "there is so great a friendship between them that they frequently accompany each other in mixed flocks." The purple grackle flies north in the latter part of March to construct mud-and-grass nests in tall cedar or pine trees, feeding upon worms, grubs and caterpillars in swamps and meadows. As soon as they spy the green blade of a corn stalk, they descend and pull up the seed. They also tear away the husk of ripening corn and consume the kernels. Grackles return south in November. Red-Winged Blackbirds return from their winter haunts in the south during the last week of March to nest in bushes, high grass or upon the ground. They scratch out corn kernels from the earth and uproot tender sprouts. Their young begin to fly about the middle of August, feeding wherever possible upon ripening corn, tearing away the husks and greedily consuming the kernels. They were said to "assemble by thousands in the corn fields and exact a heavy tax." Bowmen were posted around maize fields to destroy the plunderers. Blackbirds were considered good eating. Crows were also known to scratch corn kernels from the earth after planting, and to greedily consume ripened grain. The Red-headed Woodpecker likewise pecked ripe ears of corn.[451]

Women seasonally gathered several varieties of wild fruits and greens, including wild gooseberry and currants, strawberries, raspberries, cranberries and Angelica. By the middle of July, those residing along the upper Delaware River harvested berries from small, creeping bushes with strong, flexible stems, growing close to the ground. These berries were black when ripe, with a small pit.

A harvest festival celebrated the new moon of August. At this time, Indians pulled up any cornstalks that produced no ears and sucked out the sap or syrup, "which is as sweet as if it were sugar-cane." Corn and beans thrived in each other's company and the two crops were harvested from the end of September through the beginning of October.[452] Women beat the ripened beans out of the pod with a stick.[453] Boiled beans were served in a gourd bowl.[454]

A mature cornstalk produced half a dozen ears of corn, each between six and nine inches in length.[455] Ears of dried corn were rubbed between the hands to strip off the kernels. To prepare maize for bread or for a porridge called *sappaen*, the kernels were boiled and then beaten flat upon a stone. This mash was next "put into a wooden mortar, which they know how to hollow out by fire, and then they have a stone pestle, which they know how to make themselves, with which they pound it small, and sift it through a small basket, which they understand how to weave of the rushes..." These small baskets, called *notassen*, were woven of wild hemp "so neatly that they serve them as sieves."[456] The finest cornmeal was mixed with lukewarm water, kneaded into dough and fashioned into small round cakes about an inch thick. Sometimes nuts, cherries, dried blueberries and sunflower seeds were admixed. Corn cakes were wrapped in a grape or corn leaf and buried in hot ashes. After baking, hot corn cakes were washed in clean water to rinse away ashes.[457] Sappaen, made from the coarsest grade of cornmeal, was their daily fare. Whatever the time of day, visitors to a native lodge would see sappaen either being prepared or consumed. Mixing in "small beans of different colors" made it "a dainty dish" for special occasions. Dried fish or meat, pounded fine, was frequently boiled with it "at the close of winter and in the spring, when the hunting season is past, and their stock of provisions is nearly exhausted."[458]

Requiring "little or no cultivation," pumpkins grew "among the maize." In the latitude of New Jersey, they ripened about the end of July, and were eaten either boiled whole or roasted in ashes. To preserve them for future consumption, women "cut them in long slices which they fasten or twist together and dry either in the sun or by the fire in a room." These dried strips kept for years, and were often boiled before eating; sometimes they were eaten dried with meat.[459]

Squashes derive their name from the Algonquian word, *quaasiens*. According to botanist Peter Kalm, writing in 1749, "The natives plant more squashes than common pumpkins." They came in a rainbow of colors and shapes, being described as "oblong, round, flat or compressed, crooknecked, small, etc." They were planted in the middle of April, growing well on "newly broken woodland when it is somewhat cleared and the weeds removed."[460] Often, Indians did not wait for squashes to ripen, but gathered them when the vegetable "attained a certain size," sometimes as early as the first of June, and placed them immediately on the fire for cooking. Otherwise they ripened in September, but could only be eaten for a month or two, after which the shell hardened and the pulp decayed.[461] Squashes were commonly boiled, then mashed into porridge.

Native gardeners raised cucumbers and gourds. Calabash vines were planted, producing "a kind of round [thing] like the figure of a pear, as large as the largest pumpkin, yeas, some as small as tobacco houses or boxes." These calabashes, or *bottle gourds*, were "yellow inside and out, shine and are smooth as glass, thin as glass, hard and tough as horn, so that even if they fall on the floor, they will not break." After the seeds had been dug out, the hard shell served as a "fine vessel," and could also be cut apart "for bowls, flasks or cups..." Some were capable of holding one-and-a-half to two gallons of liquid.[462]

Indians planted melons on newly cleared woodland, freed from weeds. They were "quite sweet and pleasant to taste…" Watermelons, native to Africa, grew "more rapidly and in greater abundance than melons, so much so that some plant them…for the purpose of clearing and bringing into subjection the wild undressed land to fit it for cultivation." They ordinarily grew to the size of a man's head," having either a red or white spongy pulp within their rinds.

For winter rations, shelled corn was stored in baskets woven from rushes or wild hemp, and buried in holes lined with mats, enabling North Americans to "keep as much as they want for the winter and while hunting." Families departed their houses in October for the fall hunt, leaving their store of buried grain in the care of the elderly until their return in December.[463] Storage pits, seldom "deeper than a fathom (that is, about six feet) and often not so deep," were lined with pieces of bark or wild grass. Corn was thrown into the hole, covered "a considerable thickness with this grass" and then covered over with earth. The "corn kept extremely well in those holes, and each Indian had several such subterraneous stores, where his corn lay safe, though he traveled far from it."[464] Eyewitness Peter Lindeström noted these larder pits were dug "down in the ground, close to their dwellings, wherein they have their maize, their beans, tobacco and other provisions, such as deer-meat, elk-meat, bear-meat, birds, fish and other such things which may serve for the sustenance of man...."[465] Having stored their harvest, women joined their husbands and children for the October hunt. Some old men participated by laying snares, but elderly women and the infirm stayed home to guard the buried food caches. With the approach of winter, native communities retired to sheltered places in the thick woods for protection from cold winds, where they found fuel, game and venison plentiful.

The North American diet was unavoidably seasonal. On July 20, 1749, Peter Kalm encountered Indians in bark canoes along the shore of Lake Champlain who did not normally inhabit that place, but who "came here only to catch sturgeons...."[466] He noted the "very singular life" of these people, stating, "At one time of the year they live on the small store of corn, beans, and melons, which they have planted; during another period, or about this time [July], their food is fish, without bread or any other meat; and another season they eat nothing but game, such as stags, roes, beavers, etc., which they shoot in the woods and rivers. They, however, enjoy long life, perfect health, and are more able to undergo hardships than other people. They sing and dance, are joyful, and always content, and would not for a great deal exchange their manner of life for that which is preferred in Europe."

Even after the development of domesticated crops, wild plant foods played a significant part in the Indian diet. All sorts of wild fruits abounded in the woods, including bullace or beach plums, medlars (apple-like fruit), wild cherries, American black currants (*Ribes americanum*), gooseberries, crab apples, blueberries or huckleberries, white and black raspberries and mulberries.[467] Peter Lindeström described the native persimmon as "peach trees on which grow skinless apples, as large as other apples, yellow and rose colored, covered only with a thin downy skin. Inside is a large kernel, as large as a prune kernel but rougher. [These] dissolve in one's mouth like plums, but are much more delicious and palatable."[468] Thriving in woods and meadows, persimmons ripen from late August to November. Peter Kalm thought the fruit of the American persimmon (*Diospyros virginiana*) became sweet enough to eat only after being frost bitten.[469] The natives quickly adopted the peach (*Prunus persica*), often planting it near their habitations. In 1683, Thomas Paschall reported, "in some places peach stones grow up to bear in three years...."[470]

Grapevines overran open fields and draped the forest, "growing to the top of the largest and loftiest trees." Travelers could "not find a district or a nook of land without [them]." Peter Kalm saw grapevines growing "on the steep banks of the [Hudson] River in surprising quantities." Vines bent the trees with their weight, veiling the shore.[471] Lindeström discovered a grapevine at White Clay on Christina Creek that was "two ells thick," the equivalent of four feet. He reported, "grapevines in great abundance, which bear large white, red, brown and blue grapes."[472] Generally harvested in the middle of August, wild grapes tended "to be sour, harsh, fleshy, and strong...."[473] While some varieties were juicy, others were fit only for drying as raisins.[474] The northern fox grape (*Vitis labrusca*) produced scant numbers of "large black grapes with a bluish bloom, tough skin and a sweet and musky flavor" that ripened in September and October. They were once common in Saddle River, New Jersey.[475] The river grape (*Vitis vulpina*) produces purple-black grapes that are sour and ripen late. The blue grape (*Vitis leconteana*) is a strong climber with small berries. The muscadine or southern fox grape (*Vitis rotundifolia*), found along riverbanks and in moist woodlands, yielded purple berries. Mustang grapes (*Vitis candicans*), tough-skinned and light purple in color, were picked from high-climbing vines. True to their name, the black berries of frost grape (*Vitis cordifolia*) were edible only after being touched by frost. Kalm confirmed, "Grapes are eaten after the frost has touched them, for they are too sour before."[476]

Gabriel Thomas mentioned "cramberries" or "craneberries" growing wild in Pennsylvania and southern New Jersey.[477] The American cranberry (*Vaccinium macrocarpon*) is a creeping evergreen shrub of the heath family, closely related to blueberries, deerberries, cowberries and whortleberries. In 1749, botanist Peter Kalm found cranberries "extremely abundant in North America."[478] Wild black raspberries were collected along woodland borders in late August and September. On September 5, 1609, when Hudson's crew landed on the south shore of Sandy Hook Bay, they were given dried black currants, "which were sweet and good." Coralberry (*Symphoricarpos orbiculatus*), known as Indian currant, is a shrub producing magenta berries. It was once common upon rocky slopes of the Delaware River. Strawberries grew plentifully "all over the country," but were especially abundant upon river flats. This fruit, "always plenty in the fields, where they grow naturally," was available from the middle of May until July.[479] Indians also picked the yellow-orange fruit or *currants* of the American hawthorn (*Cratægus tomentosa*), a shrub growing in wet ground and near swamps, whose white flowers appeared in late April.[480] Describing Pennsylvania in 1683, Thomas Paschall noted, "Here grows in the woods abundance of Wortleberries or Whorts [bilberries], Strawberries and Blackberries ... as also three sorts of Grapes and Plums..."[481] Whortleberry (*Vaccinium myrtillus*) is a small shrub which produces black edible berries. These are closely related and often confused with so-called huckleberries or bilberries, specifically Lowbush blueberry (*Vaccinium pennsylvanicum*) and Highbush blueberry (*Vaccinium corymbosum*). Blueberries were collected in small splint-baskets woven from sycamore bark. The Indians "plucked them in abundance every year, dried them either in the sunshine or by the fireside, and afterwards prepared them for eating in different manners."[482]

The floor of the hardwood forest was "in autumn covered with acorns and all kinds of nuts which drop from the numerous trees."[483] Women gathered and dried nuts, particularly chestnuts, for food. American chestnut favored mountainsides. Its brown seeds or nuts, encased in a prickled ball, ripened about the middle of October. Indians were known to cut down chestnut trees "and cut off the limbs to gather the nuts, which also lessens [the number of] trees."[484] North Americans also collected and consumed groundnuts (*Apios tuberosa*) or ground-acorns, ground beans, artichokes (*Helianthus tuberosus*), wild onions and leeks (*Allium tricoccum*), together "with several other kinds of roots and fruits, known to the Indians, who use the same which are disregarded by the Netherlanders."[485] Groundnuts are the edible, tuberous roots of a climbing vine found growing on low, damp ground. The so-called Jerusalem artichoke, with its golden flowers, thrives in damp soil and yields an edible root. Wild leeks were harvested in rich woodlands. Hazel nuts, acorns, hickory nuts, filberts, walnuts and beechnuts were gathered. Women took great pains in ferreting out the store holes of squirrels and door mice, "whether in trees or in the ground, as all the nuts they contain are choice and not only quite ripe but untouched by worms."[486] Indians prepared "a kind of liquor like milk by gathering a great number of hickory and black walnuts, dried and crushed them." The nutmeat was pounded into flour and mixed with water to make a sweet liquid.

Adriæn van der Donck included sunflowers among the "flowers of native growth."[487] The Iroquois were known to bake sunflower seeds into corn cakes. The root of one species, Jerusalem artichoke, was collected in the wild. Wild rice (*Zizania palustris*), described as a "tall, thick grass, which grows here [in the region near Philadelphia] in brooks and other bodies of water and has long, grain-bearing seeds," reached ten feet in height. Women began to gather its seeds in August and prepared them "in different ways and chiefly as groats, which taste almost as good as rice." Harvesting Indian rice was tedious work because "it ripens unevenly and not all simultaneously." Because of its fondness for this food, the bobolink was called the ricebird.[488]

From aged Swedish planters at Raccoon Creek, Peter Kalm learned that Indians "planted but little corn, for they lived chiefly by hunting, and throughout the greatest part of the summer *hopniss, katniss, taw-ho* and whortleberries were their chief food."[489] Eaten "instead of bread," the roots of hopniss (*Glycine apios*) were gathered from meadows and boiled. Peas from the hopniss pod were similarly prepared. Roots of katniss (Arrowhead, *Sagittaria sp.*) were harvested from "low, muddy and very wet ground." These were either boiled or roasted in hot ashes. Indian women traveled to islands in the Delaware River in early June to dig these roots.[490] As many as forty on a rhizome, each the size of an egg, might be found only two inches below ground. Natives also boiled and ate the spadix (spike with small flowers) and berries of a bog flower known as *Tahim, Taw-ho, Tuckah, or Tuckahoe*—also called wake-robin, *Arum Virginicum*, by Kalm—which they regarded "as a great delicacy." This plant, better known as Indian turnip or Jack-in-the-pulpit (*Arisaema triphyllum*), is commonly found in woodland swamps and marshes. The exceedingly peppery bulb became edible only after boiling or baking. Sun-dried, it was ground into meal. Because of its pungent flavor when raw, Indians also "gathered a great heap of these roots, dug a great long hole, sometimes two or three fathoms and upwards in length, into which they put the roots, and covered them with the earth that had been taken out of the hole; they made a great fire above it, which burnt till they thought proper to remove it and then they dug up the roots and consumed them with avidity." They rarely dried or preserved them, preferring to dig them fresh from the marshes.[491] Peter Lindeström, describing the islands or reed flats in the Delaware River between Oldmans and Repaupo Creeks, mentions "a species of roots which grow along the land in abundance and which are called hog turnips by us Swedes, in appearance and taste almost like artichokes, which the savages collect and subsist upon, when bread and grain give out."[492] Indians also plucked the green, bladder-like fruit of Taw-kee or Taw-kim (golden club, *Orontium aquaticum*), another aquatic plant found plentifully "in marshes, near moist and low grounds," especially along the coast. Its seeds had to be dried and boiled repeatedly in water before they were fit for eating. Swedish settlers in the Delaware Basin ate several wild greens, after learning their use from the natives, including lambs-quarters (*Chenopodium album*) and the young shoots of pokeberry (*Phytolacca americana*). Wild herbs included pennyroyal, mint, mustard, sage, rue, and tansy.[493]

Established patterns of seasonal migration between resource stations developed a network of trails used for trade and cultural exchanges of every description. Certain ceremonial assemblies or ritual feasts attended the gathering of dispersed bands into family alliances, either for the fall/winter hunt or for the vernal run of anadromous fish. Such seasonal congregations facilitated courtship, trade and political discussions.

When and where northeastern Indians resided in "fixed places of abode," they built dwellings "with beams in the form of an oven, covered above with the bark of trees, so large that they are sufficient for several families."[494] Hudson visited a Mahican dwelling in the Catskills, coming ashore "with an old man, who was the headman of a tribe, consisting of forty men and seventeen women," near the outlet of Stockport Creek. Their wikwam was "well constructed of oak bark, and circular in shape, with the appearance of having a vaulted ceiling."[495] Horticulture contributed substantially to the diet of this community. Besides what remained growing in the fields, they stored a great quantity of corn and beans of the previous season's growth. Further quantities—"enough to load three ships" —dried near the house. Woven mats provided seating and food was served from "red wooden bowls."[496]

Along the Middle Atlantic Coast, native peoples fashioned dwellings from "hickory saplings, placed upright in the ground and bent arch-wise; the tops are covered with barks of trees, which they cut for this purpose in great quantities." Van der Donck's *Beschrijvinge van Nieuw Nederlant* (1656) includes a detailed description of building wikwams, which could be more than a hundred feet in length, but seldom more than twenty feet wide.[497] Builders set two rows of long slender hickory saplings with the bark stripped off into the ground as far apart as they intended the width of the house to be, continuing the rows until reaching the intended length. These saplings were bent over and tied to form arches, much like a garden arbor. Split poles were fastened horizontally to the upright posts for laths; the heaviest laths were attached near the ground. The crown of the arch was left open about a foot wide to let out smoke, and a single doorway was framed in the center of the house. Laying the smooth side inwards, they covered the framework with sheets of bark peeled off in pieces about six feet long from ash, chestnut, and other species of trees. Van der Donck commented, "chestnuts would be more plentiful if it were not for the Indians, who destroy the trees by stripping off the bark for covering their houses."[498] Making allowance for shrinkage, builders carefully overlapped the side edges and ends of wide bark shingles, using withes to attach the covering to the laths. For weatherproofing, they stuffed any cracks or splits with clay. When the bark of ash and chestnut trees was not loose enough to peel, they substituted bark from trees growing along brooks, which they could peel off during the entire summer season. Durability was "a primary object." Painted "representations of canoes and animals" ornamented the rail work of some houses.[499] Rough carvings of faces and images sometimes decorated a sachem's house.

In some places, from sixteen to eighteen families, comprising a hundred or more people, dwelt under one roof. No partitions divided the interior. Fires burned along the centerline of the earthen floor with smoke venting through the slit in the crown of the roof. People slept along the sides, near their fire and each family had its own assigned place. Engineer Peter Lindeström observed Renappi sachems using a similar method to build winter houses for their families, noting how they planned the length of the house "according to the multitude of people, that they can all be accommodated under one roof, about 100, 200, or 300 ells in length. But the width is on each side of the fireplace the length of a man, that they can lay lengthwise between the fire and the walls; for they have always the fire made lengthwise along the house, right in the center under the ridge, which burns night and day while the winter lasts."[500] Renappi wikwams had a door on each gable rather than one centered in the sidewall. After trading with the Swedes and Dutch, natives hung copper and brass kettles of every size "on a pole along their hut or house from the one door to the other, below which the fire is made up…."[501]

The use of bark-covered longhouses crossed linguistic and ethnic frontiers. In 1683, William Penn described local dwellings as "mats, or barks of trees set on poles … out of the power of the winds, for they are hardly higher than a man; they lie on reeds or grass."[502] While traveling, Indians lodged in the woods about a great fire, using the duffels they wore as clothing for blankets with "a few boughs stuck round them" for a windbreak. According to a 1698 description, the Unami of West Jersey resided in houses "for the most part, covered with chestnut bark, but very close, and warm, insomuch that no rain can go through."[503] Francis Pastorius, writing in 1700, reported natives planting "corn and beans round about their huts, but they take no thought for any more extensive farming or cattle-raising; they are rather astonished that we Christians take so much trouble and thought concerning eating and drinking and also for comfortable clothing and dwellings, as if we doubted that God were able to care for and nourish us."[504] He also claimed "there is no one among them so inexperienced in the art of building that he cannot build such a hut for himself and his family, in three or four hours."[505] In September 1679, Jasper Danckærts visited a plantation of Nyack Indians, situated near present-day Fort Hamilton in Brooklyn.[506] Accompanied by an eighty-year-old Indian woman, he and his companions found "the whole troop together, consisting of seven or eight families, and twenty or twenty-two persons," occupying a wikwam about sixty feet long and fourteen or fifteen feet wide, covered with chestnut bark. Danckærts stooped down to squeeze through one of the low entrances, situated at either end of the dwelling, lifting doors made either of reed mats or a sheet of flat bark. The roof was so low along the sidewalls "that you could hardly stand under it." The astute guest noted, "All who live in one house are generally of one stock or descent, as father and mother with their offspring." Each family tended a fire in the middle of the earthen floor, "so that from one end to the other, each of them boils their own pot, and eats when they like, not only the families by themselves, but each Indian alone, according as he is hungry, at all hours, morning, noon and night. By each fire are the cooking utensils, consisting of a pot, a bowl, or calabash [bottle gourd], and a spoon also made of a calabash. These are all that relate to cooking." Smoke escaped through the vent along the ridge, which "was open about half a foot wide, from one end to the other." Residents slept "upon mats with their feet towards the fire, on each side of it." They did not sit "upon anything raised up, but, for the most part, sit on the ground or squat on their ankles." Other household articles consisted of "a calabash of water, out of which they drink, a small basket in which to carry and keep their maize and small beans, and a knife." The inventory of implements comprised "for tillage, a small, sharp stone, and nothing more; for hunting, a gun and pouch for powder and lead; for fishing, a canoe without mast or sail, and without a nail in any part of it, though it is sometimes full forty feet in length, fish hooks and lines, and scoops to paddle with in place of oars."

In 1635, Father Jean de Brebeuf compared Huron dwellings "to bowers or garden arbors, —some of which, in place of branches and vegetation, are covered with cedar bark, some others with large pieces of ash, elm, fir, or spruce bark; and, although the cedar bark is best, according to common opinion and usage, there is, nevertheless, this inconvenience, that they are almost as susceptible to fire as matches. Hence arise many of the conflagrations of entire villages. There are cabins or arbors of various sizes, some two brasses [10.6'], others of twenty [106.36'], of thirty [159.50'], of forty [212.72']; the usual width is about four brasses [21.27'], [regardless of length] their height is about the same. There are no different stories; there is no cellar, nor chamber, nor garret. It has neither window nor chimney, only a miserable hole in the top of the cabin, left to permit the smoke to escape."[507]

When the air turned cold in autumn, many native communities erected a pihmoakan, or sweat lodge. Shaped like "a small oven, large enough for three or four men to lie in it," some were built of saplings and covered tightly with clay, always near a running brook or bubbling spring.[508] Peter Lindeström described such a hut "made of stone and clay and arched like a bake oven with a hole above, large enough to crawl through." Heated stones were placed inside the enclosure until it was sufficiently warm. The interior was large enough so that bathers could lie lengthwise around the pile of hot stones. The entrance hole was then plugged, and water poured upon the hot stones to produce steam. This was accompanied by "an unspeakable crying and noise, that one may really be fearful of it, each one imitating the animal from which his *Pååhra* or idol has been taken, upon which they believe, the one [crying] like a lion, the one like a bear, another like a bull, a third like a wild boar, wolf, dog, goose, rooster, etc."[509] Afterwards, men, women and children "come out so perspiring, that every hair has a drop of sweat on it." They then plunged into the cold waters of a stream for a thorough cleansing.[510] One crowd followed another into the steam bath until everyone had a turn. Patients also sat in sweat lodges, "naked and singing," as a treatment for various illnesses.[511]

Villages depended upon alluvial horticulture, supplemented with intensive hunting and gathering in surrounding woodlands.[512] Otherwise, hunter-gatherers congregated seasonally, wherever and whenever small gardens and abundant food resources extended the natural carrying capacity of the land. Summer villages were best situated "near the water sides, at fishing places, where they plant some vegetables; but they leave those places every year on the approach of winter, and retire to their strong places, or into the thick woods, where they are protected from the winds, and where fuel is plenty, and where there is game and venison."[513] According to Lindeström, fine lowland flanking the Schuylkill, being "good land for maize," was "occupied in greatest force by the most intelligent savages of several nations of savages, who own this River and dwell here. They have their dwellings side by side one another, wherefore also this land is thereby being cleared and cultivated with great power. And six different places are settled, under six sachems or chiefs, each one commanding his tribe or people under him, and each with its own peculiar language, being several hundred men strong, under each chief, counting women and children, some being stronger, some weaker."[514] If there were 250 people per group under six sachems, then the population of the Schuylkill flats in present-day Philadelphia would have been about 1,500 in 1650. The surrounding brushwood offered "an abundance of various kinds of rare, wild animals, which, however, now begin to become somewhat diminished, through the continual visits of the savages with devastation by hunting and shooting." Renappi horticulture, even as practiced on fertile river flats, was not sufficiently productive to alleviate dependence upon wild plants and animals in the diet. Consequently, the Schuylkill Indians were compelled to relocate within a decade or so.

Despite their somewhat transitory existence, villages could accommodate relatively large numbers of people under favorable circumstances, and on certain occasions. In late winter 1644, an expedition of Dutch and English soldiers landed at Greenwich and destroyed a large Siwanoy village called Petuguepaen, nearly wiping out its entire population of about six hundred persons who had gathered there to celebrate their New Year festival.[515] This community consisted of houses "set up in three rows, street fashion, each row eighty paces long, in a low recess protected by the hills, affording much shelter from the northwest wind."[516]

Speaking generally in 1625, Van Wassenaer indicated that, in times of war, some "fortify their tribe or nation with palisades, serving them for a fort, and sally out the one against the other."[517] Sentinels and sharpshooters mounted a tree at the center "to observe the enemy and discharge arrows." In particular, the Iroquois enclosed "their villages and castles" with "strong firm works, adapted to the places" to protect "against the sudden invasion of their enemies."[518] Some Indian castles surrounded "twenty or thirty houses," including houses measuring "a hundred and eighty yards long."[519] Maize fields and woods ringed such fortified villages. Other communities erected small forts near their plantations to guard women and children "against the sudden irruption of the small marauding parties of their enemies." They usually chose "a situation on the side of a steep high hill, near a stream or river, which is difficult of access, except from the water, and inaccessible on every other side, with a level plain on the crown of the hill, which they enclose with a strong stockade work in a singular manner." Large logs, laid upon the ground and frequently firmed by a layer of smaller logs, served as a strong foundation. Two roughly parallel lines of vertical oak palisades were planted in the ground, one line on each side of the log foundation, with their upper ends being crossed and joined. Tree trunks or logs were then set into the notch formed near the top of the crossed palisades.[520]

In 1614, Johann De Laet described the Sequins as a tribe residing along the Quinnipiac or Connecticut River near present-day Windsor. They cultivated maize and "had a village resembling a fort" for protection against their enemies, the neighboring Nawaas.[521] In 1626, when war broke out with the Mohawks, the Mahicans built a fort opposite Fort Orange, now Albany, New York. In 1644, "three castles" at Wickquaesgeck, probably near Stamford, Connecticut, were "constructed of plank five inches thick, nine feet high, and braced around with balk full of port-holes."[522] Speaking of the Renappi of the Schuylkill estuary, Peter Lindeström states categorically, "they know nothing of taxation and they are entirely ignorant of architecture and fortifications." Only the neighboring Susquehannocks were known to build palisades around their dwellings.[523]

There are two references to "Indian castles" in northern New Jersey. According to the Minutes of the Council of New Netherland, the great Hackensack elder, Oratam, appeared at Fort Amsterdam accompanied by Weswatewchy (Kakwatcheky), Meninger and Wemessamy (Memmesame), chiefs of the Menissincks (i.e., Minisinks), on August 15, 1663. These Minisink sachems, speaking through Oratam, stated "that they have no connection with the Esopus savages regarding the present war."[524] They desired peace with the Dutch, "for they are afraid, that the Sinnekus (Senecas) might kill them." Accordingly, the sachems requested "a small piece of ordnance (cannon), to use it in their fort against the Sinnekus and protect their corn." The Director-General responded that "our small pieces of ordnance had altogether been sent off and the others were too large, to bring into their country and that the Sinnekus were our friends as well as they..." The second reference to a castle comes from a deed, dated January 6, 1676, whereby Tantaqua joined Cusquehem, Nechtamcepepeaw, Wansoughham, Kanagions, Anesachore and Poughquickquarae in the sale of New Hackensack, extending from the bounds of Old Hackensack (Cedar Lane in Teaneck) north to "a small kill or Vale adjoining to the Great Indian Field—called the Indian Castle" to Laurence Andriessen Van Boskerk & Company. It apparently stood above the Hackensack River in "the Great Indian Field" immediately south of French Creek at New Bridge.

A defensive posture was often essential to the wellbeing of the natives, for conflict was rife. If any Indian killed someone from another family or nation, then the sachem of the offended party sent one of his men to the murderer's community "and stealthily has one of them killed, whereby at once war is caused between them."[525] As Van der Donck observed, "The principal command and authority among the Indians is developed in war, and in their councils on war."[526] Native warriors proved "artful in the measures, furious in their attacks, and unmerciful victors."[527] North Americans differed greatly from Europeans in their military tactics in that "they are not straight forward as soldiers but perfidious, accomplishing all their enterprises by treachery, using many stratagems to deceive their enemies, and usually ordering all their plans, involving any danger, by night." Stratagems involved the use of "hindrances, deceptions, and ambuscades against their enemies."[528] The Renappi used a sort of code language in battle to conceal their intentions from any enemies who could understand their language.[529] But it was difficult to keep a large number of warriors together to accomplish any grand strategy. Unlike Europeans, they were loath to slaughter women and children, and prisoners were taken to villages where families might adopt them, "who have previously lost connections by blood in war." Whenever possible, their own women and children were "removed to places of safety."[530]

Lindeström regarded native warriors as "brave" in military matters, using no other arms "but rifles, bows, spears, arrows and quarrels, which are set with sharp flint, and they use helmets which are made of sticks and wood, so strong that no quarry [i.e., projectile point] is able to go through it."[531] They painted their faces "in such a manner that it is difficult to recognize one known before" and some wore snakeskin headbands with a fox or wolf's tail hanging down.[532] Others carried a square shield that covered their body up to the shoulders. Attired and accoutered for war, they walked "as proud as peacocks."[533]

FOLKWAYS AND TECHNOLOGY

North Americans were "by nature a healthy people ... rarely subjected to disease, before death surprises them..."[534] Verrazano claimed, "They live by hunting and fishing, and they are long lived. If they fall sick they cure themselves without medicine, with the heat of fire. Death comes to them at last from extreme old age."[535] Most did not hold Western medicines and purgatives in high regard, preferring fasting as the primary remedy for sickness and, if that failed, "then they have recourse to sweating and drinks; but the latter they take very sparingly."[536] Feeling unwell, they might drink "a *Teran* or decoction of some roots in spring water; and if they eat any flesh, it must be of the female of any creature."[537] Other European commentators, such as Wassenaer, claimed, "there is not an ailment they have not a remedy for; but in other areas they are altogether devoid of succor, leaving the people to perish like cattle."[538]

North Americans developed botanical medicines, learning "how to cure very dangerous and perilous wounds and sores by roots, leaves and other little things."[539] Choice medicinal roots included sassafras, wild sarsaparilla, black snakeroot (either black cohosh or sanicle), rattlesnake root (*Prenanthes altissima*) and pokeroot.[540] Since ancient times, Indians used northern maidenhair, a fern found growing upon shaded, rich woodland soil, "instead of tea, in consumption, cough, and all kinds of pectoral diseases."[541] The root of blue flag, a wild swamp iris, boiled and crushed between stones, was applied as a poultice over sores. A decoction of the root of the woodland orchid, moccasin flower (*Cypripedium acaule*), also called stemless lady's-slipper, was formerly used to ease childbirth.[542] Some pregnant women also tied the skin of a rattlesnake around themselves to be "immediately relieved of their severe childbirth."[543] Pith scraped from young slips of sassafras (*Sassafras variifolium*), the aromatic deciduous tree, was boiled and the water applied as eyewash.[544]

Syphilis, also known as the French disease (*Morbus fransman*), raged among the inhabitants of the Delaware Basin, being treated with "a white kind of ointment" that supposedly wiped away the disease and its symptoms.[545] Peter Kalm related the story of an Indian who applied pulverized charcoal, made from the beaver-tree (*Magnolia virginiana*, sweet or swamp bay), mixed with fat, to an open sore on the leg of a Swedish settler, Lars Låck, and so cured him.[546] True snakeroot or snakewort "grows spontaneously in the country" and was "highly esteemed by the Indians as an unfailing cure" for the venomous bite of the rattlesnake.[547] They held this cure "in such high estimation that many of them always carry some of it, well dried, with them to cure the bites of those serpents."[548] Delaware *devil-chasers* chewed snake grass roots, which "grew very much intertwined, like a very fine and close comb," applying their medicated spittle to the wound as a "splendid medicine" against the deadly bite of rattlesnakes.

Observing coastal communities, Verrazano noted, "Their arrows are reeds, in the ends of which they fasten the bones of fish and of animals."[549] Animal intestines or sinew provided bowstrings. Where and when suitable stone was available, knappers fashioned narrow, angulated pieces of flint or quartz into projectile points, though "the bones of animals or the claws of birds and beasts" were similarly employed. Some arrowheads were "very sharp and well made," but others "very blunt," probably from breakage, and capable of killing only "birds and small quadrupeds."[550] Fishing hooks were also "made of bone or birds' claws." Indians cut and scraped with "little sharp pieces of flint or quartz, or else some other hard kind of stone, or with a sharp shell, or with a piece of bone, which they had sharpened."[551]

Peter Kalm studied and collected ancient Indian tools during his stay in the region in 1748-51. He noted that stone hatchets were generally shaped like narrow wedges, about half-a-foot long, but with the sharp end "rather blunter than our wedges."[552] To affix the handle, a notch or furrow was made around the thick end of the hatchet by which it could be inserted into the split-end of a stick and fastened by rope or cord, thus securing the head to the handle. Some stone hatchets—actually mauls or crushers— lacked furrows for handle attachment and were clutched in the bare hand during use. Some early observers saw hatchets made of "hard flint stone."[553] Most of the hatchets which Kalm studied were fashioned from "a hard rock-stone; but some are made of a fine, hard, black, apyrous [i.e., appyretic, made without application of heat] stone."[554]

Since blunt stone hatchets would not cut wood, but merely crush bark, fire was used to fell trees and to excavate or shape hollows in wood. Kindling was piled around the base of a tree and set ablaze. Washing the tree with wet rags attached to the end of a pole controlled burning. The chief use of the stone hatchet was to clear garden plots by crushing the bark in a circular pattern a few feet up from the base of a tree, especially when the sap was running—a technique called girdling. Girdled trees eventually died, allowing sunlight to reach the ground. Small trees or saplings were then pulled from the ground by brute force and the ground "turned up with crooked or sharp branches."[555]

Many tribes manufactured canoes from "one piece of wood, hollowed out by fire from the solid trunks of trees."[556] Surveying the North American coast in 1524, Verrazano wrote, "We saw many of their boats constructed of a single tree, twenty feet long and four feet wide, fabricated without the use of stone or iron or other metal.... To hollow out the log they burn as much of it as will form the concave part of the boat, and also form the ends which are to be the prow and stern, to make the boat float well."[557] On January 8, 1633, near the site of Fort Nassau, in what is now Gloucester City, Gloucester County, New Jersey, Captain David De Vries saw a boat, which the natives had hollowed out of a tree. To make a dugout canoe, dry branches were laid on a felled tree trunk and ignited. Water was poured onto the sides and ends of the log to control burning. Stone hatchets, sharp gouges of flint or quartz, or sharp shells were used to scrape out the charred wood and to smooth the interior walls. Pointed at both ends, the average canoe was thirty or forty feet long. Oarsmen standing at the bow and stern controlled and propelled the vessel, while passengers sat on the bottom.[558] Readily adopting this technology, Europeans farmers plied the Delaware River in dugout canoes throughout the eighteenth century. Eastern red cedar, Atlantic white cedar, chestnut, white oak and tulip tree were the woods of choice. Cedar was preferred because it floated lightly upon the water and lasted upwards of twenty years, whereas the heavier white oak was less buoyant and lasted but six years or so. White pine was used in the Albany area, where no other wood was fit for this purpose.[559]

For coastal voyages down the Delaware River to Virginia or New York, Indian boatmen lashed "two punts together broad wise with timbers over them, right strongly put together, the deck made completely tight and side boards of planks; sails of rugs and frieze joined together; ropes and tackle made of bast [i.e., inner bark] and slender spruce roots; [and they] also mason for themselves a little fireplace on deck, where they can thus make a fire, when necessary. These miserable vessels look like large sloops in the sea, and thus they scrape themselves along with these [ships] the best they can." Such craft, though hardly seaworthy, allowed short voyages within sight of the coast, though such trips were unavoidably hazardous without instruments of navigation.[560]

Within the range of suitable species, native craftsmen also fashioned canoes of birch bark.[561] According to Peter Kalm, who studied their manufacture, six lengths of bark went into making a canoe, two underneath and two on either side. Since bark strips usually measured three fourths of a canoe's length, two pieces were needed to complete the bottom. The inner side of the bark or that nearest the tree was utilized for the outer side of the boat. White cedar was used for ribs and binding strips. Spacing between ribs ranged from the width of three fingers to the width of a palm. Strips were placed "so close to one another that one cannot see the birch-bark between them."[562] The canoe maker sewed all seams with spruce roots or ropes made of the same material split, using "a tailor's cross-stitch."[563] The bark was double-folded at the seams, and melted resin

Museum of the American Indian
DUGOUT DREDGED UP IN THE
HACKENSACK RIVER

Figure 20. Dugout canoe unearthed in Hackensack, New Jersey, in
1868, now in the collections of the Bergen County Historical Society.
Photographed 1902 for the Museum of the American Indian.

was dabbed on the outside seams in place of pitch. Melted resin was also
employed to repair small holes. Birch-bark canoes were light enough to
carry at portages, but could be dangerous and unsafe in stormy weather or
rough water. Sharp or rough stones could easily split or rip out the bottom.
Since repairs were frequently required en route, Peter Kalm recommended
carrying a handy supply of "resin and even birch-bark along, though the
latter can generally be procured wherever one goes." Spruce roots were
also found "nearly everywhere, and, lacking these, pine roots are said to
be equally serviceable."[564]

In contrast to their eastern and southern neighbors, Minisinks on
the upper reaches of the Delaware River used bark canoes, rather than the
dugout canoes, which most of their Algonquian relatives preferred. While
on the Delaware River at Cochecton, New York, on July 10, 1719, West
Jersey Boundary Commissioner John Reading and his surveying party
rode their horses "over the River into Pennsylvania to view some bark

canoes the Indians were making."[565] A week later, while traveling south to Mahekkameck (Mackhackamack, now Port Jervis), they "saw a bark canoe with Indians in it come down, as was supposed, from the Indian town from whence we came."[566]

Flint tubes for smoking tobacco were "ingeniously perforated."[567] Pipes were also manufactured from clay, potstone or serpentine. Pottery pipes had a thick tube, "hardly an inch long, but sometimes as long as a finger; its color comes nearest to that of our tobacco pipes which have been long used." Others were "made with great ingenuity of a very fine, red potstone or a variety of serpentine marble." Kalm found such pipes to be "very scarce and are seldom used by any other than the Indian sachems or elders." The red potstone, commonly used to make the *calumet de paix*, or peace pipe, was "found only in the country of the Ajoues, south of the Missouri River."[568] An outcrop of serpentine on the Palisades at Castle Point in Hoboken, New Jersey, underlies the name, *Hobokan Hackingh*, meaning, "smoking-pipe place." Peter Lindeström spoke of tobacco pipes a fathom long, screwed together with leather, the head of green or black stone. The typical pipe-head was large enough to hold a handful of tobacco.[569]

In September 1609, Henry Hudson testified, "The people had copper tobacco pipes, from which I inferred that copper must exist there...."[570] In 1749, Peter Kalm disclosed, "some Dutchmen who lived here [at New York] still preserved the old account among them, that their ancestors on their first settling in New York had come upon many of the Indians who had tobacco pipes of copper, and who made them understand by signs that they got them in the neighborhood. Afterwards a fine copper mine [i.e. the Schuyler Mine in North Arlington, New Jersey] was discovered, upon the Second River, a tributary of the Passaic River] between Elizabeth and New York.[571] On digging in this mine the people found holes made in the mountain, out of which some copper had been taken, and they found even some tools, which the Indians probably made use of when they endeavored to get the metal for their pipes."[572] Whether or not these tools and mine-holes were of Indian origin, it is conceivable that nodules of nearly pure copper were collected on the surface. Kalm also commented upon copper coming from Lake Superior, where it was gotten "almost pure, so that it does not need melting over again, but is immediately fit for working." Loose pieces and, more rarely, large slabs, were found.[573]

Women skillfully wove "Indian mats, ropes, hats, and baskets (some of curious workmanship) of their hemp, which there grows wild, and natural, in the woods, in great plenty."[574] Aquamachuques women brought wild hemp (*Apocynum cannabinum*), a perennial species of Dogbane, to trade with Henry Hudson's crew. Botanist Peter Kalm watched Iroquois women roll the filaments upon their bare thighs, thereby making thread and string, which they then dyed red, yellow or black. Cord was woven "into goods with a great deal of ingenuity."[575] Indian hemp ropes "were stronger and kept longer in water than such as were made of common hemp."[576] Consequently, this natural fiber was used to make fishing lines and nets as well as bags and pouches.[577] The tough, fibrous bark and shoots of the marsh shrub, Eastern leatherwood (*Dirca palustris*), were also "used for ropes, baskets, etc. by the Indians, while they lived among the Swedes." Indians boiled linden bark and pounded it with wooden clubs to soften the fibers, which they then twisted by rolling it against their thighs to make a fine cord. They used this to sew their shoes.[578] The grass-like leaves of bulrush (*Scirpus* sp), the coarse sedge found in bogs and shallow water, were woven into mats for sleeping or seating.[579] Native women also worked "very fine, strong and artistic mats of finely painted spruce roots and strong straw, with all kinds of figures, to decorate and cover the walls with, and to place below their bed clothes."[580] Peter Lindeström particularly admired the artistry of native craftsmanship "in neatly working by drawing, painting and glazing, as for instance their bags, which they make so large that 1 quart, 1/2 gallon, yes, 1, 1-1/2, 2, 2-1/2, 3 up to 6 gallons can go into them, to keep grain and all kinds of other such [things] in. These they elaborate with all kinds of figures of painted pine roots and also split, painted sticks, unspeakably strong."[581]

North Americans made small dishes out of sycamore bark for gathering whortleberries. Women also wove strips of this bark, "a line in thickness," into berry-baskets.[582] Known as buttonwood or plane tree, sycamore favored low wetlands along riverbanks; the riverbank near Anderson Street, Hackensack, was anciently known as Warepeake, derived from *woapak*, meaning, "water beech or sycamore." The Swedes referred to mountain laurel as spoon tree, "because the Indians used to make their spoons and trowels of its wood." Bowls were fashioned from the aromatic wood of sassafras.[583] The bottle gourd or *calabash* was used for making all kinds of vessels such as large spoons, ladles, funnels, bowls and dishes. After drying, the seeds and pulp were removed and the interior of the hard shells scraped clean. Polishing the outside before opening them was said to make them "as hard as bone." Occasional washing restored their white color. The hard and durable shell served "to hold seeds, spices, &c," and as "the common water-pail of the natives." Seeds stored in bottle gourds supposedly retained viability longer than seeds stored in other containers.[584] One gourd vessel was reportedly large enough to "contain more than a schepel [that is, about three pecks]."[585]

Previous to the introduction of pottery, Indians carved vessels from "a kind of serpentine stone" or *talcum*.[586] Potstone is a type of soapstone, known as steatite or *Lapis ollaris*. In 1750, elderly Swedish settlers remembered seeing Indians boil meat in pots made either of clay or potstone. Many pots had "two holes in the upper margin, one on each side, through which the Indians put a stick and hold the kettle over the fire, as long as is needed."[587] Most pots had no feet. Some were hollowed out of blocks of a greenish or grey potstone and others were fashioned "of another species of fire-proof stone; the bottom and the margin are frequently above an inch thick."[588]

Pottery was a feminine invention and craft. In 1750, Peter Kalm inspected "an earthen pot, which had been found in a place where the Indians formerly lived" and concluded, "I could perceive no glaze or color upon it, but on the outside it was very much ornamented and upon the whole well made."[589] Inspecting fragments of Indian pots, he noticed that the clay was tempered with different materials "according to the nature of the place where they had been made."[590] Indians along the seashore used pulverized shells of mussels and snails as raw material, whereas inland potters used pulverized rock. Native potters did not fire their wares at any great temperature. Still, although the body of the pottery remained somewhat soft, the workmanship was "very good" and people commonly found "whole vessels or pieces in the ground, which are not damaged."[591]

Figure 21. Perfect earthenware jar found in the mound at a Minisink Cemetery. From George G. Heye and George H. Pepper, *Exploration of a Munsee Cemetery near Montague, New Jersey*, New York: The Museum of the American Indian, 1915.

MNEMONIC DEVICES

In August 1749, Peter Kalm noted, "Europeans have never been able to find any alphabetical characters, much less writing or books among the Indians, who have inhabited North America, since time immemorial, and comprise several nations and dialects."[592] When Nils Gustafson's father purchased land from the Indians, an agreement was drawn and signed, whereby one of the Indians, "whose name signified a beaver, drew a beaver; another of them drew a bow and arrow; and a third a mountain, instead of his name."[593] In June 1759, Peter Williamson published "A Short Account of the Indians of North America" in *The Gentleman's and London Magazine*, describing his captivity among the Indians. He reported that some Indians, presumably Delawares, recorded the number of their warriors and battle casualties by cutting notches on the handles of their tomahawks. He added the rather curious statement, "Their tomahawk is also the register of their time: the returns of the moon, and remarkable events are thereupon distinguished; as will appear upon conversing with any of their wise men, who will account for 6000 moons past."[594] Petroglyphs marked with a pattern of circles may also represent lunar calendars.

Native storytellers used mnemonic devices: Tantaqua, alias Jasper, a Hackensack sachem, when asked by Jasper Danckærts to explain the genesis of the world, "began to write on the floor" with a piece of coal from the fire, first drawing a small oval with four paws, a head and a tail, to represent a turtle.[595] He next stood a piece of straw upright in the midst of his drawing to represent the first tree growing in the middle of the earth. These were mnemonic pictographs. In 1643, the chosen orator for sixteen sachems on Long Island, speaking to Captain David De Vries, held a "small bundle of sticks," laying down a stick for each point made in his oration.[596] Peter Kalm reported how Indian ambassadors meeting with the governor of Pennsylvania listened intently to a long list of demands, "yet they have only a stick in their hand and make their marks on it with a knife, without writing anything else down." Returning the next day to give their decisions, they answered "all the governor's articles in the same order in which he delivered them, without leaving one out, and give such accurate answers as if they had a full account of them in writing."[597] The Iroquois also employed various devices to aid their memory, "such as bundles of sticks, and that system of signs, emblems, and rude pictures, which they shared with other tribes."[598] Wampum belts incorporated pictographs and motifs to aid recall of treaty provisions.

In 1679, Danckærts noted how Indian burial places were found "everywhere in the woods, but especially along the banks of rivers or streams near where they live or have lived."[599] Near Claverack, New York, he saw graves with "some markers hanging in a tree, such as a child's carrying plank or board ... And it signifies that there lies or sits buried there a woman with a small child or a pregnant woman." Speaking vaguely of another type of grave marker, he claimed, "Or it is one or another marker signifying what kind of person it was who is buried there. However, this is uncommon."[600]

TRADE GOODS

In September 1609, the "people of the country" offered Henry Hudson's crew green tobacco, hemp, corn, pumpkins, beans, grapes, oysters, and beaver or otter skins in exchange for knives, hatchets, and beads. North Americans coveted clothes in exchange, but eagerly bartered for knives, adzes, axes, choppers, kettles and iron household utensils.[601] In 1632, David De Vries made "some presents of duffels, bullets, hatchets and various Nuremberg trinkets" to chiefs along Delaware Bay.[602] A month later, he exchanged duffels, kettles and axes for maize.

Native communities traded furs, hides and skins; foodstuffs including corn, beans, game, fresh fish and all kinds of birds, wild fruits and nuts, including "peaches or skinless apples, watermelons, chestnuts, walnuts, plums, bullace-plums, grapes and wild hops" as well as various handicrafts.[603] Peter Lindeström, in his *Geographia Americæ*, provided the following inventory of prices paid in New Sweden to Indians for their merchandise, circa 1655.[604] The trade was mostly reckoned in Holland *florins* and *styvers*, 1 *florin* being worth 20 *styvers*.

A quilt of painted feathers	2 ells of white *sewan* or 1 ell of blue *sewan*, made by the Minquas
A quilt of Turkey feathers	1 ell of white *sewan*
A wolf-lynx skin	6 to 9 *florins*
A beaver skin	7 to 8 *florins*
A lion skin	6 *florins*
An otter skin	4 to 6 *florins*
A lynx skin	4 *florins*
A bear hide, pitch black	3 to 4 *florins*
A wolf skin	2 to 3 *florins*
A raccoon skin	1 *florin*
A mink skin	1 *florin*
36-checkered fox skins	1 *florin*
A muskrat skin	1 *florin*
A mat, according to size, beauty and skill of workmanship	1 to 6 *florins*
Bags, according to size, beauty and skill of workmanship	1 to 6 *florins*
A fisher skin	24 *styvers*
A deer skin	24 *styvers*
A swan	6 *styvers*

A turkey	4 *styvers*
A goose	4 *styvers*
A wood grouse	4 *styvers*
A black grouse	2 *styvers*
A duck	2 *styvers*
A partridge	2 *styvers*
Tobacco	2 *styvers* per pound
A hazel grouse	1 *styver*
A pigeon	1 *styver*

On December 28, 1656, Vice-Director Jan Jacquet promised several local sachems at Fort Casimir [near today's New Castle, Delaware], who sought an increase in the prices they received for peltries, "that every one is at liberty to act herein according to his pleasure and that every one could go where his purse enabled him and the goods pleased him."[605] But this free-trade policy did not sit well with colonists who, on January 10, 1657, made public complaint "that *whereas* some people do not hesitate to ruin the trade with the Indians, by running up the price of deerskins by more than one third, while most likely it will run up higher still to the great and excessive disadvantage of the poor community here, as the inhabitants, who must gain their living by their hands' work, have to pay more for the goods, as they can sell them to others and *whereas* this is as yet unimportant compared to what is to come, as when in the spring a trade in beavers should be opened in which case the community living here runs the risk of being entirely ruined and *whereas* several complaints have already been made to the Honorable Commandant [Jacquet], though the naming of persons, nobody has come yet, to be properly looked after in this respect." Without representation from the Indians, the colonists then decided to fix prices:

> For a merchantable beaver, two strings of wampum,
> For a good bearskin, worth a beaver, two strings of wampum,
> For an elk skin, worth a beaver, two strings of wampum,
> Otters accordingly;
> For a deer skin, one hundred and twenty wampum;

Foxes, catamounts, raccoons and other to be valued accordingly.[606]

In exchange, Indians sought red and blue Holland frieze, guns, gunpowder, lead shot, copper and brass kettles, axes, hoes, picks, spades, shovels, glass beads, awls, bodkins, small common scissors; knives, small mirrors (looking glasses) and needles.[607] In June 1657, Director Jacob Alrichs of New Amstel reported red duffels were "most asked for by the savages."[608] In November 1658, he complained that Amsterdam merchants had not yet sent wide duffels to New Amstel, "which is very inconvenient, as without duffels it is hard to get deer meat or maize from the savages." He also requested a few pieces of duffels for the purchase of land about Horekil, "for without having [duffels], and they are not to be had here from anybody, one should hardly dare to speak of it, because one would thereby show an inability, besides that it would not give any respect or esteem, if in wintertime we came without duffels to negotiate something of importance [with the local sachems], so that hereby we are already somewhat hindered."[609] In December 1658, duffels, coats, kettles, mirrors, knives, corals and trumpets were still needed to purchase lands about Horekil. According to Peter Lindeström's report for 1655, trade items cost the natives:

A gun	10 to 20 beaver skins
An ell of Holland frieze	9 *florins*
One handful of powder	3 *florins*
An axe	3 *florins*
A shovel	3 *florins*
A hoe	3 *florins*
A pick	3 *florins*
A small common pair of scissors	3 *florins*
A knife	1 or 2 *florins*
A bodkin	1 *florin*
A small mirror	1 *florin*
A pin	1 *florin*
A common sewing needle	1 *florin*

A string of glass beads, wrapped
three times around the arm   1 *florin*

At first, North Americans "were accustomed to fall prostrate on the report of the gun," but quickly learned to "stand still from habit..."[610] The first adventurers to come ashore discovered "whole troops [of native warriors] run before five or six muskets."[611] Swedes claimed the English colonists of Virginia first sold guns to the Indians, and that the Swedes subsequently sold powder and lead to operate them.

Cultural crosspollination was inevitable. Clearly, Europeans could not have maintained their foothold on the continent without the sustenance and ingenuity of native peoples, based upon their long adaptation to local environments. This is well recognized. In the other direction, Indians equally absorbed beneficial aspects of their new neighbors' culture. They purchased hogs from the earliest Swedish settlers and "taught them to follow them like dogs, and whenever they moved from one place to another their pigs always went with them."[612] They also grew "extremely fond of milk and drank it with pleasure when the Swedes gave it to them."[613] Peter Lindeström told how the sachems and their peers had "begun to buy shirts from the Christians, reaching to the knees; but they do not know enough to let them be washed, but let them stay on unwashed as long as there is a single piece left."[614] As merchandise for the sachems, Swedish colonists began making coats, reaching to the knees, of frieze cloth, "the one side of the breast and back, red, the other side, blue, likewise on the arms, as the cloths of the orphan children in Stockholm are made." Ells of broad Dutch frieze, red or blue, were held in "high esteem" for body wraps. The natives did not buy more than an ell's length at a time, for this length was sufficient to wrap around a person.[615] Trade goods listed as payments in twenty-three deeds recording land sales in East and West Jersey made over a period of thirty-seven years (between 1677 and 1714) comprised:[616]

720 fathoms (4,320 feet) of wampum or sewan, 185 fathoms (1,110 feet) of white wampum, 50 fathoms (300 feet) of black wampum, 6 pounds of

black and white wampum, £63 and 120 Shillings in silver money, 400 Guilders of silver money.

291 guns, 12 pistols, 760 flints, 1 barrel of shot, 185 lbs. of shot, 2-3/4 barrel of powder, 15 small barrels of powder, 5-1/2 ankers of powder, 456 lbs. of gunpowder, 10 quarts of powder, 1/2 hundred weight of powder, 230 hands of powder, 895 bars of lead, 100 lbs. of lead, 1 gun bore, 4 cutlasses, 5 swords.

829 matchcoats, 28 striped matchcoats, 12 blue and red matchcoats, 20 Stroudwater red and blue coats, 96 Stroudwater matchcoats, 4 coats Strouds, 20 Frieze coats,[617] 6 Kersey coats,[618] 2 calico matchcoats, 10 coats made up, 19 coats, 3 coats of cotton, 30 Duffel coats, 30 coats of red and blue Duffel, 320 shirts, 293 pairs of stockings, 70 pairs of hose, 200 blankets, 10 Stroudwater blankets, 26 Strouds [blankets?], 6 pair of Strouds, 14 white blankets, 10 Duffel blankets, 45 Duffels, 10 striped Duffels, 25-1/2 yards of Duffel, 74 fathoms (444 feet) of Duffel, 10 yards of Stroud, 20 yards of Stroudwater, 10 yards of red cotton, 10 yards of white cotton, 30 petticoats, 12 pairs of shoes, 15 hats, 4 caps.

5 great kettles, 2 brass kettles, 30 tin kettles, 282 kettles, 58 glass bottles, 14 small bottles, 312 glasses, 60 bowls, 100 small bowls, porringers.

28 lbs. of red lead, 2 grasps of red paint, 20 pewter spoonfuls of paint, 146 looking glasses, 60 tinshaw looking glasses, 224 combs, 1 razor, 28 lbs. and one-half handful of beads, 5 pairs of spectacles, 200 bells, 72 rings, 60 bracelets, 172 and one double-handful of jaw harps.

1,542 knives, 880 needles, 720 fishing hooks, 506 hatchets, 346 awls, 278 hoes, 250 pairs of scissors, 128 axes, 57 handsaws, 22 drawing knives, 19 adze, 6 fine files, 4 harpoons, 3 rasps, 1 auger, 1 frying pan, 1 pot hinge, one hatful of nails.

114 gallons of rum, 2 barrels of rum, 1 cask of rum, 12 ankers of rum, 40 quarts of rum, 14 ankers of brandy, 1/2 barrel of wine, 5 gallons of wine, 9 barrels of cider, 1 gallon of molasses, 10 barrels of beer, 5 half vats of beer, 2 ankers of beer, 15 gallons of beer.

153 lbs. of tobacco, 6 ankers of tobacco, 1 roll of tobacco, 2,431 tobacco pipes, 114 tobacco boxes, 416 tobacco tongs, 5 steels.

Overall, there were 1,106 coats of various descriptions; 291 guns; 278 hoes; 224 combs; 293 pairs of stockings and 70 pairs of hose; 289 blankets; 320 shirts, and 319 kettles. In 1749, Kalm listed French trade goods as muskets, gunpowder, shot, cloth, iron hatchets, knives, scissors, needles, flint, copper or brass kettles (ironware being too heavy to conveniently transport), cinnabar and verdigris for body paint, mirrors, burning-glasses, tobacco, wampum, glass beads, brass and steel wire and brandy.[619]

GENDER

As hunters, fishermen and warriors, males claimed a superior position in North American society. According to Wassenaer's *Historisch Verhæl*, published in 1624, "The men never labor, except to provide some game, either fowl or other wild sort, for cooking, and then they have provided everything."[620] From the perspective of European farmers, Indian males were "so inclined to freedom that they cannot by any means be brought to work."[621] Adriæn van der Donck thought, "To all bodily exertions they are very competent, as far as their dispositions extend; but to heavy slavish labor the men have a particular aversion, and they manage their affairs accordingly."[622] While women worked long and hard sowing and tending cornfields, it was said, "the men would not once look to it, for it would compromise their dignity too much, unless they are old and cannot follow the chase."[623] Without a comparative experience of the relative efficiency of a hunting-and-gathering lifestyle, Europeans disparaged native men as "generally lazy, [who] do nothing until they become old and unesteemed, when they make spoons, wooden bowls, bags, nets and similar articles; beyond this the men do nothing except fish, hunt and go to war."[624] As in many cultures, young men were regarded as "the most courageous, and do for the most part what they please."[625]

Described as "rather tall, well proportioned in their limbs," Indian males "let their hair grow on one side of the head into a braid; the rest is cut off" or "shorn on the top of the head like a cock's comb."[626] They shaved their heads with sharp flints, "allowing tufts to remain here and there, and the bare places they color with red paint." Lindeström thought, "their hair is by nature coal black and long grown, so that their locks at the ears, which they allow to hang uncut, reach down to the knees, which they, together with the other hair, anoint with bear fat, that it shines so that one can see one's reflection in it." Speaking of New Sweden and its environs, Lindeström specifically observed males who bound up their locks "with braids and ribbons and their threaded money and tie a knot to [it]." They also wore a headband of sewan, measuring "the width of a hand, strung in the form of figures."[627] Facial hair was considered "shameful" and consequently "when the first hairs appear they sit and always pull and pluck out the hair with the roots, so that it never gets to grow, but they look smooth on the chin as the women."[628] Consequently, men displayed little or no hair "on the breasts and about the mouth."[629]

Males painted themselves "in all kinds of ways in the face with all kinds of colors, so that they look inexpressibly horrible, when they think themselves to be adorned in the best manner."[630] They wore brass and tin rings or small bunches of money (*sewan*) in their ears, fixed "long and large painted bird feathers" on their heads and wore strings of sewan "like a lot of chains" around their necks. They also hung their *Pååhra* or idol among these sewan necklaces, and wore their bags or *notasser* down their backs. These bags were "very skillfully and neatly made, in which they have their things, such as food, money, tobacco, tobacco pipes...." Broad belts of *sewan*, "strung in the form of figures," were worn about the waist to fasten pieces of red or blue frieze or deerskin, which they draped about their bodies. These pieces of cloth or skins were "everywhere sewed on with their money, and around the edges which hang down, lightly fastened with hanging narrow strips, like thick long fringes on the ends of which they also have money strung." Belts of money "threaded into figures" were worn over the shoulders like a sash.[631]

Native women were "fine looking, of middle stature, well proportioned and with finely cut features; with long and black hair, and black eyes set off with fine eyebrows."[632] Other than fishing, hunting and soldiering, exclusively the domain of males, women were "compelled to do the rest of the work ... whatever else there is to be done," although old men and children "will do some labor under the direction of the women."[633] Corn was "pounded by the women, made into meal, and baked into cakes in the ashes, after the olden fashion, and used for food."[634] Because of their responsibility as gardeners and foragers, females became "the most skilful star-gazers," knowing the risings, settings and movements of heavenly bodies and constellations and "closely observing the seasons."[635] They were also weather forecasters, being "great observers of the weather by the Moon."[636] Speaking of the Indians of Narragansett Bay in 1525, Verrazano said, "In the time of sowing they are governed by the moon, which they think effects the sprouting of the grain. They have many other ancient customs."[637]

Upon their first menstruation, girls had their hair "shaved all around."[638] They occupied "a separate house, where food is furnished them on a stick" until their next menstruation.[639] Thereafter, they appeared among their relatives, dressed their hair for the first time since their isolation and were "sold" in marriage. Menstruating women usually secluded themselves and did "not appear abroad or permit themselves to be seen of men; if they are at one of their great feasts or public assemblies, and the fountain springs, they retire immediately if possible, and do not appear abroad again until the season is over."[640] According to William Penn, menstruating women "touch no meat, they eat, but with a stick; lest they should defile it; nor do their husbands frequent them, till that time be expired."[641] Newly married women were "very nice and shy," not suffering "the men to talk of any immodest or lascivious matters."[642] Married women grew their hair to their waist, letting it hang loose, but dressed it with oil or grease.[643]

Females were supposedly "more inclined to dress and to wear ornamental trinkets than the men are," but otherwise dressed basically the same, "the only difference being in the adornment of the hair, in that the females braid their hair in 4 locks, which they allow to hang down the back or they tie it up in a square pouch on the back."[644] This bun at the back of the head was arranged by coiling hair "in a club about a hand long, in the form of a beaver's tail; over which they draw a square cap, which is frequently ornamented with wampum."[645] Finely dressed women wore bands of sewan "on the forehead under the hair," which kept "the hair smooth, and [was] fastened behind over the club [of hair], in a beau's knot."[646] In the Delaware Basin, women stylistically distinguished themselves from men by neither shaving their heads nor wearing headbands of sewan.[647] Women did wear wampum necklaces, bracelets, girdles and "costly ornaments in their ears."[648] They sometimes painted their faces or drew "a black ring around their eyes."[649] They also greased their bodies to condition their skin, to protect against sun damage and to repel insects, which made them "smell very rankly." Their common garb consisted of "a leathern girdle, which is usually ornamented with pieces of whales' fins, whale bones, or sewan."[650] When cloth became available, women wrapped it "around their bodies, fastened by a girdle which extends down below their knees, and is as much as an undercoat; but next to the body, under this coat, they wear a dressed deerskin coat, girt around the waist. The lower border of this skirt they ornament with great art, and nestle the same with strips, which are tastefully decorated with wampum."[651]

Women did not ordinarily participate in public affairs. For example, in October 1744, when Reverend David Brainerd preached to "about seventy souls, old and young," at Opeholhaupung, an Indian village on the Susquehanna River consisting of twelve houses, he noted, "The men, I think universally (except one) attended my preaching. Only the women, supposing the affair we were upon was of a public nature, belonging only to the men, and not what every individual person should concern himself with, could not be readily persuaded to come and hear; but, after much pains used with them for that purpose, some few ventured to come, and stand at a distance."[652]

Women usually married upon reaching sexual maturity, at thirteen or fourteen years of age, while men married after attaining success in hunting, usually at seventeen or eighteen years of age. It was rare to postpone marriage much beyond these ages.[653] Relatives arranged adolescent marriages to strengthen familial alliances and to maintain status. Widows and widowers married according to their convenience and desires.[654] Men could purchase wives, "generally in a neighboring village."[655] They calculated consanguinity to the eighth degree and marriage or intercourse "with those of their own family within the third degree" was considered "an abominable thing."[656]

Sexually mature women, available for marriage, "veil their faces completely and sit covered as an indication of their desire; whereupon propositions are made to such persons and the practice is common with young women who have suitors, whereby they give publicity of their inclination."[657] According to custom, "when there is one who resolves to take a particular person for his wife, he collects a fathom or two of *sewan*, and comes to the nearest friends of the person whom he desires, to whom he declares his object in her presence, and if they are satisfied with him, he agrees with them how much he shall give her for a bridal present; that being done, he then gives her all the Dutch beads he has, which they call *Machampe* [wampum], and also all sorts of trinkets."[658] Men, however, seldom initiated "the first overtures, unless success is certain and they hope to improve their condition in life."[659] If a man chose a virgin, he waited "six weeks more before he can sleep with her, during which time she bewails or laments over her virginity, which they call *Collatismarrenitten*. All this time she sits with a blanket over her head, without wishing to look at any one, or any one being permitted to look at her."[660] In 1683, William Penn described this head covering as "an advertisement, but so as their faces are hardly seen, but when they please…."[661] During this time, the bridegroom went hunting not only to furnish "a feast called a *Kintikaen* for their friends, with dancing and singing," but also to provide "some proofs of their manhood, by a good return of skins, [then] they may marry, [otherwise} it is a shame to think of a wife." [662] At the proper moment, his chosen was "delivered to him by two or three other women, carrying on the head meal, roots, corn or other articles, to the young man's hut and he receives her."[663] Thereafter, "the bride must bedeck [herself] for a year and a day, although they do not know what a year means, yet a period of about that length is designated, during which she must go the whole time in her bridal attire, completely covered with their money, strung into the form of all kinds of figures, with which the ears, the arms and the body, down to the knees, are ornamented; with oiled hair, and face painted with all kinds of colors like a fearful scare-crow face."[664]

Except for chiefs, who kept several wives in order to entertain visitors, men took "one wife whom they frequently change according to caprice." Peter Lindeström thought them rather promiscuous, claiming no one knew "rightly who is the father of the child."[665] Shameless promiscuity was said to be "the cause of the men so often changing their wives and the women their husbands." Men, however, were more often blamed than women were in this regard.[666] Either party could dissolve a marriage. In instances of divorce, children followed their mother, since kinship was determined by matrilineal descent.[667] However, it must be said, that parties in stable, enduring marriages were "esteemed and honored."[668]

Whether married or not, pregnant women naturally took cares "that they do no act that would injure the offspring," and they commonly refrained from intercourse.[669] Delivery dates were closely calculated. If a woman was about to deliver her first child, or if she expected a difficult delivery, they drank "a decoction of roots that grow in the woods, which are known to them."[670] In some places, pregnant women tied rattlesnake skins around their bodies to promote "an immediate and easy delivery."[671] When birth was imminent, they chose "a secluded place near a brook or stream of water, where they can be protected from the winds, and prepare a shelter for themselves with mats and covering, where, provided with provisions necessary for them, they await their delivery without the company or aid of any person."[672] Because of their "well-formed bodies, and their manner of living," women rarely suffered sickness or death in childbirth.[673] Soon after birth, they washed the infant, plunging the baby into warm water to make him or her grow strong. Some immersed newborns in cold rivers "to harden and embolden them."[674] Adriæn van der Donck claimed only males were subject to coldwater immersion, even in freezing weather, "which, they say, makes them strong brave men and hardy hunters."[675] Thereafter, the infant was wrapped in warm clothing, nursed and cuddled. After several days, mother and child returned home.

To provide straight bones and easy carriage, infants were fastened "on a straight thin board, a little more than the length and breadth of the child ... wherefore all Indians have flat heads; and thus they carry them at their backs."[676] Customarily a newborn was bound to this carrying board without "the smallest particle of clothing under or above the child."[677] For this purpose, mothers used three long and broad braids: the first braid she wrapped over the baby's forehead and around the board, the second braid was tied around the board at the arms, while the third was tied around the board at the knees. They supposedly pressed the child "over the forehead with her hands the hardest she is able against the board, as well as the breast and knees."[678] Consequently, the children grew to be "as straight as a candle and flat in the neck as a board." Jasper Danckærts

Figure 22, "Representation of two warriors, a man wearing snow shoes and a woman carrying a child." From David P. deVries, *Korte Historiael, ende Journaels Aenteyckeninge*, Hoorn: Symon Cornelisz Brekegeest, 1655.

also noted the head, back and buttocks of an infant were entirely flat from being fastened to a board. When placing a papoose on the ground, the mother bent a sapling over it, sticking the two ends into the ground to form an arched frame over which she draped a deerskin canopy. Children remained fastened to the board even while nursing, and were only removed "for sanitary reasons." They began to toddle "very young, at nine months commonly."[679] Once released from their boards, they were carried on their mothers' backs.[680] Danckærts observed a woman carrying a toddler with the child clinging "tight around her neck like a cat, where it was kept secure by means of a piece of duffels, their usual garment."[681] Mothers never engaged nursemaids, and abstained from sexual relations while nursing. It was the accepted norm to wean babies when they reached a year old.[682]

In 1628, Reverend Jonas Michælius observed, "Parents have a strong affection for their children and are very loathe to part with them."[683] Throughout native societies, children were ardently loved and treated with "great laxity."[684] Mothers showed considerable tenderness, rocking crying children "rapidly to and fro" to quiet them.[685] European observers consequently thought Indian children "much spoiled."[686] But parents were also dutiful. In 1700, Pastorius observed, "the women bring up their children honestly, under careful oversight and dissuade them from sin."[687] Divorced or separated parents often reconciled out of mutual affection for their offspring.

As soon as boys were old enough for more active pursuits, they exercised with "cross bows and slings, and when they become somewhat larger with the shooting of guns; and then names are given to them, how they are to be called."[688] Boys learned in their infancy to catch fish with hooks. At about fifteen years of age, they were trained to hunt."[689] Girls, on the other hand, remained with their mothers, learning "to hoe the ground, plant corn and carry burdens; and they do well to use them to that [purpose] young, [what] they must do when they are old; for the wives are the true servants of their husbands, otherwise the men are very affectionate to them."[690] Nearly all natives learned to "swim like ducks from their childhood."[691] When children turned fifteen years old, they selected and adopted their "*Pååhra* or idol, faith and religion...." This idol was either a "child of skin," that is, a doll or figurine made of skin, or the claw of a lion or bear, or an eagle's talon, the tooth of a lion or bear, or a bird's bill. Whatever animal or fish token was chosen, this *pååhra* was hung from a wampum chain on their breast; it was considered a sacred object that no one else was allowed to touch. When the wearer dreamed of his *pååhra*, he would succeed the next day in shooting as much game or catch as much fish as he might want.[692]

NATURAL DEMOCRACY

Adriæn van der Donck thought "distinguishing names" in the native languages for various kinship relationships and for differences between married and unmarried persons was "strong evidence of their attachment to their relatives and of their preference to marriage connections."[693] Kinship bonded communities. Verrazano concurred, writing upon return to France in 1525, "We judged them to be very affectionate and charitable toward their relatives, for they make loud lamentations in their adversity, and in their misery call to remembrance all their good deeds. When they die their relations mutually join in weeping mingled with singing for a long while."[694]

Along the Middle Atlantic Coast, North Americans formed "tribes, mostly of one consanguinity" with "no form of political government, except that they have their chiefs, whom they call *sackmos* and *sagamos*, who are not much more than heads of families, for they rarely exceed the limits of one family connection."[695] Each tribe lived pretty much "by itself" with "one of its number as a chief, though he has not much power or distinction except in their dances or in time of war."[696] The Renappi along the Schuylkill, for example, occupied six different villages "under six sachems or chiefs, each one commanding his tribe or people under him, and each with its own peculiar language, being several hundred men strong, under each chief, counting women and children, some being stronger, some weaker."[697] This state of affairs led Nicolaes Van Wassenaer to conclude there was "little authority known among these nations," inferring natives lived "almost all equally free."[698] For the most part, North

Figure 23. Indian family. From Peter Lindeström, *Geographia Americæ*, 1654-56.

American natives showed "no reverence or honor to their ruler, which their sachem does not require of them, but their sachem may come to sit just as soon last as first, thus and in other such things [they show no preference for their sachems]."[699] But Isaack De Rasieres, Provincial Secretary of New Netherland, was emphatic in saying, "These tribes of savages all have a government." It perhaps seemed otherwise to Europeans because, as he noted, "their political government is democratic" and the chief was chosen by "election." A sackima or sachem might be the "richest in sewan, though of less consideration in other respects."[700] By observation and experience, Adriæn van der Donck further described indigenous egalitarianism, claiming "they are all free by nature, and will not bear any domineering or lording over them; they will not bear any insult, unless they have done wrong, and they will not bear chastisement without resentment."[701] This seems very similar to what we describe as the *American spirit*, its origins firmly rooted in native societies.

Nevertheless, social distinctions were "supported and observed" in certain times and places. Some North American tribes recognized "those among them whom they hold as nobles, who seldom marry beneath their rank, and they also have their commonality."[702] Accordingly, "rank descends in families, and continues as long as any one in the family is fit to rule, and regents frequently govern in the name of a minor."[703] To Peter Lindeström, native "government and household exists as under a family."[704] Among some tribes he noted greater respect for hereditary rulers, writing, "those who are rulers retain the mastery and command, children after children, those who are male persons, whose subjects are to be submissive and obedient, which they are, attempting nothing else than to live up to that [which] they are commanded, and in case they do otherwise, then he without pardon, when [someone is] caught in the act, consigns the same to death."[705]

Essentially, a chief or sackima was "the oldest and first of a household or family."[706] Often the evidence is contradictory, perhaps describing differing practices and opinions among various communities. In 1630, some "Saccimaes" were perhaps too grandly described as "the Lords of the Country," but most Europeans were of the opinion that "a chief who is general and generally called *Sackema*" possessed "not much authority and little advantage, unless in their dances and other ceremonies." In general, common folk did "not regard them much, unless they are distinguished for understanding, activity and bravery; and then they honor them greatly."[707] When merited, communities did pay "some respect" to those in authority, fearing and obeying their headman "as long as he is near," but the sachem was "no wise richer than others" and had to "shift for himself like others."[708] To a large degree, elders were respected for the sum of their knowledge and experience. In September 1679, Jasper Danckærts described Indian *patroons* or sachems as "their medicine-men and surgeons as well as their teachers...."[709] Because of their responsibility for entertaining guests and strangers, "the Sackimas generally have three or four wives, each of whom has to furnish her own seed-corn." A sachem's wife "must manage his entire household like a matron who always, in the absence of the sachem, must guard his property, which becomes her possession after his death."[710] The sachem's wife was "the housekeeper for the whole crowd," assigning women to cook and to distribute meals.[711]

Chiefs were naturally "proud of their stations," but not nearly as much as European nobles or colonial governors.[712] In 1694, Pastorius remarked, "these very kings go forth with the others to the hunt, shoot the wild animals and support themselves by the work of their own hands."[713] Customarily, upon receiving presents at a conference or payment in goods for a sale of land, a sachem "sub-divides it in like manner among his dependents, they hardly leaving themselves an equal share with one of their subjects: and be it on such occasions, at festivals, or at their common meals, the Kings distribute, and to themselves last."[714] On June 17, 1653, when Swedish Director Johan Rijsingh assembled the principal sachems of the Renappi at Tenneconk, now Tinicum Island, the hosts fed their guests from large kettles of sappaen. On this occasion, Peter Lindeström observed, "the superior Sachems remained sitting and the lesser people ate their stomachs full of it. But when the great Sachems went away, they asked permission to pour the rest into two kettles and carry them out on the ground to eat, which was granted them."[715]

In August 1634, Captain Thomas Young met eight sackimas near present-day Trenton. One sackima apparently headed a family of from forty to sixty Indians. In some instances, the sackimas appeared to be paired: an elder and a younger man; in one instance, the elderly sackima was described as the father-in-law of the younger man; in other instances, a sackima was attended by his brother. These figures of authority seem to represent divisions in the native community where younger males, being hunters and warriors, were headed by a war captain or youthful sackima—one of their own generation—while old men, who appear to have lived separately from the women of the village at least part of the year, were represented by the elder sackima. It appears that most sackimas claimed their position by matrilineal descent, although the clan may have ratified their elevation.[716] In 1683, William Penn confirmed the office of sackima passed by matrilineal succession, that is, "the children of him that is now King, will not succeed, but his brother by the mother, or the children of his sister, whose sons (and after them the children of her daughters) will reign; for no woman inherits; the reason they render for this way of descent, is, that their issue may not be spurious."[717]

William Penn also observed, "nothing of moment is undertaken, be it war, peace, selling of land or traffic," without advice from a council "of all the old and wise men of his Nation, which perhaps is two hundred people…."[718] As a model for Europeans, Indians did "not resolve and decide hastily and by a small number, but on all important matters, all the chiefs and persons of any distinction in the nation assemble in their councils, when each of them express their opinions freely on the subject before the council, as briefly or as extendedly as they please without any molestation. If the speaker even digresses from the matter in hand, or opposes others, he is heard with attention; if they approve of what has been said, at the conclusion they shout and cheer the orator."[719] Such councils convened "in the morning while the sun is ascending, and if the business is not done before noon they adjourn until the next morning."[720] Traditionally, the sackima "sits in the middle of an half moon, and hath his council, the old and wise on each hand; behind them, or at a little distance, sit the younger fry, in the same figure."[721] The sackima was fact-finder, arbiter, spokesman and justice of the peace. His role, as first among equals, was to poll opinion and build a consensus for action or inaction. After eliciting testimony in either a dispute or proposal concerning his family, the sackima announced his opinion. If his male relatives agreed, "they give all together a sigh— 'He!' —and if they do not approve, they keep silence, and all come close to the sackima, and each sets forth his opinion until they agree…." Once a consensus was achieved, the sackima "then announces what they have determined, with the reasons moving them thereto."[722] He also presented their decision to outsiders.[723]

The sackima presided at divorce court. The plaintiff, whether husband or wife, summoned him and he listened to accusations of infidelity. If a woman was found guilty, he ordered her to cut off her hair as a public sign of contempt. She lost her possessions and was driven from her house, though her children usually remained in her care. When a man was found guilty, his wife removed his right shoe and stocking, together with his lappet, and then "gives him a kick behind, and so drives him out of the house…."[724] The sackima also acted as magistrate in cases of injury or death, imposing "his fixed fine of sewan for fighting and causing blood to flow."[725]

Because the numerous tribes or families "often engaged in wars among themselves, they are fearful and timid."[726] The sachem or sackima of each family, who normally was "somewhat above the others," would command absolutely when warriors gathered from several villages to go to war.[727] According to Van der Donck, "the principal command and authority among the Indians is developed in war, and in their councils on war."[728] In times of conflict, a war captain was selected "by merit, without regard to families or birth." This rank or office might be conferred upon "the lowest among them ... but the rank dies with the person, unless his posterity follow in the footsteps of the parent; and then, the rank of the parent and his situation will descend in the family."[729] Van der Donck speculated, "that such is the origin of the rank and distinction which prevails among them."[730]

On January 8, 1633, Captain De Vries met with nine chiefs, sachems from nine different places on the site of Fort Nassau, opposite today's Philadelphia. These chiefs "seated themselves in a circle," making peace by presenting "ten beaver-skins, which one of them gave us, with a ceremony with each skin, saying in whose name he presented it; that it was for a perpetual peace with us, and that we must banish all evil thoughts from us, for they had now thrown away all evil."[731] These chiefs then refused presents from the Dutchmen, "declaring that they had not made us presents in order to receive others in return, but for the purpose of a firm peace...."[732]

LAND OWNERSHIP AND SALES

Indians only sold land to European agents with community consent, arrived at through discussions moderated by an elder or sackima. This procedure was largely hidden from European eyes and ears, but at least one example of the process has entered the historical record. Oratam, a Hackensack sachem, Waerhen van Couwe, of Hespatingh on Bergen Neck, and their interpreter, Sarah Kiersted, appeared at the Council Chamber at Fort Amsterdam on July 20, 1663. Oratam said, "he has come to bring an answer to the proposition made by his Honor, the [Director] General [Peter Stuyvesant], namely, whether the savages would sell us the hook of land behind the Kil van Kol, etc., to which he answers, that most of the young men of the tribe are out hunting, so that he has not been able to speak with them, but he has talked with the old warriors, who say, that they would not like to sell, preferring to keep a portion of it to plant, for they dare not go further inland for fear of being robbed by their enemies. He says further, that there is land enough both for us and for them divided by the Kil and that it is as good as the land on the Esopus."[733]

The generation gap was not uncommon. The Esopus Indians sent Kessachauw, one of the chiefs of the Wappings, to New Amsterdam on May 18, 1660, to sue for peace. Peter Stuyvesant told him "that the Esopus chiefs had before this frequently declared to us, they, the chiefs, were quite willing to continue in peace with us, but that the young people always wanted to fight and they, as chiefs, had no command or power to punish the barebacks and young people and we see no occasion and safety in making peace with the chiefs only; therefore it would first be necessary, that he first and above all informed the Esopus Indians, old and young, Sachems and barebacks, hereof and if they altogether desire peace, they must come themselves."[734] On June 3, 1660, Oratam stated that Seweckenamo, an Esopus chief who met with him on Staten Island, told him "that just before he came here he had spoken with the soldiers, that is the fighting savages, who camp by themselves, and had asked them, what they desired; they had answered: We do not want to fight any more; then he had spoken with the women about what they thought best; they had answered, that we may peacefully plant the land and live in peace; then he had gone to the inexperienced young men, who camp alone upon another place, to ask them, what they thought and they said, to make peace with the Dutch and that they would not kill a pig nor a chicken."[735]

Speaking of the Minisinks and Delawares in 1744, Reverend David Brainerd concluded, "they are almost continually roving from place to place; and it is but rare, that an opportunity can be had with some of them for their instruction. There is scarce any time of the year, wherein the men can be found generally at home, except about six weeks before, and in the season of planting their corn, and about two months in the latter part of summer, from the time they begin to roast their corn, until it is fit to gather in."[736] He pronounced "their wandering to and fro in order to procure the necessaries of life" a great impediment to missionary work.

Payment for a real estate transaction was "not hoarded by the particular owners, but the neighboring Kings and their clans being present when the goods were brought out, the parties chiefly concerned consulted, what and to whom they should give them? To every King, then, by the hands of a person for that work appointed, is a proportion sent, so sorted and folded, and with that gravity, that is admirable. Then that King subdivides it in like manner among his dependents, they hardly leaving themselves an equal share with one of their subjects…."[737]

VENDETTA: LIKE FOR LIKE.

Steeped in social stratification, Dutch colonial officers thought that either the natives possessed "no law, no justice," or, at best, that there was "hardly any law or justice among them, except sometimes in war matters, and then very little."[738] Adriæn van der Donck believed "common rules of order in the administration of justice" were not observed among them and that minor offenses such as stealing, adultery, lying, and cheating were generally disregarded. He even cited examples of rape and murder that went unpunished, though capital offenses were rare among Indians.[739] Generally they were peaceable, "so long as no injury is done them," but grudges were long held and revenge taken "even after a long lapse of time," and sometimes at great risk. Justice was a personal matter and vengeance "highly prized."[740] Natives followed "no other law or justice, but in whatever manner anyone unjustly suffers from the other, they immediately revenge on one another, like for like."[741] In 1683, William Penn described North Americans as "great concealers of their own resentments, brought to it, I believe, by the revenge that hath been practiced among them…."[742]

By custom, if an Indian killed another, it was not punished; rather the aggrieved party "sets vengeance on foot; if not, nothing is done."[743] The nearest of kin was the avenger.[744] Algonquian tribes reckoned "consanguinity to the eighth degree and revenge an injury from generation to generation unless it be atoned for; and even then there is mischief enough, for they are very revengeful."[745] Proper payment might atone for an injury, even murder, and reconcile the parties to a grievance; in such cases, where settlement was possible, the sackima imposed "his fixed fine for fighting and causing blood to flow."[746] William Penn noted, "the Justice they have is pecuniary: In case of any wrong or evil fact, be it murder itself, they atone by feasts and presents of the wampum, which is proportioned to the quality of the offence or person injured, or of the sex they are of: for in case they kill a woman, they pay double, and the reason they render, is, that she breeds children, which men cannot do."[747] In instances of murder, if the victim's kin apprehended the culprit within twenty-four hours, he was slain. After a day had expired, friends attempted "to reconcile the parties, which is frequently agreed to, on condition that the nearest relatives of the murderer, be they men, women, or children, on meeting the relatives of the person murdered, must give way to them."[748] Atonement for murder required "heavy payment."[749]

On December 6, 1632, Captain David De Vries visited the ruins of his settlement at Swanendæl, now Lewes, Delaware, where he discovered "the skulls and bones of our people … and the heads of the horses and cows."[750] An Indian later informed De Vries of the cause of the massacre: One of the Indian chiefs removed "a piece of tin, whereon the arms of Holland were painted" from a wooden post "for the purpose of making tobacco-pipes, not knowing that he was doing amiss."[751] Those in command "made such an ado about it, that the Indians, not knowing how it was, went away and slew the chief who had done it, and brought a token of the dead to the house to those in command, who told them that they wished they had not done it, that they should have brought him to them, as they wished to have forbidden him to do the like again."[752] The family and friends of the slain chief soon "set about the work of vengeance." Consequently, several Indians entered the settlement, under pretense of trade, and slew the inhabitants. Exhibiting his own cultural bias, Captain De Vries stereotyped Indians as "a people like the Italians, who are very revengeful."[753]

In March 1642, a Wickquaesgeck Indian appeared at the East River house of Clæs Smits, wheelwright, seeking to trade beavers for duffel cloth. Smits' son had formerly employed this Indian.[754] When Smits stooped over to retrieve some cloth from a chest, the Indian fatally struck him on the neck with an axe, cutting off his head. The native then proceeded to plunder his trade goods. Upon inquiry, the murderer explained "that, while the fort was being built [in 1626], he came with his uncle and another savage to the Freshwater, bringing beavers, in order to trade with the Dutchmen, that some Swannekes (as they call the Netherlanders) came there, took away from his uncle his beavers, and then killed him. He was then a small boy, and resolved that, when he should grow up, he would revenge that deed upon the Dutch, and since then he had seen no better chance to do so than with this Clæs Rademaker [Dutch for "wheelwright"]."[755]

In August 1642, at Winkelman's trading post on the Hackensack River in present-day Bogota, a sackima's son was sold brandy that had been adulterated with water, and was then robbed of his beaver-coat. Inebriated, the cheated Indian returned shortly thereafter, and fatally shot one of the Dutch traders as he sat thatching the roof. Captain David De Vries, who lived in the neighborhood, accompanied several chiefs from Ackinghsack and Reckawawanck to Fort Amsterdam, where they offered payment of one or two hundred fathoms of sewan to the murdered man's widow, "if thereby they would be at peace ... they desired in a friendly way to make the widow contented, and to pay for the man's death with sewan, which is their money; it being a custom with them, if any misfortune befall them, to reconcile the parties with money."[756]

In 1683, William Penn published an account of a sackima's daughter who felt slighted when her husband allowed another woman "to lie down between them." She committed suicide by eating a poisonous root, forcing her widower to make "an offering to her kindred for atonement and liberty of marriage; as two others did to the kindred of their wives, that died a natural death: For till widowers have done so, they must not marry again."[757]

Tchipai Meskenau, The Path of Souls

North Americans held beliefs and rituals "transmitted to them by tradition, from ancestor to ancestor."[758] Yet most Europeans, trapped within their own deadly history of sectarian intolerance and religious certitude, could detect "no religion whatever, nor any divine worship" among Indians.[759] Of seven North Americans brought from Newfoundland to Rouen, France, with their canoe, clothing and weapons, in 1509, it was said, "they form a dialect with their lips; religion they have none."[760] Drawing upon logs and journals of the earliest Dutch explorers, Van Wassenaer vacillated, surmising, "Respecting Religion we as yet cannot learn that they have any knowledge of God, but there is something similar in repute among them."[761] Recognizing the complexity of North American beliefs, *The Representation of New Netherland*, published at the Hague in 1650, reported "not the least knowledge of God," among some tribes, "and among others very little, though they relate many strange fables concerning Him."[762] In 1656, Adriæn van der Donck described North Americans as heathens "without any religious devotions," who did not worship idols nor offer prayers nor honor any particular day over others.[763] Obviously, a spirituality that did not evidence *devotions*, *worship*, *prayer* or *holy days* was beyond his comprehension. He expressed the almost universal pejorative European opinion when he recorded: "They neither know or say any thing of God; but they possess great fear of the devil, who they believe causes diseases and does them much injury."[764] Hardly an open-minded observer, Quaker William Penn decided Indians were "under a dark night in things relating to Religion, to be sure, the tradition of it; yet they believe a God and Immortality, without the help of Metaphysics…."[765]

The testimony of European commentators is thus self-serving and contradictory: some said Indians "neither know or say any thing of God," while others claimed Indians acknowledged "that there is a God in heaven from all eternity, who is almighty."[766] Wishful thinking played a part in these perceptions, as did ignorant contempt. Opinions obviously depended on whether or not a particular European observer found any correspondence between the Great Spirit of some native belief and their own Biblical God. In addition, there was another cultural barrier to mutual respect—no systematic *credo* or written scripture existed that all Indians shared and disputed. On more common ground, both North Americans and Europeans were fully capable of imagining a better condition or place beyond the capricious material plain of existence with its sudden and often unpleasant twists of fate. Yet both—in their own ways—attributed natural events and the direction of human affairs to a regulation by hidden powers.

Another possible explanation for discrepancies of opinion about native religions is that the varied linguistic and cultural stock of peoples who inhabited the Middle Atlantic Coast were receptive to a broad range of beliefs covering the existence, source and strength of unseen or possibly unseeable influences upon their lives. Even members of the same band were not compelled to any conformity or standard of belief. As with most humans, many North Americans were pragmatic, borrowing and blending different traditions to meet their own circumstances. Reverend Brainerd visited mixed communities of Indians along the Susquehanna River, where Algonquian-speaking Minisinks and Delawares lived beside Iroquoian-speaking Senecas and Tutelas. Communicating through interpreters, he learned "that in ancient times, before the coming of the white people, some supposed that there were four invisible powers, who presided over the four corners of the earth. Others imagined the sun to be the only deity and that all things were made by him. Others, at the same time, have a confused notion of a certain body or fountain of deity, somewhat like the *anima mundi*, so frequently mentioned by the more learned ancient Heathens, diffusing itself to various animals, and even to inanimate things, making them the immediate authors of good to certain persons, as before observed, with respect to various supposed deities."[767] Some of these traditions may be traced to their sources. Regarding sun-worship, for example, Captain De Vries claimed to have encountered a nation of Indians "at the north" —most likely Iroquois—who looked upon the sun as a god "for in summer he drew the leaves from the trees, and all the fruits from the ground."[768] Indians also told European visitors "that mention was made by their forefathers for many thousand moons, of good and evil spirits, to whose honor, it is supposed, they burn fires or sacrifices."[769] As do peoples everywhere, they understandably wanted "to stand well with the Good Spirits." An original heavenly power or Great Spirit was called "*Menutto* or *Menetto*; and whatever is wonderful and seems to exceed human capacity, they also call *Menetto*."[770] Some attributed sickness and death to "*Manitto*, that is the Devil ... who sends him all evil things."[771] As a result, sacrifices and feasts cultivated the favor of *Manitto*, seeking success in hunting and other activities.

Manitto apparently derives from the Algonquian verb *maniton*, meaning, "to make."[772] It would seem, therefore, that native spirituality recognized an invisible causality, that is to say, some force that either shaped events in the past or that shapes them in the present. Manitou, however, was not necessarily or exclusively identified as maker of the material universe, but rather as the governor of fate and animator of both mundane and extraordinary events. Manitou was imminent in the natural world and, so far as it concerned its inhabitants of all species, existed without beginning. The Ottawas, resident on the southwest borders of Lake Superior, recognized "no sovereign master of Heaven and Earth, but believe there are many spirits—some of whom are beneficent, as the Sun, the Moon, the Lake, Rivers, and Woods; other malevolent, as the adder, the dragon, cold, and storms. And, in general, whatever seems to them either helpful or hurtful they call a *Manitou*, and pay it the worship and veneration, which we render only to the true God."[773]

Reverend Jonas Michælius thought that by the word *Menetto* the natives "comprehend everything that is subtle and crafty and beyond human skill and power." Ironically, given European inclinations, he likewise perceived North Americans as practitioners of "so much witchcraft, divination, sorcery and wicked arts."[774] Many Europeans similarly assumed that Indians were deceived into worshipping a sham-god or devil. De Laet, while compiling his *Nieuwe Wereldt*, summarily dismissed native spirituality by claiming Indians "indeed pay homage to the Devil; but not so solemnly nor with such precise ceremonies as the Africans do."[775] Van der Donck, in his *Representation of New Netherland*, found the natives "in general much afraid of the Devil; who torments them greatly; and some give themselves up to him, and hold the strangest notions about him."[776] Apparently, these "devils" would "have nothing to do with the Dutch," who of course had demons of their own.[777] Van der Donck specifically noted a sacrificial offering of *first fruits*, relating, "When they go on a hunting or fishing excursion they usually cast a part of what was first taken into the fire, without using any ceremony on the occasion, then saying, 'stay [away] thou devil, eat thou that.'"[778] Such offerings were generally made with "few solemnities." Peter Lindeström describes a similar ritual among the Renappi, remarking that the first hunt of the year was consecrated to Manitto: "When they first have eaten their fill of it and enjoyed their feast they make a burnt offering of the remaining, which they sacrifice to Manitto, i.e., the Devil, but not one animal of it do [they] sell, believing that they through this later will get in their hunt so much the greater blessing." The festivities concluded with a dance and a chant: "*Hägginj, hä, hä, hä; Hägginj hä; Hägginj hä; Hägginj hä, hä, hä, hä*"[779]

Tantaqua, alias Jasper, a Hackensack Indian, went fishing daily and regularly provided some of his catch to Dutch settlers on Long Island during "a very dear time; [when] no provisions could be obtained, and they suffered great want, so that they were reduced to the last extremity...."[780] When asked many years later, why he had done so much kindness, he answered, "I have always been inclined, from my youth up to do good, especially to good people known to me. I took fish to these people because Maneto said to me, 'you must take fish to these people,' whispering ever in my ear, 'you must take fish to them.' I had to do it or Maneto would have killed me." According to Tantaqua, Maneto killed those who did evil and left those who did good works at peace. Again, suggesting a dualism, he thought there might be a *Great Sackemaker* who remained aloof, not troubling himself with the world. But Maneto, also a *sackemaker*, governed earthy affairs, punishing and tormenting those who do evil or "drink themselves drunk."[781] Tantaqua's beliefs seemed to reflect a popular outlook and understanding. Many natives considered the Great Spirit benign and remote, saying, "God is good, kind, and compassionate, who will not punish or do any injury to any person and therefore takes no concern himself in the common affairs of the world, nor does he meddle with the same, except that he has ordered the devil to take care of those matters. For they say that all that happens to persons on the earth is ordered and directed by the devil as he pleases. God, the chief of all, who dwells in heaven, is much greater and higher than the devil, over whom he has power, but he will not meddle in, or trouble himself with, those concerns."[782]

Some had a very pragmatic explanation for this divine aloofness from worldly affairs—the Supreme Spirit was distracted by "a goddess, a female person, the most beautiful ever known and beheld," whereby, he was "so much engrossed that the time is passed away and forgotten."[783] Providing a mythological origin for clans, this goddess was also involved in creation, having descended from heaven, whereupon land appeared beneath her as by the ebbing of the tide. Thereafter, vegetation sprouted as the land became unbounded. The goddess gave birth to three distinct and different creatures, a deer, a bear and a wolf, which she suckled to maturity. From her cohabitation with these creatures, all further species originated, including humanity. Having assured the great variety and abundance of nature, this "Common Mother" ascended to heaven. In the meanwhile, "all mankind, wherever they be, are always born with the nature of one or the other of the aforesaid animals"—like deer, some folks are "doe-in-the-headlights," timid and innocent; like bear, some are brave, revengeful and just of hand; like wolves, some are deceitful and bloodthirsty. [784]

The Iroquoian Hurons believed "that a certain woman named Eataensic is the one who made earth and man."[785] She governed the world with her young son named Jouskeha. Eataensic has "care of souls; and because they believe that she makes men die, they say that she is wicked." Jouskeha has "care of the living and of the things that concern life, and consequently they say that he is good." According to Huron mythology, "Eataensic fell from the Sky, where there are inhabitants as on earth, and when she fell, she was with child."[786] *The Jesuit Relations* tell us the Hurons thought, "This God and Goddess live like themselves, but without famine; make feasts as they do, are lustful as they are; in short, they make them human and corporeal, they seem nevertheless to attribute to them a certain immensity in all places."[787] It almost seems the Hurons saw their Common Mother and her lordly Son with pretty much the same eyes as French Catholics regarded the Virgin and her Incarnate Son—these are the Hurons' Great Intercessors, assisting with their daily hopes and cares. According to Reverend Johannes Megapolensis, Iroquoian Mohawks confirmed this "theory of the Creation, for they think that a pregnant woman fell down from heaven, and that a tortoise (tortoises are plenty and large here, in this country, two, three and four feet long, some with two heads, very mischievous and addicted to biting) took this pregnant woman on its back, because every place was covered with water; and that the woman sat upon the tortoise, groped with her hands in the water, and scraped together some of the earth, whence it finally happened that the earth was raised above the water."[788]

The Iroquois shared this belief of the role of a goddess or divine consort in creation with some of their Algonquian neighbors. According to the *Relation* of Father Paul Le Jeune, written in 1634, the Montagnais, the previously-mentioned Algonquian-speaking nation of eastern Canada, believed the *Manitou*, "whom we may call the devil," was regarded as "the origin of evil; it is true that they do not attribute great malice to the Manitou, but to his wife, who is a real she-devil."[789] The Manitou was "only present in wars and combats, and those whom he looks upon are protected, the others killed ... As to the wife of the Manitou, she is the cause of all the diseases which are in the world. It is she who kills men; otherwise they would not die; she feeds upon their flesh, gnawing them upon the inside, which causes them to become emaciated in their illnesses. She has a robe made of the most beautiful hair of the men and women whom she killed; she sometimes appears like a fire; she can be heard roaring like a flame, but her language cannot be understood."[790] With Manitou distracted by his fiery consort, "the devil plays tyrant and does what he pleases." This "devil" (so called by Christian equation with the dark side of their own belief) is deceitful and wicked, taking pleasure in using his powers "in the most wicked and injurious ways," causing "all accidents, infirmities, and diseases…." Those suffering misfortune and illness complained, "that the devil is in them."[791] To deserve his friendship and favor, they would "cast a piece [of meat] to him into the fire."[792]

The Iroquoian legend perhaps is related to an Algonquian creation story, and both may derive from a clan-bonding belief in descent from a common mythological ancestor. In October 1679, Tantaqua, who resided on Tantaqua's Plain at New Bridge, where the towns of Teaneck, River Edge, Hackensack and New Milford now intersect, spoke to Jasper Danckærts about human origins and a seemingly godless act of creation. He explained how a tortoise raised its back above the water, creating the first dry land. A tree grew in the middle of the earth and from its root the first male sprouted. To produce a female companion, the tree bent over and another root sprouted the first woman. All humankind descends from these two.[793] Algonquian-speaking Sawanoos of southern New Jersey recounted a similar tale seventy years later, telling Peter Kalm in 1750, "A large turtle floated on the water. Around it gathered more and more slime and other material that fastened itself to it, so that it finally became all America. The first savage was sent down from heaven and rested on the turtle. When he encountered a log he kicked it and behold, people were formed from it. In every city (of the Red Men) there is ordinarily one family, which takes the name of 'Turtle.' "[794] The turtle has a dual nature, being able to live in or out of water and thus readily explained the origin of all creatures. In a related matter, another old Indian told Kalm, "that when God had created the world and its people, he took a stick, cast it on the ground, and spoke unto man, saying, 'Here thou shalt have an animal, which will be of great service to thee, and which will follow thee wherever thou goest,' and in that moment the stick turned into a dog."[795]

A Sanhican spiritual healer once spoke of a Prime Mover. In March 1680, Hans, an Indian sackemaker and medicine-man residing near Constable's Hook on Newark Bay, explained that all North Americans, whether Manhattans, Senecas, Mohawks or Susquehannocks, Southern or Northern Indians, acknowledge the existence of "a supreme first power … the first and great beginning of all things," whose true name was "*Kickeron*, who is the origin of all, who has not only once produced or made all things, but produces every day."[796] It was Kickeron who "made the tortoise, and the tortoise had a power and a nature to produce all things, such as earth, trees and the like, which God wished through it to produce, or have produced." Hans further elaborated, "All that we see daily that is good, is from him; and every thing he makes and does is good. He governs all things, and nothing is done without his aid and direction." Sickness was an evil visited upon those who were bad, and Hans believed medicines would only work if Kickeron wished to work a cure. A wicked spirit or "devil" urged people to commit "all kinds of evil, drunkenness and excess, to fighting and war, and to strife and violence amongst themselves, by which many are wounded and killed."

The Maker seemed indifferent to some native observers, being neither benign nor malicious. Good and evil simply acted as weight and counterweight in maintaining a cosmic equilibrium. Evil required immediate retribution or correction. Good received no reward other than enjoyment of life and health through the cyclical replenishment and proper distribution of natural bounty. The cosmic scales were largely self-adjusting; priests and judges were not needed to right wrongs among humans or between god and humans. Manitou maintained stability either by bestowing or withholding his favors. To this end, Manitou, the *anima mundi*, acted through all creation.

For many North Americans, encountering one's Spirit Guide and thereafter respecting its Totem brought spiritual protection and favor. Writing in his *Geographia Americæ* about the Renappi, Peter Lindeström contended, "...they adopt their *Pååhra* or idol when they are about 15 years old. Thus the one makes for his self a child of skin with head, body, arms, hands, legs and feet to believe in. The other selects a lion claw, that [one], a bear claw, this one, an eagle claw, that one, a bear claw, this one, an eagle claw, that one, a lion tooth, this one, a bear tooth, this one, a bird bill, etc. In fine, whatever limb of any animal, bird, fish, or other [living thing] they desire to choose for their god or *Pååhra*, as they call [it], which is hung on a chain of their money on their breast, they consider this their god, so sacred that no one is allowed to touch it, —the one who attempts it, he becomes his chief enemy. In this their god they have such a strong faith, that the night he dreams about him, he will at once the following day be

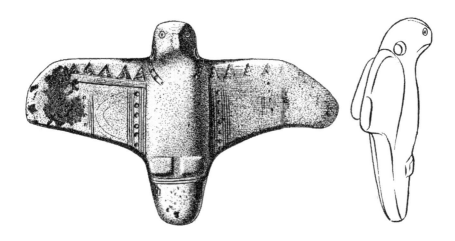

Figure 24. Shell Pååhra or bird Totem. From George G. Heye and George
H. Pepper, *Exploration of a Munsee Cemetery near Montague, New
Jersey*, New York: The Museum of the American Indian, 1915.

able to shoot as much game and catch as much fish as ever he wants to,
—the evil one, undoubtedly helps him to it"[797]

Reverend Brainerd concurred, saying, "So far as I can learn,
they had a notion of a plurality of invisible deities and paid some kind
of homage to them promiscuously under a great variety of forms and
shapes. It is certain that those who yet remain Pagans pay some kind of
superstitious reverence to beasts, birds, fishes, and even reptiles; that is,
some to one kind of animal, and some to another. They do not indeed
suppose a divine power essential to, or inhering in, these creatures; but
that some invisible beings—I cannot learn that it is always one such being
only, but divers; not distinguished from each other by certain names, but
only notionally; —communicate to these animals a great power; either
one or another of them, just as it happens, or perhaps sometimes all of
them; and so make these creatures the immediate authors of good to
certain persons. —Whence such a creature becomes sacred to the persons
to whom he is supposed to be the immediate author of good, and through
him they must worship the invisible powers, though to others he is no
more than another creature. Perhaps another animal is looked upon to

be the immediate author of good to another; and consequently he must worship the invisible powers in that animal. I have known a Pagan burn fine tobacco for incense in order to appease the anger of that invisible power, which he supposed presided over rattlesnakes, because one of these animals was killed by another Indian near his house."[798] To confirm this, Nils Gustafson, ninety-one years of age in 1749, told Peter Kalm that he "once walked with an Indian and they encountered a red-spotted snake on the road: the old man therefore went to seek a stick in order to kill it, but the Indian begged him not to touch it, because it was sacred to him. Perhaps the Swede would not have killed it, but on hearing that it was the Indian's deity, he took a stick and killed it, in the presence of the Indian, saying: 'Because thou believe in it, I think myself obliged to kill it.'"[799]

Belief that spiritual instruction came through dreams was widespread in North America. On March 2, 1639, and over several succeeding days, Father François Du Peron, a Jesuit missionary, observed a "carnival" of "deviltry and masquerading at that time throughout the Huron country."[800] This may have been a New Year's celebration following the Dark Moon, denoting the arrival of spring. Father Du Peron noted, "all their actions are dictated to them directly by the devil, who speaks to them, now in the form of a crow or some similar bird, now in the form of a flame or a ghost, and all this in dreams, to which they show a great deference. They consider the dream as the master of their lives; it is the God of the country. It is this which dictates to them their feasts, their hunting, their fishing, their war, their trade with the French, their remedies, their dances, their games, their songs." In 1635, Father Brebeuf reported, "Their superstitions are infinite, their feasts, their medicines, their fishing, their hunting, their wars, —in short almost their whole life turns upon this pivot; dreams, above all have here great credit."[801] Renappi and Minisinks also gave "much heed to dreams, because they suppose these invisible powers give them directions at such times about certain affairs, and sometimes inform them what animal they would choose to be worshipped in."[802]

Near-death experiences reinforced belief in the significance of dreams. In 1745, one man told missionary David Brainerd that he had been dead for four days.[803] His burial had been delayed to accommodate relatives traveling from a great distance, but before they arrived, "he came to life again." While dead, "he went to the place where the sun rises; imagining the earth to be a plain; and directly over that place, at a great height in the air, he was admitted, he says, into a great house, which he supposes was several miles in length, and saw many wonderful things…." Another woman who was believed dead for several days claimed, "her soul went southward and feasted and danced with the happy spirits, and that she found all there exactly agreeable to the Indian notions of a future state." It was widely believed that departed souls of those "who have been good and valuable in this life" traveled southward to a moderate climate "where they will be satisfied and have an abundance of good things, without any trouble or labor for the same, forever."[804] Some thought the souls of evildoers were excluded from this afterlife of plenty and contentment. "Voices or noises in the woods at night … they declare, with fear and astonishment, are made by the wicked, the souls of whom are thus doomed to wander at night in the woods and solitary places for punishment in unhappy situations."[805] For this reason, some Indians refused to travel alone at night, unless they carried a firebrand to "keep off those evil spirits and prevent them from doing them any injury, which, they say, are always disposed to frighten them and do them wrong."[806] Opinions in this matter differed, and many natives believed that once a person's shadow or soul departed, "no haunting of spirits and the like are heard among them."[807]

In 1628, Reverend Jonas Michælius claimed, "If we speak to them of God, it appears to them like a dream; and we are compelled to speak of him, not under the name of Menetto, whom they know and serve—for that would be blasphemy—but of one great, yea, *most high Sackiema*, by which name they—living without a king—call him who has command over several hundred among them, and who by our people are called Sackemakers…."[808] Blinded by cultural prejudice and religious intolerance, Dominie Michælius regarded his stoic audience as "strangers to all decency, yea, uncivil and stupid as garden poles, proficient in all wickedness and godlessness; devilish men, who serve nobody but the Devil." The amazement was mutual—some natives responded by muttering and shaking their heads at Christian belief "as if it were a silly fable," while others responded with polite regard and friendship, perhaps enjoying a well-told tale.[809] Clearly something had been lost in the translation.

Interpreters from both communities moved between languages with sufficient skill for purposes of trade, but, as Jonas Michælius readily admitted, "this cannot be done in religious matters."[810] Much like himself, missionary David Brainerd found the Delawares "extremely attached to the customs, traditions, and fabulous notions of their fathers." He noted, "divers miracles ... were anciently wrought among the Indians, which they firmly believe, and thence look upon their ancestors to have been the best of men."[811] Their principal objection to Christianity was that "'it was not the same God made them, who made the white people,' but another, who commanded them to live by hunting, &c. and not to conform to the customs of the white people."[812]

Despite great differences, Adriæn van der Donck was convinced the natives "know that there is a distinction between the body and the soul and believe, as they actually do, that the one is perishable and the other immortal."[813] The soul was defined as "that spirit which directs all the actions of the body and is the producing cause of all good and evil conduct, which when the body dies, separates from it and removes to a place towards the south, where the climate is so fine that no covering against the cold will be necessary and where the heat will never be troublesome." Indians believed "that the soul proceeds from God and that the same is his gift."[814]

This enduring soul, spirit-mind, or *animus* inhabited all things, and may perhaps be compared to ancient Western notions of Platonic idealism. The *shadow* or spirit of an individual existed before his birth, entering the physical body after Manito determined its destiny. The Montagnais of Canada believed "all animals, of every species, have an elder brother, who is, as it were, the source and origin of all individuals, and this elder brother is wonderfully great and powerful."[815] The elder brother of the beaver was supposedly as large as a cabin. When the skeleton of a large Pleistocene mammal was discovered in a swamp by the Illinois River, they thought, "that it must be the skeleton of the chief or father of all the beavers."[816] Dreaming of the Elder or archetype of a species was regarded as betokening "a fortunate chase" for members of that species—the hunter "possessing the juniors through the favor of their senior whom he has seen in the dream." Though uncertain as to the location of these elders or progenitors, it was thought, "the elders of the birds are in the sky and that the elders of the other animals are in the water."[817]

According to the *Jesuit Relations*, the Montagnais "persuade themselves that not only men and other animals, but also all other things, are endowed with souls and that all souls are immortal: they imagine the souls as shadows of the animate objects: never having heard of anything purely spiritual, they represent the soul of man as a dark and somber image, or as the shadow of the man himself, attributing to it feet, hands, a mouth, a head, and all other parts of the human body."[818] Consequently, they believed that "souls drink and eat, and therefore they give them food when any one dies...." Furthermore, "the souls of men, of animals, of hatchets, of knives, of kettles, —in short, the souls of all things that die or that are used..." journeyed to the world or dwelling-place of the dead. For this reason, certain grave goods were "ritually killed" or broken so that the deceased could use them in the great beyond. A Jesuit missionary observed, "several stripped, or almost so, of all their goods, because several of their friends were dead, to whose souls they had made presents. Moreover, dogs, fish, deer, and other animals have, in their opinion, immortal and reasonable souls."[819] Some Algonquians believed departed souls traveled southward, where good souls were admitted "into a beautiful town with spiritual walls" and where bad souls "would for ever hover around these walls, in vain attempts to get in."[820] Delawares believed, "There is a great King that made them, who dwells in a glorious Country to the southward of them, and that the souls of the good shall go thither, where they shall live again."[821] In 1697, Pastorius confirmed that natives of the Delaware Basin "say that God dwells in the most glorious southern land, to which they also shall attain at some future time, after death."[822] The Algonquian-speaking Mahicans held a variant belief —at least in regard to compass orientation—saying the soul "goes up westward on leaving the body. There it meets with great rejoicing the others who have died previously; there they all wear black otter or bearskins, which among them are signs of gladness. They [the living] have no desire to be with them."[823] The Montagnais, another northerly tribe, also believed that departed souls journeyed "very far away, to a large village situated [westward] where the Sun sets." Souls of the deceased traveled thither via "the Milky Way, *Tchipai meskenau*, the path of souls...."[824]

Burial customs indicate belief that some aspect of the individual survives after death. With great empathy, natives were "faithful to sustain and take care of each other," even in cases of "deadly disease."[825] Survivors poured out their grief at the moment of death, when "they set themselves down to bawl and howl, weep and lament over their good comrade's deathly departure."[826] Immediately afterwards, "the nearest relatives extend the limbs and close the eyes of the dead; and after the body has been watched and wept over several days and nights, they bring it to the grave...."[827] A messenger was sent out "around the country, crying, calling and lamenting, who runs around everywhere and makes this known to the good friends of the dead savage."[828] Friends and relations of the departed traditionally offered this messenger hospitality and gifts. The deceased was buried after a few days, allowing time for the gathering of those who received and responded to the death announcement. Burial grounds were "secluded and preserved with religious veneration and care" and natives considered it "wicked and infamous to disturb or injure their burial places."[829] All residents of a place assembled at funerals, whether the deceased be a friend, relative or stranger.[830] In some cultures, a corpse was interred in "a large grave lined with boughs, supplied with grave goods, and covered with clay, piled seven or eight feet above ground level," in a conical mound "the shape of a sugar-loaf," surrounded by a palisade.[831] Mohawks were known to place their dead "upright in holes, and do not lay them down, and then they throw some tress and wood on the grave, or enclose it with palisades."[832] This matches the description of natives who heaped wood, stone or earth into a large pile or cairn atop the burial, surrounded by a "palisades resembling a small dwelling."[833]

Mahicans buried their dead in a squatting position, facing east. Adriæn van der Donck observed such an interment where the corpse was placed "in a sitting posture upon a stone or a block of wood, as if the body were sitting upon a stool; then they place a pot, kettle, platter, spoon, with some provision and money, near the body in the grave; this they say is necessary for the journey to the other world."[834] Some placed wood around the body to keep the earth from it. Peter Lindeström described a "seated" burial as temporary, and recounted subsequent rituals attending disposal of the corpse, its possessions and even memory. He related, "A few days after [the death] he is buried, and then a round deep pit is dug in the ground and a stool is placed in the hole upon which the dead man shall sit. Then the dead man's money is placed upon him and he is set down in the pit upon the stool with a tobacco pipe, a fathom long, in his mouth, screwed together with leather, the head of green and black stone, which is lighted through by the fire in the pipe, so that we can see how the tobacco is consumed, and this pipe-head is so large that a handful of tobacco will go into it, which is to be his food on the journey. This pipe they dig down into the ground from the mouth of the man. Afterwards they throw earth upon him and fill up the hole. When this is done they dig down in the corners of a square four very long poles upon which they make three shelves, and decorate the poles with long strips of blue, red or green frieze, hanging like fringes. Then those who have been the dead man's relatives and best friends set themselves down for about the period of a month to lament the departure of the dead one, singing, crying, howling and lamenting, so that it is heard for a long distance. Now when this time is past they dig up the dead one and take all his money off him, which they put in a box and place on the lowest rack or shelf, then each one takes a knife and thus cuts the flesh off the bones of the dead one, wrapping the flesh in chestnut bark [and] placing them on the upper shelf or rack; but the entrails they dig down in the hole. Afterwards they still set themselves down for about the period of 14 days and further lament the departure of the dead, and when now that time is over, then their sorrow and lamentation are gone. Those who then are the relatives and best friends of the dead take the money-chest, dividing it between themselves, and therewith go their way; but the scaffolding together with the other [things] remains standing as a monument until; it falls and rots away. When now the savage is thus buried the savages do not wish to hear him mentioned by name again or to speak further about him."[835]

Captain De Vries saw widows on daily pilgrimages to their husbands' graves, laying prostrate in grief, weeping. Families customarily gave "a party when any one is dead in the house."[836] The nearest of kin, especially women, kept "periods of lamentations, when they make dreadful and wonderful wailing, naming the dead, smiting upon their breasts, scratching and disfiguring their faces, and showing all possible signs of grief. But where a mother has lost a child, her expressions of grief exceed all bounds, for she calls and wails whole nights over her infant, as if she really were in a state of madness."[837] The death of a young hunter or warrior required "a particular kind" of lamentation, whereby "women shave off their hair, which they keep the customary time, and then burn the hair upon the graves of the deceased or slain, in the presence of the relations."[838] When a spouse died, it was customary for the survivor to shave off his or her hair; widows painted their "whole countenance black as pitch" and widowers wore "a buckskin vest next to their skin."[839] The customary period of mourning lasted "a whole year, even if they have not been long married, or if the connection had not been happy—still they observe the ceremonies religiously, without marrying again until the season of mourning is over." Tokens of mourning were common, "which usually are black signs upon their bodies."[840]

The deceased was usually buried "with their apparel, be they men or women, and the nearest of kin fling in something precious with them, as a token of their love; Their mourning is blackening of their faces, which they continue for a year; They are choice of the graves of their dead; lest they should be lost by time and fall to common use, they pick off the grass that grows upon them, and heap up the fallen earth with great care and exactness."[841] Speaking of West Jersey in 1698, Gabriel Thomas noted the inclusion of grave goods, such as "house-utensils, and some money, (as tokens of their love and affection) with other things, expecting they shall have occasion for them again in the other world." He found the natives "very curious, nay, even nice in preserving and repairing the graves of their dead."[842] He observed, "they don't allow of mentioning the name of a friend after his death; for at his decease, they make their face black all over with black lead; and when their affairs go well with them, they paint their faces with red lead, it being a token of their joy, as the other is of their grief."[843] Pastorius noted, "When they recall the death of their parents and friends, they begin to wail and weep most pitifully."[844] He also saw survivors of the deceased throwing "something costly into the grave with the dead by which they wish it to be understood that their affectionate good will toward the dead shall not fail."[845]

Captain De Vries described a Death Feast "at the North," when multitudes assembled who had "collected together the bones of their ancestors, cleaned them, and bound them up in small bundles" for reburial in a "square grave, the size and length of a person," surrounded by four pillars, which they covered with bark.[846] Friends and allies from neighboring tribes were invited to feast, frolic and dance for ten days. This ceremonial commingling of ancestral bones provided the occasion for contracting new alliances and affirming old friendships. The sackima or *kichkenet*, standing over the bones, proclaimed "that if they remain thus united, their enemies can have no power over them." Sewan, arrows, kettles, knives, and other goods were placed in the grave and the bones covered with earth and the whole surrounded by palisades. De Vries noted, "Such is the custom on the coast in regard to the dead," but he does not reconcile this observation with the claim that he had witnessed such ceremonies "at the North." The ritual, which De Vries described, resembles the Feast of the Dead practiced by the Hurons, Neutrals and kindred Iroquoian tribes at intervals of ten or twelve years, perhaps when they relocated their villages.[847] It is unclear whether or not any native communities in the Hudson Valley or Delaware Valley engaged in bundled-bones reburial.[848] In West Jersey, Gabriel Thomas noted, "If a person of note dies very far off from the place of his own residence they will carry his bones home some considerable time after, to be buried there."[849]

There are several large prehistoric cemeteries in the Minisink country. A burial ground covering several acres is situated on a bluff or terrace that rises thirty feet above the Delaware River, just south of Minisink Island. In 1719, surveyor John Reading reported a land fort, which the Shawnees built adjacent to the Minisink Burial Ground when they first entered the area in 1692.[850] Near the beginning of the twentieth century, Benson Bell, while plowing his field, uncovered a grave that yielded twelve dark blue beads, eight white stone tubes and two carved "banner stones."[851] Dr. Charles Philhower, who purchased forty-five acres, including the Minisink Burial Ground, in 1922, excavated between 175 and 200 Indian graves. Dr. William A. Ritchie excavated the same site in 1947.[852]

Another burial ground was situated on the Van Etten farm, on the Neversink River near Port Jervis, where, for many years, spring floods eroded the banks, exposing skeletal remains and grave goods. In 1909, Everett R. Burmaster conducted archaeological excavations there for the New York State Museum at Albany, eventually retrieving a large quantity of artifacts from this site. A number of beads were unearthed and described as flat beads, manufactured in Venice, Italy, having a Moorish crescent inscribed on one face. An antique silver spoon, a bronze bell and a shell gorget were found in a child's grave. Archaeologists recovered a string of opalescent beads that glittered with iridescent hues from another burial. Several skeletons were found in a fetal position, lying on their sides with knees drawn up to their chin. Jesuit rings were also discovered around the necks of their former owners, indicating that they had been worn upon necklaces.[853] This area was originally known as Mackhackamack.

Of relevance, perhaps, seventeenth-century planters noted the Patuxent Indians, an Algonquian tribe resident upon the Maryland coast and Potomac River, referred to their ceremonial place or "temple" as a *Matchcomaco*. Early traders among the Patuxents witnessed a ceremony "in the Matchcomaco, or temple of the Patuxans," wherein "at a day appointed the towns about met together and built a great fire, then standing all about the same, lifted up their hands to heaven, crying, *Taho Taho,* after this was brought forth a bag of *Poate*, which is their tobacco, with a great tobacco pipe, and carried about the fire, a young man following it, crying *Taho Taho,* with a great variety of gesture of body, this done they filled the pipe, and gave to every one a draught of smoke from it, which they breathed out on all parts of their bodies, as it were to sanctify them to the service of their god."[854] In another reference, Indians of coastal Virginia called "their place of Council," Match-comaco.[855] Mackhackamack, now Port Jervis, may be similarly named from the Minisink word, *Machtschikamik*, meaning *hole, grave*. It is unknown whether the Minisinks also congregated seasonally at their burial grounds for similar rituals of purification.

While plowing a field near his house in Sparta Township, New Jersey, seven miles east of Newton, on April 25, 1842, William Gunderman struck "some hard substance, which proved to be a human skull."[856] Four or five other skeletons, nearly entire, each "contracted in a narrow space, as if drawn up together and not deposited at length," were found, all buried in the light, dry sandy soil, not more than two feet below the surface. Grave goods included "a number of small pieces of pottery, figured and rudely ornamented, bucks-horn, arrowheads, shells, &c." Once the remains were determined to belong to "the aborigines of our country, which were here inhumed after the Indian fashion," the excavations were respectfully discontinued.

In April 1744, workmen digging a cellar in East Jersey accidentally unearthed an Indian grave. A large quantity of human bones and a cake of corn was found about four feet below a "great stone, like a tombstone," said to be "eight feet long, four feet broad, and even some inches more where it was broadest, and fifteen inches thick at one end, but only twelve inches at the other."[857] The stone was "of the same coarse material that is to be found everywhere in this locality" and had no visible "letters nor other characters" inscribed upon it. The discoverers concluded, "that this was a grave of a person of note among the savages."[858]

In March 1871, a number of men in the employ of station-master Jacob Van Buskirk were taking down an embankment opposite to an old mill, on the west of the railroad track near the New Milford Depot on New Milford Avenue, Oradell, New Jersey, when they unearthed sixteen or seventeen skeletons that "lay in different directions" but were "all in an excellent state of preservation." The workmen also turned up "a stone such as the Indians used for mashing corn and the remains of an old stone pot." This "half of an old pot [was] extensively decorated in true Indian style." Mr. Van Buskirk re-interred the skeletons in a field located about a quarter of a mile lower down the track.[859]

Other mysterious burials have been uncovered over the years. On September 28, 1886, preparatory to placing pillars under the north part of a building occupied by William S. Lozier, situated on the west side of Main Street, Hackensack, a little south of Camden Street, workmen uncovered a human skeleton about two and a half feet below the surface. The skull showed teeth in a good state of preservation, but for reasons never explained, someone crushed the upper jaw and stole the teeth before the coroner made his appearance. The spot where the skeleton was unearthed had been the garden of the late Abraham Berry, who dwelt in a house torn down in 1865 by J. J. Anderson. The burial stood just beside the site of a former out kitchen and only a few feet from the Main Street sidewalk. The oldest neighbors could not remember any person having suddenly disappeared, and so could not explain the unexpected find. This confirmed the possibility that this had been an Indian burial. On May 17, 1900, John Smith and John Gallagher, who were grading the property on the southeast corner of Railroad Avenue and Atlantic Street for the Hackensack Land Company, unearthed five skeletons. The bones fell apart, however, as soon as they were handled. One skull was gathered up in good shape and was placed in a local doctor's case of curiosities. As the heads all pointed toward the west, these were believed to be Indian skeletons. The property was part of the old Van Giesen farm, and the bodies were found only a few feet north of the Muldoon house. One of the jawbones, full of well-preserved teeth, suggested, "the original possessor must have been a giant." Relic hunters took the teeth from the skeletons, which were in remarkably good shape.[860]

In 1624, Nicolæs Van Wassenaer noted, "all the natives pay particular attention to the sun, the moon and the stars, as they are of as great interest to them, as to us, having like summer and winter."[861] Van der Donck said, "They think much of the moon, and believe it has great influence over vegetation."[862] There is evidence to indicate that Hurons practiced a similar spiritual regime, also counting the years, days, and months by the moon.[863] Synchronized with their lunar computation of changing seasons, Delawares conducted "feasts, which they eat in honor to some unknown beings, who, they suppose, speak to them in dreams, promising them success in hunting, and other affairs, in case they will sacrifice to them. They oftentimes also offer their sacrifices to the spirits of the dead; who, they suppose stand in need of favors from the living, and yet are in such a state as that they can reward all the offices of kindness that are shown them. And they impute all their calamities to the neglect of these sacrifices."[864] Among the tribes of New Netherland, one major feast honored the arrival of the first moon following its occurrence at the end of February, which was "a harbinger of the summer." This new moon of spring, Chwame gischuch, or the Smelt Moon, was watched "with great devotion" and celebrated as people "collect together from all quarters, and revel in their way, with wild game or fish, and drink clear river water to their fill."[865] Again, Jesuit missionaries observed Hurons celebrating a "carnival," similar to Mardi Gras, on the days succeeding March 2, 1639. The Montagnais recognized only ten Moons in the year and believed that the February Moon was longer by several days than the others, and therefore they call it the great Moon. The moon was considered a feminine entity, the sun being her husband.[866] The Dark Moon of August, Winu gischuch, or the Ripe Corn Moon, marked the approaching harvest and was the sign for another great festival. In 1626, Nicolæs Van Wassenaer made a curious report: "In the month of August a universal torment seizes them [i.e., the natives], so that they run like men possessed, regarding neither hedges nor ditches, and like mad dogs resting not until exhausted. They have in such men a singular sight."[867] This apparently describes the Huron festival of Ononharoia or "Upsetting of the Brain."[868]

In 1683, William Penn wrote of Indian worship that "their sacrifice is their first fruits; the first and fattest buck they kill, go to the fire, where he is all burnt with a mournful ditty of him that performs the ceremony, but with such marvelous fervency and labor of body, that he will even sweat to a foam."[869] He also noted another feast held in autumn, "when the corn cometh in." He attended one festival, held in a shady clearing beside a spring of water, where twenty bucks were consumed, together with "hot cakes of new corn," mixed with beans, "which they make up in a square form, in the leaves of the stem and bake them in ashes." After the meal, they "fell to dance." Those attending were required to make presents of wampum.[870] In 1700, Pastorius observed, "they accompany their own worship of God with songs, during which they make strange gestures and motions with the hands and feet…."[871]

Reverend David Brainerd described a festival held at Juncauta Island in the Susquehanna River on September 20, 1745.[872] He wrote, "In the evening they met together, nearly a hundred of them, and danced around a large fire, having prepared ten fat deer for the sacrifice. The fat of the innards they burnt in the fire while they were dancing and sometimes raised the flame to a prodigious height, at the same time yelling and shouting in such a manner that they might easily have been heard two miles or more. They continued their sacred dance nearly all night, after which they ate the flesh of the sacrifice and so retired each one to his own lodging."[873]

The Natchez, a Mississippian mound-building culture, were dependent for their food supply upon communal horticulture. The people assembled each spring to plant a vast field of Indian corn, beans, pumpkins, and melons. They gathered again in fall to harvest these crops. At the end of July, the great chief ordered his people to attend a grand feast lasting three days and nights. The fathers of the families carried "the first of their fruits, their corn and the vegetables" to the gates of the mound Temple, where a Temple Guardian presented them to the spirits and then conveyed them to the chief's house, where after the chief distributed them among the people.[874] In 1656, Adriæn van der Donck reported such feasts and great assemblages were only held "on the subjects of peace, war, alliances, treaties, and devotions, or to counsel the devil [that is to say, the Manitou] on some approaching event, or in relation to the fruitfulness of the seasons, or to celebrate some successful occurrence by frolicking and dancing, as at the conclusion of peace, or to make war with some neighboring people."[875]

In 1683, William Penn imagined North Americans were "of the Jewish Race, I mean, of the stock of the Ten Tribes," who had crossed "from the Eastern-most parts of Asia, to the Western-most of America."[876] He thought the Delawares and the Jews "agree in rites, they reckon by moons: they offer their first fruits, they have a kind of Feast of Tabernacles; they are said to lay their Altar upon twelve stones; their mourning a year, customs of women, with many things that do not now occur."[877] This supposition gained currency, for Gabriel Thomas repeated it in 1698, saying the natives "resemble the Jews very much in the make of their persons, and tincture of their complexions: They observe New Moons, they offer their first fruits to a Maneto, or supposed Deity, whereof they have two, one, as they fancy, above (good), another below (bad,) and have a kind of Feast of Tabernacles, laying their Altars upon Twelve Stones, observe a sort of mourning twelve months, [and] customs of women...."[878] Elaborating further, Thomas noted that the natives of West Jersey, like those of Pennsylvania, also "observe the New Moons with great devotion and reverence: And their first fruits they offer, with their corn and hunting-game they get the whole year, to a False

Deity or Sham-God, whom they must please, else (as they fancy) many misfortunes will befall them and great Injuries will be done them."[879]

Probably repeating accounts of the Mahicans, Nicolæs Van Wassenaer wrote in 1624 that "ministry of their spiritual affairs is attended to by one they call *Kitsinacka*."[880] He treated the sick by sitting alongside the patient, bawling, crying and roaring, "like one possessed." He lodged "where he pleases, or where he last officiated," having no house of his own. Only an unmarried maiden or old woman prepared his food and he supposedly remained celibate.[881] Among Hurons, these healers had to "be deprived of all their possessions, [and] they must abstain from women."[882] A family could determine whether a child was s *kitsinacka* or *kichkinet* (a dialectal variant) when he arrived at twelve years of age. If "he says so, then he is brought up to such office," but he could only exercise his powers when he attained maturity. In 1745, Reverend Brainerd reported a person might be endowed with such special powers either in infancy or as an adult, generally through no desire or agency of their own, though it was claimed that parents might induce the gift by various means such as "to make the child swallow a small living frog, after having performed some superstitious rites and ceremonies upon it."[883]

Kichkinet signifies "one who understands the marks or signs," based upon the root "kichkican," meaning "a mark or sign."[884] The verb *kuhkinneau* or *kehkinoo* has also been translated, "he marks, observes, takes knowledge, instructs or imitates"; hence, "he interprets."[885] The Montagnais of eastern Canada believed "there are certain Genii of light, or Genii of the air, which they call *Khichikouai*, from the word *Khichikou*, which means 'light' or 'air.' The *Kichikouai* are acquainted with future events, they see very far ahead; this is why the Savages consult them, not all [the savages] but certain jugglers, who know better than the others how to impose upon and amuse these people."[886] The Montagnais believed these *Khichikouai* might inhabit a body of stone, cone-shaped, about as large as a fist, with power of flight. The *Khichikouai* taught them where to hunt eels or moose, and rendered them "a thousand other good offices."[887] They were honored in feasts by throwing a few spoonfuls of grease into the fire, while requesting, "Make us find something to eat."[888]

One Delaware prophet and healer, whose spiritual gifts departed upon conversion to Christianity, reflected upon his prenatal endowment with shamanic powers, claiming, "He was admitted into the presence of a great man, who informed him, that he loved, pitied and desired him to do good. It was not in this world that he saw the great man, but in a world above at a vast distance from this. The great man, he says, was clothed with the day; yea, with the brightest day he ever saw—a day of many years, yea, of everlasting continuance! This whole world, he says, was drawn upon him, so that in him, the earth and all things in it, might be seen ... that everything that was beautiful and lovely in the earth was upon him and might be seen by looking on him, as well as if one was on the earth to take a view of them there. By the side of the great man, he says, stood his *shadow* or spirit; for he used (*chichung*) the word they commonly use to express that part of the man that survives the body, which word properly signifies a shadow. This shadow, he says, was as lovely as the man himself and filled all places, and was most agreeable as well as wonderful to him. —Here he tarried for some time, and was unspeakably entertained and delighted with a view of the great man, of his shadow or spirit, and of all things in him. What is most astonishing, he imagines all this to have passed before he was born. He never had been, he says, in this world at that time. What confirms him in the belief of this, is, that the great man told him, that he must come down to earth, be born of such a woman, meet with such and such things, and in particular, that he should once in his life be guilty of murder. At this he was displeased and told the great man he would never murder. But the great man replied, 'I have said it and it shall be so.' Which has accordingly happened. At this time, he says, the great man asked him what he would choose in life. He replied, First to be a hunter, and afterwards, to be a powwow or diviner. Whereupon the great man told him, he should have what he desired and that his shadow should go along with him down to earth, and be with him forever. There was, he says, all this time, no words spoken between them. The conference was not carried on by any human language, but they had a kind of mental intelligence of each other's thoughts, dispositions, and proposals. After this, he says, he saw the great man no more; but supposes he now came down to earth to be born, but the spirit or shadow of the great man still attended him and ever after continued to appear to him in dreams and other ways, until he felt the power of God's word upon his heart; since which it has entirely left him."[889]

"The spirit, he says, used sometimes to direct him in dreams to go to such a place and hunt, assuring him he should there meet with success, which accordingly proved so. The great man accordingly fulfilled his promise to make him a great hunter. On occasions, the spirit visited him 'in a special manner, and he was full of what he saw in the great man.' The diviner was 'all light, and not only light himself, but it was all light around him, so that he could see through men and knew the thoughts of their hearts.'"[890]

Shamans were "supposed to have a power of foretelling future events, or recovering the sick, at least oftentimes, and of charming, incanting, or poisoning persons to death by their magic divinations."[891] When Hurons summoned their "sorcerer" to cure a sick person, he danced and shook a tortoise shell, then gazed into water or into fire to discover the nature of the disease. It was the desire of the soul for some object or present—the gift "of a canoe, for example, of a new robe, a porcelain [wampum] collar, a fire-feast, a dance, etc." —that caused the wasting or disease of the physical body. Recovery began with satisfying this subconscious longing. Hurons also carried "charms, to which they speak and make feasts, in order to obtain from them what they desire."[892]

The community singularly favored these gifted individuals even though the powers only came upon them at times. Along the Delaware River, Peter Lindeström described how the "devil-chaser," as a doctor of medicine, "first makes use of all kinds of medicines and when he finds that they do not help, he pretends to be worse than the Devil himself, intending thus to chase the evil one out of body of the savage, wherefore he is called the devil-chaser."[893] To chase the evil spirit, he ran back and forth while making loud cries, rolled naked into the fire and then built a wall of firebrands around the patient.[894] Among the Sickenanes or Sequins, an Algonquian community residing along the Connecticut River, the kichkinet officiated at a curious ceremony, described as a sacrifice. The Sickenanes had "a hole in a hill in which they place a kettle full of all sorts of articles that they either have by them or can procure, as part of their treasures. Then a snake comes in, then they all depart, and the Manitou, that is the Devil, comes in the night and takes the kettle away, according to the statement of the Koutsinacka, or devil-hunter, who presides over the ceremony."[895]

Special assemblies for the purpose of *devil hunting* or *devil driving* were held "in the afternoon towards evening and then some of them do, most singularly indeed, endeavor to enchant and charm the devil and carry on witchcraft, wherein the common people believe."[896] Such ceremonies began "with jumping, crying, and grinning, as if they were possessed and mad."[897] The participants "kindle large fires and dance around and over the same, lengthwise and across; they roll, tumble overhead and bend themselves, and continue their violent exercises until the sweat pours out and streams down to their feet."[898] The kichkinets or devil-drivers "join in the rolling and howling, when they altogether appear to be crazy." Eventually, the spirit or devil appeared in the form of a beast: "if the beast be a ravenous animal, it is a bad omen; if it be a harmless creature, the sign is better; the animal gives them strange answers to their inquiries, but seldom so clear and distinct that they can comprehend or interpret the same, which, however, they strike at, as a blind man does at an egg."[899] The kichkinets could "sometimes bewitch some of their common people and cause them to appear possessed or besotted, which otherwise is not seen, when they cast themselves into glowing fires without feeling it." After a spell, the kichkinet could calm the possessed individual by whispering in their ear.[900]

One and a half centuries later, kichkinets still practiced their art, but they were then "called powwows." They were "supposed to have a power of enchanting, or poisoning them to death, or at least in a very distressing manner." One afternoon after witnessing the sacred dance on Juncauta Island, Reverend Brainerd reported, "Near noon they gathered together all their powwows, or conjurers, and set about half a dozen of them playing their juggling tricks and acting their frantic distracted postures in order to find out why they were then so sickly upon the island, numbers of them being at that time disordered with a fever and bloody flux. In this exercise they were engaged for several hours, making all the wild, ridiculous and distracted motions imaginable; sometimes singing; sometimes howling; sometimes extending their hands to the utmost stretch and spreading all their fingers, —they seemed to push with them as if they designed to push

Figure 25. "Representation of them when they dance and have a Feast." From David Pietersz deVries, *Korte Historiael, ende Journaels Aenteyckeninge*, Hoorn: Symon Cornelisz Brekegeest, 1655.

something away, or at least put it off at arm's-end; sometimes stroking their faces with their hands, then spurting water as fine as mist; sometimes sitting on the earth, then bowing down their faces to the ground; then wringing their sides as if in pain and anguish, twisting their faces, turning up their eyes, grunting, puffing, &c."[901] According to Brainerd, a highly biased observer, these rites "tended to excite ideas of horror...." Some participants were "more fervent and devout in the business than others and seemed to chant, peep and mutter with a great degree of warmth and vigor as if determined to awaken and engage the powers below." These "charms and incantations" lasted "for more than three hours, until they had all wearied themselves out although they had in that space of time taken several intervals of rest, and at length broke up..."[902]

Mohawks called their doctors, *simachkoes* or *sinachkoo*. According to a description recorded in 1635, they entered the house of a sick person, singing, and lit a large fire. They then wrapped their heads in snakeskins, washed their faces and hands, and laid the patient beside the fire. They washed a stick, measuring about half a yard in length, in a bucket of water mixed with medicine. The doctors repeatedly swallowed the entire length of the stick, then spat on the patient's head and body. The ceremony concluded with "all sorts of farces, as shouting and raving, slapping of the hands...."[903] The Oneida used even more elaborate curative techniques—in one reported instance, a dozen "devil-hunters," mostly old men with their faces painted red, spread bark on the floor of a lodge and laid a patient, whose illness had defied previous treatments, in the middle of the room. Three of the devil-hunters wore deer-hair wreaths, braided with the roots of a green herb, upon which five white crosses were stuck. An elderly woman shook a turtle-shell rattle, filled with "a good many beads," accompanying the doctors' chants. They then proceeded "to catch the devil and trample him to death; they trampled the bark to atoms so that none of it remained whole, and wherever they saw but a little cloud of dust upon the maize, they beat at it in great amazement and then they blew that dust at one another and were so afraid that they ran as if they really saw the devil; and after long stamping and running one of them went to the sick man and took away an otter that he had in his hands; and he sucked the sick man for awhile in his neck and on the back, and after that he spat in the otter's mouth and threw it down; at the same time he ran off like mad through fear." The other men went over to the otter and began "to throw fire and to eat fire," scattering hot ashes and red-hot coals...."[904]

Reverend Brainerd encountered a Minisink shaman who saw himself as a "restorer of what he supposed was the ancient religion of the Indians."[905] This shaman wore a costume, not allowing "any part of his body, not so much as his fingers, to be seen," covering himself in a "coat of bear skins, dressed with the hair on, and hanging down to his toes; a pair of bear skin stockings; and a great wooden face painted, the one half black, the other half tawny, about the color of an Indian's skin, with an extravagant mouth, cut very much awry; the face fastened to a bear-skin cap, which was drawn over his head." While dancing, the shaman "beat his tune with the rattle" made of "a dry tortoise shell with some corn in it, the neck of it drawn on to a piece of wood, which made a very convenient handle." Brainerd observed, "no one would have imagined from his appearance or actions that he could have been a human creature, if they had not had some intimation of it otherwise ... his appearance and gestures were so prodigiously frightful."[906] This shaman "had a house consecrated to religious uses, with divers images cut upon the several parts of it." Inside, the ground had been beaten as hard as a rock by frequent dancing.

Van der Donck said, "among some nations the word Sunday is known by the name of *Kintowen*. The oldest among them say that in former times the knowledge of God had been known among them and they remark, that since they can neither read nor write, in process of time the Sunday will be forgotten, and all knowledge of the same lost."[907] For important assemblies, the community gathered at midday. An orator first delivered "an address on the occasion and the cause of their meeting; this they also do sometimes at their councils." Then the people gorged themselves on ample provisions brought for the occasion, leaving no morsel to be carried home afterwards. After eating, "the old and middle-aged conclude with smoking and the young with a *kintecaw*, singing and dancing, which frequently is continued until morning."[908]

Captain David De Vries claimed to have witnessed a dance "at the north" where the participants "stand two and two beside each other," dancing "in two, three, and four pairs." He said, "the first pair carry a tortoise in their hands, as this nation say that they have descended from a tortoise-father...."[909] In 1683, William Penn described a similar *Cantico* or kintekoy, "performed by round-dances, sometimes words, sometimes songs, then shouts, two being in the middle that begin, and by singing and drumming on a board direct the chorus: Their postures in the dance are very antic and differing, but they all keep measure."[910] In 1697, Francis Pastorius similarly described native festivities, noting, "When they sing, they dance in a circle; while two, in the centre, lead the dance and raise a dirge, the entire chorus carries on a pitiful lamentation, weeps in addition, at one time gnashing the teeth, at another snapping with the fingers, at another stamping with the feet, and they execute this laughable spectacle quite ardently and seriously."[911]

Under great cultural stress, native belief systems either altered or publicly faded. Fortunately, many were kept in the heart and passed from generation to generation. Nils Gustafson, the nonagenarian interviewed by Peter Kalm in 1749, dismissed the religion of the original natives as "very trifling, and even believed that they had none at all." He said they interpreted loud claps of thunder to be a sign that the evil spirit was angry. Some natives informed him, however, "that they believed in a God, who lives in heaven."[912] By 1700, Pastorius wrote, "They know of no idols, but they worship a single all-powerful and merciful God, who limits the power of the Devil."[913] Perhaps some native narrators simply molded their communications to satisfy Christian expectations. In 1745, one shaman, devoted to the ancient customs of his people, "denied the existence of a devil, and declared there was no such creature known among the Indians of old times, whose religion he supposed he was attempting to revive." Apparently, it was the Schwonack—"those who came from the salt sea"— who brought this devil and so much mischief and misfortune to the shores of the North Americans.

On May 10, 1744, Reverend David Brainerd, traveling toward the Forks of the Delaware River [Easton, Pennsylvania], "met with a number of Indians in a place called *Miunissinks* (Minisinks)." Requesting permission to preach Christianity, he met first with their king, who "laughed, turned his back upon me, and went away." Brainerd next spoke to one of their principal men who appeared more receptive. In a subsequent conversation with a spokesman for the sachem (who declined talking), the missionary was politely informed that the conduct of the Christians was generally reprehensible, replete with lying, stealing and inebriation. The spokesman added that his people "would live as their *fathers* lived, and go where their *fathers* were when they died."[914]

Beyond 1609

If Henry Hudson was not the first of his kind to reach our shores, why commemorate the quadricentennial of his visit? His exploration marked a turning point; thereafter, his Amsterdam patrons sent a steady stream of traders and planters, colonizing New Netherland and founding the world we now see around us. It is not that Hudson or other daring European navigators discovered a New World, but for better or for worse they did expand human horizons. Experience teaches that nothing begins without an ending and nothing ends without loss.

At the middle of the seventeenth century, survivors of the original North American population estimated, "that before the arrival of the Christians, and before the small pox broke out amongst them, they were ten times as numerous as they now are, and that their population had been melted down by this disease, whereof nine-tenths of them have died."[915] Lindeström observed, "whole nations could die out" from contagious diseases, unknown before European contact, "as has happened formerly among them here."[916] In 1698, some of the earliest Dutch and Swedish settlers in the Delaware Valley informed Gabriel Thomas that the natives "are greatly decreased in number to what they were when they came first into this country: And the Indians themselves say, that two of them die to every one Christian that comes in here."[917] By 1750, Peter Kalm told how the Indians sold their lands with the advance of European settlement and retired into the country, adding, however, that "in reality few of the Indians really left the country in this manner; most of them ended their days before, either by wars among themselves, or by the small-pox, a disease which the Indians were unacquainted with before their commerce with the Europeans, and which has since that time killed incredible numbers of them."[918] Kalm noted the horrific toll inflicted by small pox, writing, "It killed many hundreds of them, and most of the Indians of the section, then called New Sweden, died of it. The wolves then came, attracted by the stench of so many corpses, in such great numbers that they devoured them all, and even attacked the poor sick Indians in their huts, so that the few healthy ones had enough to do to drive them away."[919] He further elaborated: "But brandy is said to have killed most of the Indians ... I have heard them say that to die by drinking heavily was a desirable thing and an honorable death; and indeed it was a very common thing to kill themselves by drinking this liquor to excess."[920]

The introduction of alcoholic beverages had a devastating impact upon native society, but alcoholism was likewise the scourge of European colonists. Some Indians, whose ancestors had commonly lived to a very great age, "found [strong liquors] so palatable, [that] those who could not resist their appetites, hardly reached half the age of their parents."[921] Peter Lindeström noted how an intoxicated native "becomes as though he were quite raving, throws and rolls himself into the burning fire, with a loud cry, and may easily strike his good friend to death or otherwise set fire to the house, not knowing what he does; for he is not accustomed to such strong drinks."[922] Louwerens Pieters complained to the Commissary at Fort Casimir that, on January 6, 1657, he witnessed five native men, two women, a big boy and a child consume three water pails of beer from Boertjen, which reportedly made them "intoxicated and insolent."[923] In this respect, the natives were no better or worse than their European neighbors, whose frequent intoxication also fed disputes and quarrels; official correspondence is filled with incidences of wife-beating, drunken soldiers, disorderly conduct and lost productivity.

The incidents surrounding even one frontier tavern illustrate the destructive impact of alcohol upon societies. Jan Juriansen Becker's tavern at Fort Altena in modern Delaware was a source of constant trouble to both Europeans and North Americans.[924] Its owner provided credit to soldiers who often "spent for drinks 2 or 3 months' wages, before they have been here 6 or 7 weeks, while he takes their bond, wherein is set forth, that he has advanced such a sum for the necessaries of life." On one occasion, two drunken soldiers from the tavern burned a little Indian canoe, prompting those wronged to threaten burning a house or killing some cattle in retaliation. Becker repeatedly sold liquor to the natives, causing considerable distress to his neighbors. On the morning of November 19, 1659, an Indian who had gotten "a two-quart measure full of liquor" from Becker's tavern was found dead in the woods, "the can with a little liquor in it lying near him." His relations placed the corpse "upon a hurdle and put it in four great prongs opposite the house of Jan Juriaenjsen in the bushes. Some say that, whereas he has drunk himself to death, he is not yet worthy of a grave, others say, that he must curse there the house, where he got the liquor...." Only a month later, neighbors reported seeing yet another Indian with a can of liquor fetched from Becker's wife. In June 1660, Commissary Beeckman noted "many drunken savages daily," being informed, "that they sit drinking publicly in some taverns." His soldiers reported a group of natives sitting and drinking "an entire anker of anise-liquor on the strand near the church...." Gerret the Blacksmith, who lived "in the back part of town near the edge of the forest" was annoyed nightly by drunken Indians and was so frightened that he felt "obliged to abandon his house."[925]

In September 12, 1681, Rathquack, a Minisink sachamaker, related how his "poor people," not having "a shirt to their back," having been out hunting, intended to purchase "good clothes for ye winter but finding rum in every house their men stayed there & drunk rum & spent their beavers, & about 60 were killed by knives in their drink in 3 years..."[926]

The land itself changed under the axe and plow. By 1750, descendants of the earliest Swedish colonists about Raccoon, New Jersey, claimed, "in little lakes, ponds, and marshes the amount of water had visibly decreased, and that many of them had dried up completely." Decimation of the beaver population for the peltry trade partly accounts for the loss of ponds and wetlands formerly drowned by their dams.[927] The chain of effects was inescapable. Peter Kalm noted, "all of the old Swedes and Englishmen born in America whom I ever questioned asserted that there were not nearly so many edible birds at present as there used to be when they were children, and that their decrease was visible." Waterfowl and woodland birds declined between 1680 and 1750. Some species such as squirrels and blackbirds thrived, owing to "the infinitely greater cultivation of corn, which is their favorite food...."[928] Deer decreased with the relentless destruction of woodlands. Wolves vanished through loss of prey, loss of habitat and to bounties paid for their destruction.

North Americans also seemed to vanish from sight. By the close of the seventeenth century, less than a century after the *Halve Maen* probed the inlets and rivers of the Middle Atlantic Coast, citizens of New York and Philadelphia had little opportunity to glimpse the original inhabitants of these shores since they had "withdrawn very far from us, into the wild forest, where, after their hereditary custom, they support themselves by the chase, shooting birds and game, and also by catching fish, and dwell only in huts made of bushes and trees drawn together."[929] By the middle of the eighteenth century, Peter Kalm informed readers, "in most parts you may travel twenty Swedish miles or about a hundred and twenty English miles, from the coast, before you reach the first habitations of the Indians."[930] Others remained, outwardly disguised in European garb and customs.

On June 11, 1774, Royal Governor William Tryon of New York reported the "Indians who formerly possessed Nassau or Long Island, and that part of this Province which lies below Albany" as being "reduced to a small number, and are in general so scattered and dispersed, and so addicted to wandering that no certain account can be obtained of them. They are remnants of the tribes Montocks and others of Long Island, Wappingers of Dutchess County, Esopus, Papagonk, &c in Ulster County, and a few Skachticokes. These Tribes have generally been denominated River Indians and consist of about three hundred fighting men—They speak a language radically the same, and are understood by the Delaware being originally of the same race."[931] By this time many of them professed Christianity and adopted European customs, but while the greater part of them attended the army during the French and Indian War, they did not enjoy "the same reputation as those who are still deemed hunters."

BIBLIOGRAPHY

Kraft, Herbert, ed. *Anthropological Series Number 4, A Delaware Indian Symposium.*
Harrisburg: The Pennsylvania Historical and Museum Commission, 1974.

A Book of Ornithology for Youth. Boston: William Hyde & Co., 1832.

Bolton, Reginald P. *New York in Indian Possession.* New York,
New York: Museum of the American Indian, 1975.

Brinton, Daniel G., and Rev. Albert Seqaqkind Anthony. *A Lenape-English Dictionary.*
Philadelphia, Pennsylvania: The Historical Society of Pennsylvania, 1888.

Brodhead, John Romeyn, ed. *Documents Relative to the Colonial History of the
State of New York.* Vols. I, VII, XII. Albany, New York: Weed and Parsons.

Carmer, Carl. *The Susquehanna.* New York, New York: Rinehart & Co., Inc., 1955.

Chrisley, Ronald L. *An Introduction to the Shawnee Language.* 1992.

Clarkson, Thomas. *Memoirs of the Private and Public Life of William
Penn.* Dover, New Hampshire: Samuel C. Stevens, 1827.

Colden, Cadwallader. *The History of the Fiver Nations Depending on the Province
of New York in America.* Ithaca, New York: Cornell University Press, 1958.

Danckaerts, Jasper. "Journal of Jasper Danckaerts 1679-1680." In *Original
Narratives of Early American History,* edited by Bartlett Burleigh James and
J. Franklin Jameson. New York, New York: Charles Scribner's Sons, 1911.

*Documents Relating to the Colonial History of the State of New York,
Documents Relating to the History and Settlements of the Towns
along the Hudson and Mohawk Rivers from 1630 and 1684.* Vol. XIII.
Albany, New York: Weed, Parsons and Company, 1881.

Donck, Andriaen van der. *A Description of New Netherland.*
Syracuse, New York: Syracuse University Press, 1968.

Driver, Harold E. *Indians of North America.* Chicago,
Illinois: The University of Chicago Press, 1970.

Edwards, Sereno Dwight. *Memoirs of the Reverend David
Brainerd.* New Haven, Connecticut: S. Converse, 1822.

Fernow, Berthold, ed. *Documents Relating to the Colonial History of the
State of New York, Documents Relating to the History and Settlement
of the Towns along the Hudson and Mohawk Rivers from 1630 to
1684.* Albany, New York: Weed, Parsons and Company, 1881.

Force, Peter, ed. *Tracts and Other Papers Relating Principally to the Origin,
Settlement, and Progress of the Colonies in North America from the Discovery
of the Country to the Year 1776.* Washington, D. C.: Peter Force, 1838.

Gerhing, Charles T., and Robert S. Grumer. ""Observations of the Indians from Jasper Danckaert's Journal, 1679-1680." *The William and Mary Quarterly, Third Series* XLIV (January 1987).

Gifford, John. *Annual Report of the State Geologist for the Year 1899, Report on Forests.* Trenton, New Jersey: MacCrellish & Quigley, 1900.

Grant, W. L., ed. *Voyages of Samuel Champlain 1604-1618.* New York, New York: Barnes & Noble, Inc., 1946.

Hall, Clayton Colman, ed. *Narratives of Early Maryland 1633-1684.* New York, New York: Barnes & Noble, Inc., 1910.

Halsey, Francis W., ed. *Great Epochs in American History.* Vol. I. New York, New York: Funk & Wagnalls, 1912.

Hanna, Charles A. *The Wilderness Trail.* Vol. Vol. I. New York, New York: AMS Press, 1971.

Hart, John P., and Hetty Jo Brumbach. "Cooking Residues, AMS Dates, and the Middle-to-Late Woodland transition in Central New York." *Northeast Anthropology*, 2005.

Haviland, William A., and Marjory W. Power. *The Original Vermonters.* Hanover, New Hampshire: University Press of New England, 1981.

Heckewelder, John. *History, Manners and Customs, of the Indian Nations.* New York, New York: Arno Press, 1971.

Henry, M. S. *A History of the Lehigh Valley.* Easton, Pennsylvania: Bixler & Corwin, 1859.

Heye, George G., and George H. Pepper. *Exploration of a Munsee Cemetery near Montague, New Jersey.* New York, New York: The Museum of the American Indian, 1915.

Jameson, J. Franklin, ed. *Original Narratives of Early American History, Narratives of New Netherland 1609-1664.* New York, New York: Charles Scribner's Sons, 1909.

Jameson, J. Franklin, ed. *Original Narratives of Early American History, The Voyages of Samuel Champlain 1604-1618.* New York, New York: Charles Scribner's Sons, 1907.

Javier, Thomas A. *Henry Hudson, A Brief Statement of His Aims and Achievements.* New York, New York: Harper & Brothers, Publishers, 1909.

Jennings, Francis. *The Ambiguous Iroquois Empire.* New York, New York: W. W. Norton & Co., Inc., 1984.

Johnson, Amandus. *The Swedish Settlements on the Delaware 1638-1664.* Vol. Vol. I. Baltimore, Maryland: Genealogical Publishing Company, 1969.

Juet, Robert. *Juet's Journal. The Voyage of the Half Moon.* Edited by Robert M. Lunny. Newark, New Jersey: New Jersey Historical Society, 1959.

Kalm, Peter. *Peter Kalm's Travels in North America.* The English Version of 1770. Edited by Adolph B. Benson. Translated by Adolph B. Benson. New York, New York: Dover Publications, 1964.

Kenton, Edna, ed. *The Jesuit Relations and Allied Documents.* New York, New York: Albert & Charles Boni, 1925.

Lenik, Edward J. "The Minisink Site as Sacred Space." *Archaeological Society of New Jersey* (Archaeological Society of New Jersey) No. 51 (1996).

Lindstrom, Peter. *Geographia America.* Philadelphia, Pennsylvania: The Swedish Colonial Society, 1925.

Linn, John B., and William H. Engle, *Pennsylvania Archives, Second Series.* Vol. V. Harrisburg, Pennsylvania: Lanes S. Hart, 1877.

Mathews, F. Schuyler. *Field Book of American Wild Flowers.* Boston, Massachusetts, 1902.

Myers, Albert Cook, ed. *Narratives of Early Pennsylvania, West New Jersey and Delaware 1630-1707.* New York, New York : Charles Scribner's Sons, 1912.

Nelson, William. *The New Jersey Coast in Three Centuries.* Vol. I. New York, New York: The Lewis Publishing Company, 1902.

O'Callaghan, Edmund B., ed. *Documents Relating to the Colonial History of New York.* Vol. II. Albany, New York: Weed, Parsons & Company, 1858.

—. *The History of New Netherland, or New York under the Dutch.* Vol. I. New York, New York: D. Appleton & Co., 1855.

—. *The Register of New Netherland; 1626-1674.* Albany, New York: J. Munsell, 1865.

Parkman, Francis. *France and England in North America.* Vol. I. New York, New York: The Library of America, 1983.

Prins, Harold E. L., and Bunny McBride. *Astou's Island Domain: Wabanaki Peoples at Mount Desert Island 1500-2000.* US Department of the Interior, Acadia National Park, Ethnographic Overview & Assessment, Vol. I, Northeast Region Ethnpgraphy Program, National Park Service, 2007.

Realm of the Iroquois. Alexandria, Virginia: Time-Life Books, 1993.

Schrabisch, Max. *Geological Survey of New Jersey, Bulletin 13. Indian Habitations in Sussex County, New Jersey.* Union Hull, New Jersey: Dispatch Printing Company, 1915.

Scott, Kenneth, and Charles E. Baker. "Renewals of Governor Nicholl's Treaty of 1665." *The New York Historical Society Quarterly*, 1953.

Skinner, Alanson, and Max Schrabisch. *Bulletin 9, A Preliminary Report of the Archeaological Survey of the State of New Jersey.* Trenton, New Jersey: MacCrellish & Quigley, 1913.

Thatcher, Benjamin B. *Indian Biography: Manners, Customs, and Wars.* New York, New York: D. M. MacLellan Book Company, 1910.

The American Magazine of Entertaining and Useful Knowledge. Vol. Vol. III. Boston, Massachusetts: The Boston Bewick Company, 1835.

Thompson, Charles. *An Enquiry into the Causes of the Alienation of the Delaware and Shawanese Indians from the British Interest.* London: J. Wilkie, 1759.

Thwaites, Reuben Gold, ed. *The Jesuit Relations and Allied Documents.* Vols. XV, Hurons and Quebec: 1638-1639. Cleveland, Ohio: The Burrows Brothers Company, 1898.

Tooker, William Wallace. *The Indian Place-Names on Long Island and Islands Adjacent.* New York, New York: G. P. Putnam's Sons, 1911.

Tyler, Lyon Gardiner, ed. *Narratives of Early Virginia 1606-1625.* New York, New York: Charles Scribner's Sons, 1907.

Warren, George C., and H. J. Burlington, . *The Outdoor Heritage of New Jersey.* Camden, New Jersey: The Haddon Craftsmen, Inc., 1937.

Weise, Arthur James. *The Discoveries of America to the Year 1525.* London: Richard Bentley and Son, 1884.

Weslager, C. A. *Delaware's Buried Past.* New Brunswick, New Jersey: Rutgers University Press, 1968.

Westervelt, Frances A., ed. *History of Bergen County, New Jersey 1630-1923.* Vol. I. New York, New York: Lewis Historical Publishing Company, Inc., 1923.

Williams, Lorraine E., Anthony Puniello, and Karen A. Flinn. *A Reinvestigation of the Late Woodland Occupation in the Delaware Water Gap National recreation Area, New Jersey.* Archaeology, US Department of the Interior, Office of Cultural Programs, Mid-Atlantic Region, National Park Service, National Park Service, 1982.

Williamson, Peter. "A Short Account of the Indians of North America." *Bulletin of the Archeological Society of New Jersey* (Archeological Society of New Jersey), No. 31 (Fall/Winter 1974).

Winkle, Daniel Van. *Reference Pamphlet 1609-1632.* Jersey City, New Jersey: The Historical Society of Hudson County, 1911.

Winsor, Justin, ed. *French Explorations and Settlements in North America and Those of the Portuguese, Dutch and Swedes, 1500-1700.* Cambridge, Massachusetts: Houghton Mifflin & Co., 1884.

ENDNOTES

1   Edna Kenton, (ed.), *The Jesuit Relations and Allied Documents*, (New York: Albert & Charles Boni, 1925), 112.

2   Bartlett Burleigh James and J. Franklin Jameson, (eds.), "Journal of Jasper Danckaerts 1679-1680," *Original Narratives of Early American History*, (New York: Charles Scribner's Sons, 1913), 77-78.

3   Algonquian name for the Hudson River, used in 1646 deed to Adriæn van der Donck for what is now Yonkers.

4   Peter Lindeström, *Geographia Americæ*, (Philadelphia: The Swedish Colonial Society, 1925), 213.

5   Adolph B. Benson (translator and editor), *Peter Kalm's Travels in North America, The English Version of 1770*, (New York: Dover Publications, Inc., 1964), 186-189.

6   Adolph B. Benson (translator and editor), *Peter Kalm's Travels in North America*, 187.

7   Adriæn van der Donck, *Description of the New Netherlands*, (Syracuse, NY: Syracuse University Press, 1968), 91.

8   Ibid., 90.

9   Ibid., 90.

10   Amandus Johnson, *The Swedish Settlements on the Delaware 1638-1664*, Vol. 1, (Baltimore: Genealogical Publishing Company, 1969), 563.

11   Ibid., 563.

12   Peter Lindeström, *Geographia Americæ*, 170.

13   John Heckewelder, *History, Manners and Customs of the Indian Nations*, (New York: Arno Press, 1971), xl-xli.

14   Edna Kenton, (ed.), *The Jesuit Relations and Allied Documents*, 71-73.

15   Ibid., 350.

16   Ronald L. Chrisley, *An Introduction to the Shawnee Language*, (Baltimore, Ohio: 1992), 54-55.

17   Charles Thomson, *An Enquiry into the Causes of the Alienation of the Delaware and Shawanese Indians from the British Interest* (London: J. Wilkie, 1759), 84.

18   Pompton may derive from *poniton*, meaning, "to remain," referring to a remnant of the Wappingers, or Oppings, who settled at Pompton under the Minisinks.

19   Peter Lindeström, *Geographia Americæ*, 203-204.

20   John Heckewelder, *History, Manners and Customs of the Indian Nations*, xxxix.

21   Ibid., 53.

22   *Rumachenanck* probably derives from *Wundchennewunk*, meaning "westerly" or "those on the west side."

23   John Heckewelder, *History, Manners and Customs of the Indian Nations*, 53.

24   Herbert Kraft, "Indian Prehistory of New Jersey," in Herbert Kraft (ed.), *Anthropological Series Number 4, A Delaware Indian Symposium*, (The Pennsylvania Historical and Museum Commission: Harrisburg, 1974). 30-46.

25   Ibid., 30.

26   Ibid., 33.

27   John P. Hart and Hetty Jo Brumbach, "Cooking Residues, AMS Dates, and the Middle-to-Late Woodland Transition in Central New York," *Northeast Anthropology, No. 69*, 2005, 6.

28   Lorraine E. Williams, Anthony Puniello and Karen A. Flinn, *Reinvestigation of the Late Woodland Occupation in the Delaware Water Gap National Recreation Area, New*, (Office of Cultural Programs, Mid-Atlantic Region, National Park Service, 1982), 56.

29   Edward J. Lenik, "The Minisink Site as Sacred Space," *Bulletin of the Archaeological Society of New Jersey, No. 51*, 1996, 55.

30   John Heckewelder, *History, Manners and Customs of the Indian Nations*, 56n.

31   Franklin Jameson (ed.), *Original Narratives of Early American History, Narratives of New Netherland 1609-1664*, (New York: Charles Scribner's Sons, 1909), "The Representation of New Netherland, 1650," *Narratives of New Netherland*, 293; Adriæn van der Donck and Thomas F. O'Donnell (ed.), *A Description of the New Netherlands*, (Syracuse, NY: Syracuse University Press, 1968), 4.

32   Adriæn van der Donck, *A Description of the New Netherlands*, 4.

33   Ibid., 4.

34   Bartlett B. James, and J. Franklin Jameson, (eds.), *Journal of Jasper Danckærts 1679-1680*, 178-179.

35   The wife of the French Dauphin, or heir to the throne, was known as *la Dauphine*. Use of the dolphin came from the Breton coat-of-arms. Claude, Duchess of Brittany, married François I in 1514. She became Queen Consort when he was crowned in 1515. She died July 20, 1524 at 24 years of age. Verrazano's ship was built in 1518. Verrazano found New York Harbor "at the end of a hundred leagues," or about 400 miles. New York City is about 400 miles north of Virginia Beach. The place, which Verrazano named *Arcadia*, would be about 200 miles from New York, or about Cape Henlopen, Delaware.

36   Arthur James Weise, *The Discoveries of America to the Year 1525*, (London: Richard Bentley and Son, 1884), 316-317.

37   Ibid., 317.

38   Ibid., 315.

39   Thomas A. Javier, *Henry Hudson A Brief Statement of His Aims and Achievements*, (New York: Harper & Brothers, Publishers, 1909), 51.

40   Arthur James Weise, *The Discoveries of America to the Year 1525*, 357-358.

41   Brodhead, John Romeyn, *Documents Relative to the Colonial History of the State of New York*, Vol. I, (Albany, NY: Weed and Parsons, 1856), 149; Edmund B. O'Callaghan, *The History of New Netherland, or New York under the Dutch*, Vol. I, (New York: D. Appleton & Co., 1855), 29.

42   The term, variously spelled, derived from the Celtic word for "scout," meaning a wanderer, pillager, or scout.

43   Emanuel Van Meteren, "On Hudson's Voyage," *Narratives of New Netherland*, 6.

44   Johan De Laet, "New World," *Narratives of New Netherland*, 37. A Norman fishing boat supposedly first visited the Grand Banks in 1504. Soon, Dutch English, Breton, Portuguese and Basque fishing fleets were harvesting cod from these waters.

45   Bands of Mi'kmaq and Eastern Etchemins, known as Tarrentines, were allied with French traders and opposed to the Abenakis on the western shore of Penobscot Bay.

46   Johannes De Laet, Director of the West India Company, composed *Nieuwe Wereldt, ofte Beschrijvinghe van West-Indien* between 1621 and 1624, borrowing from the journals of early navigators such as Henry Hudson, Adriæn Block, Hendrick Christiænssz and Cornelis May.

47   Interestingly, Penobscot Bay was the outlet for Bangor, Maine, once styled "the lumber capital of the world."

48   The *scute* or *scooter* was a two-masted fishing boat designed for shallow water.

49   It is possible that the raiders pillaged Chief Asticou's village at Precante, located near Ellsworth Falls on the Union River at the head of tidewater. See Harald E. L. Prins and Bunny McBride, *Astcou's Island Domain: Wabanaki Peoples at Mount Desert Island 1500-2000*, Acadia National Park, Ethnographic Overview & Assessment, Vol. I, (Boston: Northeast Region Ethnography Program, National Park Service, US Department of the Interior, 2007), 25-26.

50   Robert Juet, *Juet's Journal*, (Newark, NJ: The New Jersey Historical Society, 1959), 24. De Laet gives the latitude as 41°43', which crosses Nauset Beach and Strong Island in Pleasant Bay.

51   Robert Juet, *Juet's Journal*, 24.

52   De Laet gives the latitude as 37° 15', which runs further south, through New Inlet, between Wreck Island and Ship Shoal Island.

53 De Laet reports that they saw land at 37° 15'. Jamestown lies between 37° 13'
and 37° 12', so it seems as if this was Hudson's destination. His Dutch crewmen
may have been unhappy with his intention to visit the English colony.

54 Johan De Laet, "New World," *Narratives of New Netherland,* 37.

55 Francis W. Halsey (ed.), *Great Epochs in American History, Vol. 1,* "The Discovery
of New York Harbor by Verazzano (1524), Verazzano's Own Account," (New
York: Funk & Wagnalls, 1912), 92

56 Indian River Inlet, Delaware, is another possibility.

57 Johan De Laet, "New World," *Narratives of New Netherland,* 37.

58 Europeans, sailing offshore, occasionally observed plumes of smoke rising
from the land at the time of the winter hunting drives. On December 2, 1632,
Captain David De Vries, while sailing off the coast of Delaware, "smelt the land,
which gave a sweet perfume, as the wind came from the northwest, which blew
off the land, and caused these sweet odors. This comes from the Indians setting
fire, at this time of year, to the woods and thickets, in order to hunt; and the
land is full of sweet-smelling herbs, as sassafras, which has a sweet smell." On
January 2, 1633, Captain De Vries anchored off Reedy Island in the Delaware
Bay, and "saw fires on land" which he "supposed...were made by Indians out
a-hunting..." September, however, would be early for purposely burning the
woods.

59 Johan De Laet, "New World," *Narratives of New Netherland,* 38.

60 Franklin Jameson (ed.), *Original Narratives of Early American History,
Narratives of New Netherland 1609-1664,* "The Third Voyage of Master Henry
Hudson, by Robert Juet, 1610," 17.

61 Robert Juet, *Juet's Journal,* 27.

62 Ibid., 17.

63 Johan De Laet, "New World," *Narratives of New Netherland,* 38.

64 Franklin Jameson (ed.), *Original Narratives of Early American History,
Narratives of New Netherland 1609-1664,* "The Third Voyage of Master Henry
Hudson, by Robert Juet, 1610," 17.

65 Johan De Laet, "New World," *Narratives of New Netherland,* 38. Interestingly,
Plum Island is a spur of Sandy Hook, nearly opposite Atlantic Highlands, at the
entrance to the Shrewsbury River.

66 Johan De Laet, "New World," *Narratives of New Netherland,* 38.

67 According to the 1630 version of De Laet's *Nieuw Wereldt,* the Sanhikans as
well as the Aquamachuques dwelt along Raritan Bay and Sandy Hook, into the
interior of the country.

68 Conaskonk has been variously spelled. Conescunke meadow is located south of
Raritan Bay, between the beach and the upland, known as Conescunke Neck.
The main stem of Conescunke Creek, later called Manashkanck Creek, flows

through Keyport and empties into Raritan Bay through Conescunke Meadow. Conaskonk Point is located across the small bay from Point Comfort. The name probably derived from Schingaskunk, *bog meadow.*

69   Aquamachuques may be an approximation of *Allamuch Ahokking*, meaning, "the land at the foot of the mountain" or possibly, "the (corn) fields under the mountain," referring to the Neversink Highlands. Luppatatong is possibly an approximation of *Chuppecat-onk*, meaning, "place of deep, high water."

70   Franklin Jameson (ed.), *Original Narratives of Early American History, Narratives of New 1609-1664*, "The Third Voyage of Master Henry Hudson, by Robert Juet, 1610," 18.

71   Johan De Laet, "New World," *Narratives of New Netherland*, 48.

72   Emanuel Van Meteren, "On Hudson's Voyage," *Narratives of New Netherland*, 1-9.

73   Possibly swamp milkweed, known as Indian hemp.

74   Franklin Jameson (ed.), *Original Narratives of Early American History, Narratives of New Netherland 1609-1664*, "The Third Voyage of Master Henry Hudson, by Robert Juet, 1610," 18.

75   Ibid., 18.

76   Now partly the site of Collect Pond Park and Foley Square, south of Canal Street in lower Manhattan. Emanuel Van Meteren, "On Hudson's Voyage," *Narratives of New Netherland*, 7.

77   Franklin Jameson (ed.), *Original Narratives of Early American History, Narratives of New 1609-1664*, "The Third Voyage of Master Henry Hudson, by Robert Juet, 1610," 19.

78   Ibid., 19.

79   Ibid., 19.

80   Ibid., 19.

81   Ibid., 19.

82   Johan De Laet, "New World," *Narratives of New Netherland*, 45, 46.

83   Franklin Jameson (ed.), *Original Narratives of Early American History, Narratives of New Netherland 1609-1664*, "The Third Voyage of Master Henry Hudson, by Robert Juet, 1610," 19.

84   Historians have generally interpreted these passages to indicate that Hudson entered the Upper Bay via the Narrows. Mention of a rather shallow, sand-banked "river" on the previous evening may well indicate they sailed through the Arthur Kill and Kill van Kull. Otherwise, they must have sailed into Gravesend Bay or Rockaway Inlet. See Robert Juet, *Juet's Journal*, 29, 30.

85   Johan De Laet, "New World," *Narratives of New Netherland,* 48-49. According to Hudson's own report, which Emmanuel Van Meteren transcribed, "they sailed along the shore until we reached 40° 45', where they found a good entrance,

between two headlands, and thus entered on the 12th of September into as fine a river as can be found, with good anchoring ground on both sides." This line of latitude runs between 11th Street in Hoboken and a hill on the Manhattan shoreline at what is now 10th Avenue and West 27th Street in New York City, so the headlands would be Castle Point in Hoboken and a vanished hill in the Chelsea neighborhood of Manhattan's West Side.

86   Johan De Laet, "New World," *Narratives of New Netherland*, 48.

87   Franklin Jameson (ed.), *Original Narratives of Early American History, Narratives of New Netherland 1609-1664*, "The Third Voyage of Master Henry Hudson, by Robert Juet, 1610," 20.

88   Ibid., 20.

89   According to Robert Juet's *Journal*, the *Halve Maen* sailed 43.5 leagues and 9 miles northward on the Hudson River. Translating the 9 miles into 3.3 leagues, the distance upstream would be 46.8 leagues. On the return from Coxsackie to Hoboken, the ship traveled 47 leagues. Thus the distances provided for the exploratory and return voyages nearly correspond. The scout boat traveled another 7 or 8 leagues to the head of navigation, which Meteren gave as 42° 40', based upon Hudson's log. This would place the northernmost point of exploration just beyond the Patroon Island Bridge in Albany, which carries Interstate 90 over the Hudson River. Thus they covered 150 miles or 55 leagues northward to Albany, making a league equivalent to approximately 2.7 miles. This corresponds with the standards of the time, a league being the equivalent of 2.67 nautical miles.

90   These visitors may have been the Tappans, who inhabited the west side of the Hudson River, "where the land is low." This describes the Piermont Marsh, an alluvial flat between Piermont Pier and Sneden Landing, where Sparkill Creek enters the Tappan Zee.

91   Franklin Jameson (ed.), *Original Narratives of Early American History, Narratives of New Netherland 1609-1664*, "The Third Voyage of Master Henry Hudson, by Robert Juet, 1610," 21.

92   The 1616 map shows the "vis school hoeck," literally, "fish school corner."

93   Franklin Jameson (ed.), *Original Narratives of Early American History, Narratives of New Netherland 1609-1664*, "The Third Voyage of Master Henry Hudson, by Robert Juet, 1610," 21.

94   Ibid., 21.

95   Since only a few latitudinal readings are available, the various locations for the ship are subject to interpretation.

96   Franklin Jameson (ed.), *Original Narratives of Early American History, Narratives of New Netherland 1609-1664*, "The Third Voyage of Master Henry Hudson, by Robert Juet, 1610," 22.

97   Johan De Laet, "New World," *Narratives of New Netherland*, 49.

98   Franklin Jameson (ed.), *Original Narratives of Early American History, Narratives of New Netherland 1609-1664*, "The Third Voyage of Master Henry Hudson, by Robert Juet, 1610," 22.

99   Franklin Jameson (ed.), *Original Narratives of Early American History, Narratives of New Netherland 1609-1664*, "The Third Voyage of Master Henry Hudson, by Robert Juet, 1610," 22-23.

100   Ibid., 23.

101   Ibid., 23.

102   Emanuel Van Meteren, "On Hudson's Voyage," *Narratives of New Netherland*, 7.

103   Franklin Jameson (ed.), *Original Narratives of Early American History, Narratives of New Netherland 1609-1664*, "The Third Voyage of Master Henry Hudson, by Robert Juet, 1610," 23. While sailing the Hudson River from New York City to Albany in 1769, Richard Smith mentioned, "Slate Stone Rocks are on the West Shore at and below Little Sopus from whence N. York has of late been supplied." The Klein or Little Esopus is the area south of Roundout Creek. Francis W. Halsey (ed.), *A Tour of Four Great Rivers, The Hudson, Mohawk, Susquehanna and Delaware in 1769, Being the Journal of Richard Smith of Burlington, New Jersey*, Part II, "A Tour of Four Great Rivers," (New York: Charles Scribner's Sons, 1906), 9.

104   Franklin Jameson (ed.), *Original Narratives of Early American History, Narratives of New Netherland 1609-1664*, "The Third Voyage of Master Henry Hudson, by Robert Juet, 1610," 24.

105   Ibid., 24.

106   Ibid., 24.

107   Ibid., 24.

108   Ibid., 24. The Long Reach, or Lange Rack, extends from Crum Elbow, above Poughkeepsie, to Danskammer Point.

109   Ibid., 25.

110   Ibid., 25.

111   Ibid., 26.

112   Ibid., 26.

113   Ibid., 27.

114   Emanuel Van Meteren, "On Hudson's Voyage," *Narratives of New Netherland 1609-1664*, 7, 8.

115   Ibid., 8.

116   Ibid., 9.

117   Johan De Laet, "New World," *Narratives of New Netherland*, 34.

118   Nicolaes Wassenaer, "Historisch Verhæl, 1624-1630," *Narratives of New Netherland,* 63.

119   Justin Winsor, (ed.), *French Explorations and Settlements in North America and Those of the Portuguese, and Swedes, 1500-1700.* (Boston: Houghton Mifflin, 1884), 2.

120   Jonas Michælius, "Letter of Reverend Jonas Michaelius, 1628," J. Franklin Jameson (ed.) *Narratives of New Netherland,* 128.

121   Ibid., 128.

122   Ibid., 128.

123   Ibid., 128.

124   Ibid., 128.

125   Since such words as tribe and nation carry heavy freight, I have invented the neutral term *affine.* For the purpose of this discussion, a *band* is one or several families with a common ancestor (probably female); an *affine* is a group of neighboring consanguine bands and a *superaffine* is a dispersed but cooperative group of contiguous, consanguine *affines.* The corresponding political organization is an inverted pyramid, which broadens as it rises from the individual to larger councils of sachems or family heads as cooperation at the levels of the *affine* and *superaffine* include more participants. In other words, there is no hierarchy of chiefs, ruled over by a single chief.

126   Johan De Laet, "New World," *Narratives of New Netherland,* 50.

127   Harold E. Driver, *Indians of North America,* (Chicago: The University of Chicago Press, 1970), 253.

128   "A Short Account of the Mohawk Indians, by Reverend Johannes Megapolensis, Jr., 1644," J. Franklin Jameson (ed.) *Narratives of New Netherland,* 178-179.

129   Johan De Laet, "New World," *Narratives of New,* 57.

130   Nicolaes Wassenaer, "Historisch Verhæl, 1624-1630," *Narratives of New Netherland,* 72.

131   Adriæn van der Donck, *A Description of the New Netherlands,* 92.

132   "Journal of New Netherland," J. Franklin Jameson (ed.), *Narratives of New Netherland,* 271.

133   Adriæn van der Donck, *A Description of the New Netherlands,* 91-92.

134   Ibid., 92.

135   Ibid., 91.

136   Ibid., 92.

137   Ibid., 92.

138   Manhattan is a transliteration of *menach'hen,* signifying "island"

139   Johan De Laet, "New World," *Narratives of New Netherland,* 45.

140 Nicolaes Wassenaer, "Historisch Verhæl, 1624-1630," *Narratives of New Netherland,* 68.

141 Isaac Jogues, "Novum Belgium, 1646," J. Franklin Jameson (ed.), *Narratives of New Netherland,* 261.

142 Isaack De Rasieres, "Letter of Isaack De Rasieres to Samuel Blommaert, 1628 (?)," J. Franklin Jameson (ed.) *Narratives of New Netherland,* 103.

143 Isaack De Rasieres, "Letter of Isaack De Rasieres to Samuel Blommaert, 1628 (?)," J. Franklin Jameson (ed.) *Narratives of New Netherland,* 103. According to Arthur James Weise, author of *The Discoveries of America to the Year 1525,* "the noun *berge,* besides meaning an elevated border of a river, a scarp of a fortification, a steep side of a moat or of a road, is a designation for certain rocks elevated perpendicularly above the water. In an old French lexicon it is said: 'They likewise call in marine phraseology *berges* or *barges* those great rocks, rugged and perpendicularly elevated, that is to say, uprightly and plumb, as the *berges* or *barges* of Clone: such rocks as are Scylla and Charybdis, toward Messina.'" (348) *Bergen* is the Dutch plural.

144 David De Vries, "Korte Historiael," *Narratives of New Netherland,* 207.

145 Isaack De Rasieres, "Letter of Isaack De Rasieres to Samuel Blommaert, 1628 (?)," J. Franklin Jameson (ed.) *Narratives of New Netherland,* 105.

146 David De Vries, "Korte Historiael ende Journals Aenteyckeninge," *Narratives of New Netherland 1609-1664,* 208.

147 Nicolaes Wassenaer, "Historisch Verhæl, 1624-1630," *Narratives of New Netherland,* 67.

148 Johan De Laet, "New World," *Narratives of New Netherland,* 46.

149 David De Vries, "Korte Historiael," *Narratives of New Netherland,* 206.

150 Ibid., 205-206.

151 In 1657, Augustine Herrman purchased a tract of land lying west of the mouth of the Raritan River running to a creek at the uppermost end of the Great Marsh called Mankachkewachky, which runs northwest up into the country. Obviously, the margins of many streams and marshes on the red sandstone piedmont would aptly be described as "the red bank of the river."

152 *Rumachenanck* is probably a corruption of *Wundchennewunk,* meaning "westerly."

153 In 1671, Balthazar De Harte's purchase of 400 acres of land and meadow on the Hudson River at Haverstraw included Newa-sink, possibly an approximation of *Nahiwi-ink,* meaning "a place downstream;" Yandakah, possibly an approximation of *Yu undach,* meaning "on this side of the river," Coquaney, possibly an approximation of *Pokawachne,* meaning "a creek between two hills," and Menisacongue, possibly an approximation of *Quenischquney,* meaning "panther."

154 David De Vries, "Korte Historiael," *Narratives of New Netherland,* 206.

155   Nicolaes Wassenaer, "Historisch Verhæl, 1624-1630," *Narratives of New Netherland*, 68.

156   Johan De Laet, "New World," *Narratives of New Netherland*, 46.

157   In 1684, Wecepwes, also spelled Weawapecon, sachem of Murderer's Creek, and Sackhewughien, also spelled Pemerawaghin, chief sachem of the Esopus Indians, sold land on the west side of the Hudson River, extending south of New Paltz to Murderer's Creek, comprehending lands, meadows and woods called Nescahock (from *Nesca-hacki*, meaning, "black dirt"), Chawangon (from *Schawanewunk*, meaning, "southward") Memorasinck, Kakogh (possibly from *Lekau*, meaning, "sand, gravel"), Getawn Arunk and Ghittawagh (possibly from *M'hittschoak*, meaning, "barren woods"). This tract extended west to the foot of the high hills, called Pechickakes and Aiashkawassing, and southwest along the hills and a river called Peakuensack to a pond lying upon the hills called Meratange (possibly from *mechouteney*, meaning, "old town").

158   Johan De Laet, "New World," *Narratives of New Netherland*, 46. Waranawankougs may be an approximation of *Achwowangeu*, meaning "steep, high bank."

159   John Heckewelder, *History, Manners and Customs of the Nations*, 53.

160   Nicolaes Wassenaer, "Historisch Verhæl, 1624-1630," *Narratives of New Netherland*, 67.

161   He also places a group known by the similar name of the "Morhicans" or Mohegans upon the Frisian River (Four Mile River), north of Long Island Sound. Shad Island is located near Castleton-on-Hudson, southeast of Albany.

162   Nicolaes Wassenaer, "Historisch Verhæl, 1624-1630," *Narratives of New Netherland*, 67. Nyack derives from *naiag* or *nayack*, "a point of land." Various bands likely were known by this name. One group known as Nyack, for example, occupied the neighborhood surrounding Fort Hamilton on the east side of the Narrows, Long Island.

163   One wonders if the "Canoemakers" shown on the 1616 map refer in some way to the Mahican sachem Kanaomack.

164   Isaac Jogues, "Novum Belgium, 1646," *Narratives of New Netherland*, 262.

165   Daniel Van Winkle, *Reference Pamphlet 1609-1632*, (Jersey City: The Historical Society of Hudson County, 1911), 20.

166   Hopatcong probably derives from *Chuppecat*, "deep, high water." Pequannock is an approximation of either *Pequabuck*, meaning "clear, open pond," or *Poquonock*, meaning "cleared land."

167   Tajapogh's name is variously spelled Taepan, Taepgan, Taphen, Tapon, Tephgan and Topheon.

168   "Journal of John Reading," *Proceeding of the New Jersey Historical Society, Vol. X, No. 2, Third Series*, April 1915, (Newark, NJ: Library of the Society, 1915), 40-44.

169   The Indian plantation of Allamuch Ahokking stood along the Trout Brook, somewhere near Lake Tranquility in Green Township, Sussex County, NJ. The historic name *Allamuchy* derives from *Allamutschi*, meaning "under (at the foot of) the hill or mountain." *Allamuchahoking* refers either to "the land at the foot of the mountain" or possibly to "the (corn) fields under the mountain." The name *Pequest* was first recorded as *Paquaessing*, most likely an approximation of *poquosin*, meaning, "drowned meadow, where the water widens and drowns the land," an obvious reference to the Great Meadows below Allamuchy.

170   "Journal of John Reading," *Proceeding of the New Jersey Historical Society, Vol. X, Third Series, 1915,* No. 3, 43.

171   The Allamuchahokking band, inhabiting the upper branches of the Pequest River, was apparently affiliated with the Sanhicans.

172   Tohockonetcong may derive from *Pokhakenikan,* meaning "grave."

173   The documentary record clearly establishes the use of fortifications by the Esopus tribe, who were closely related to the Minisinks. On July 26, 1663, Captain Lieutenant Martin Crieger led a small army of Dutch soldiers and Indian mercenaries against an abandoned Esopus fort, which they destroyed along with the surrounding maize. On September 3, 1663, Crieger led a second military expedition against the Esopus Indians' new fort, killing thirty of its defenders including sachem Papoquanaehem, capturing fourteen others and routing the rest. Since the Esopus Indians were relations, neighbors and allies of the Minisinks, the use of such forts was apparently common to both groups. The location of the Minisink fort remains undiscovered.

174   Edmund B. O'Callaghan, *Documents Relating To The Colonial History of New York*, Vol. II, (New York: Weed, Parsons & Company, 1858), 63.

175   John B. Linn and William H. Egle, M. D., (eds.), *Pennsylvania Archives, Second Series, Vol. V.*, (Harrisburg: Lane S. Hart, 1877), 313-314.

176   Henri and Barbara Van der Zee, *A Sweet and Alien Land*, (New York: The Viking Press, 1978), 354.

177   Edmund B. O'Callaghan, *The Register of New Netherland; 1626-1674*, (Albany, NY: J. Munsell, 1865), 133.

178   "Indian Cemetery," *The Sussex Register*, May 5, 1842

179   *T'Schepinaikonk* is possibly a corrupted form of Wentschipennassiechen, *where the road goes down the hill*. It may be related to a later place name, Machippacong, Shipeconk or Shabacong, given to an island in the river, lying between Carpenters Point and Montague. (2) *Meoech konck* may derive from Megucke konk, *where there is a wide plain*, on what may be the Neversink Branch. The West Branch of the Delaware River was called the Mohoch River on a map of the *Province of Pennsylvania,* printed by James Nevil in April 1770. (3) *Mecharienkonck* may derive from Mechaquiechen konk, *where there is high water or a freshet*. It appears to be situated at or near present-day Matamoras, Pennsylvania, opposite the confluence of the Neversink and Delaware Rivers;

and (4) *t'Schichte Wacki,* located in the Jersey Minisink, may derive from Kschiechpecat, *clear water.*

180   Cochecton probably derives from *kschiechton,* meaning "to wash, to cleanse" It presumably refers to a bathing-place in the Delaware River.

181   Sandiunquin may derive from Schindikeu, *a hemlock forest*; it was later corrupted to Shandaken.

182   Totinquet may be an approximation of tachanigeu, *a woody place,* later corrupted to Topatcoke, now near Napanoch, New York, on Roundout Creek.

183   Oquekumsey probably derives from Ochquechum, *female of beasts,* later corrupted to Oquwage, now Deposit, New York.

184   Wendianmong may derive from Wendamen, meaning, *"to fish with hook and line."*

185   The islands were originally known as Great and Little Minisink Islands, but the smaller, southerly one was later called Namanack.

186   According to a description of the site published in 1915, "a low, broad mound" stood at the eastern end of the burial area. See George G. Heye and George H. Pepper, *Exploration of a Munsee Cemetery near Montague, New Jersey,* (The Museum of the American Indian: New York, 1915), 15.

187   "Relation of Captain Thomas Young, 1634," Albert Cook Myers (ed.), *Narratives of Early Pennsylvania, West New Jersey and Delaware 1630-1707,* (New York: Barnes & Noble, Inc., 1912), 31-40.

188   Mattaloning may derive from *mauwallauwin,* meaning, "to go hunting."

189   Francis Parkman, *France and England in North,* Vol. I, (New York: The Library of America, 1983), 420.

190   This "evil spirit "was probably the same epidemic sickness that had recently made the rounds at Fort New Amstel. From the *Documents Relating to the Colonial History of the State of New York* Vol. XII, 312.

191   This according to Rathquack, sachamaker of the Minnissinke, as told in Berthold Fernow, *Documents Relating to the History and Settlements of the Towns along the Hudson and Mohawk Rivers from 1630 to 1684,* (Albany: Weed, Parsons and Company, 1881), 551; See also Francis Parkman, *France and England in North America, Vol. I,* 913-915.

192   Berthold Fernow, *Documents Relating to the History and Settlements of the Towns along the Hudson and Mohawk Rivers from 1630 to 1684,* 551; Francis Parkman, France and England in North America, Vol. I, 913-915.

193   Berthold Fernow, *Documents Relating to the History and Settlements of the Towns along the Hudson and Mohawk Rivers from 1630 to 1684,* 551.

194   Francis Jennings, *The Ambiguous Iroquois Empire,* (New York: W. W. Norton & Co., Inc., 1984), 197-198.

195 Charles A. Hanna, *The Wilderness Trail*, Vol. I, (New York: AMS Press, 1971), 139.

196 In a letter to George Clark, dated August 4, 1737, James Logan the Proprietary Secretary of Pennsylvania, wrote: "At the time of the arrival of the Shawonoe Indians, in 1698, when they came into Pennsylvania from the South — they were always a rough, ungovernable, and cruel people, more so than any other Indians — they were placed by the Delawares at such places where there was something to take care of or watch over." See M. S. Henry, *A History of the Lehigh Valley* (1859), 164.

197 Their ownership of this land was proven in 1695, when Taepan joined other Minisink sachems in selling 5,500 acres near Pekquanack and Pompton to Captain Arent Schuyler.

198 Charles A. Hanna, *The Wilderness Trail, Vol. I*, 140.

199 Ibid., 140.

200 Ibid., 119-160.

201 *Warensaghskennick*, largely a parcel of fresh meadow or bottomland, is possibly a corruption of *Menenachkhasik*, meaning *garden*. This place was "otherwise" known as *Maghawaemus*, a word evidently derived from *mawenemen* or *mawewi*, signifying a *meeting* or *assembly place*. The "certain Island called *Menayack*" probably derives its name from *menachk*, referring to a *fort*. Could this have been the location of the fort for which the Minisink sachems requested a small cannon from Peter Stuyvesant in August 1663? An island or high point of land in the fork of confluent rivers was a favored location for fortification.

202 The earliest reference to this place-name occurs in 1649, when the Dutch were negotiating peace with Indians around Fort Amsterdam. Pennekeck, sachem of the natives residing around Newark Bay, reported, "an Indian of Mechgachkamic had involuntarily or unknowingly lately done mischief at Paulus Hook, which they requested us to excuse."

203 The nine purchasers were Ebenezer Willson, Dirck Vandenburgh, Daniel Honan, Philip Rookeby, William Sharpass, John Cholwell, Hendrick Tenykee, Lancaster Symes and Benjamin Aske, all of New York City.

204 *Shawenkonk* is an approximation of *Schawanewunk*, meaning "southward," and survives in the name of the Shawangunk Mountains.

205 The seven were Hendrick Tenyke, Derrick Vandenburgh, John Cholwell, Lancaster Symes, Daniel Honan, Philip Rookeby, and Benjamin Aske, who joined Doctor John Bridges, Christopher Denn, John Merret, Peter Matthews and Cornelius Christianse in purchasing the Wawayanda Patent.

206 Is Wawayanda a corruption of Wawastawaw's name?

207 Chingapaw is probably the same individual previously referred to as Kisekaw and Oshasquemenus is likely the same individual as Orackquehowas.

Rapingonick, Moghopuck, Nanawitt, Arawimack, Jan Clauss, Chouckhass and Quilapaw also appear as native grantors.

208   East Jersey Deeds, *Liber E2*, 152; Pemrachquinming is perhaps a corruption of *Kipachgiminshi*, meaning "upland hickory." *Remopock*, better known as *Ramapo*, derives from *Pemapuchk*, meaning, "a rock." *Japock*, now *Yapough*, in Oakland, Bergen County, derives from *Japewi* or *Yapewi* and aptly means "on the high bank of the river."

209   The purchasers were Philip French, Esquire, Mayor of New York City, Matthew Ling, Stephen De Lancey, John Corbett and Caleb Cooper, all New York merchants.

210   Keskentems is also given as Kakentecus, Tendemunge is also given as Tendemundge and Abraham Mametukquim is also given as Mametackquim. Magockamack is also Mahackamack. *Magascoot* is possibly a corruption of *Massipook*, which means, "The river drifts with ice."

211   Matasit is rendered as Mahwtatatt and Kakowatcheky is rendered as Cohevwichick.

212   Matasit is rendered as Mastewap.

213   A version of the *Dutch Figurative Map* (1616) shows them occupying the tidal shores of Bergen Neck, while an earlier version shows them on what may be the Raritan, Passaic or Hackensack River. The Sankikans were included as a nation of Indians inhabiting the South (Delaware) River, according to De Laet's *Nieuwe Wereldt* (1625, 1630).

214   Adolph B. Benson (translator and editor), *Peter Kalm's Travels in North America*, 325.

215   Isaack De Rasieres, "Letter of Isaack De Rasieres to Samuel Blommaert, 1628 (?)," J. Franklin Jameson (ed.) *Narratives of New Netherland*, 103. *Achter* meaning "after" and *col*, meaning, "neck" (as in). This is the origin of the modern toponym *Arthur Kill*.

216   Johan De Laet, "New World," *Narratives of New Netherland*, 53.

217   Ibid., 45.

218   Isaack De Rasieres, "Letter of Isaack De Rasieres to Samuel Blommaert, 1628 (?)," J. Franklin Jameson (ed.) *Narratives of New Netherland*, 104.

219   Wickquaesgeck derives from *wiquajeck*, meaning "the head of a creek," and probably refers to the head of the Saw Mill River, northeast of Tarrytown in Westchester County, New York. In 1628, Isaac De Rasieres described the east bank of the Hudson River above Manhattan as a place "where formerly many people have dwelt, but who for the most part have died or have been driven away by the *Wappenos*." (See "Letter of Isaac De Rasieres to Samuel Blommært, 1628," *Narratives of New Netherland*, 105) At a peace conference with the Dutch in 1649, Pennekeck, sachem of Achter Col (Newark Bay), "said the tribe called Raritanoos, formerly living at Wisquaskeck had no chief, therefore he spoke

for them, who would also like to be our friends..." The Raritans may specifically have come from Roaton, a territory bordering the Noroton River and Long Island Sound in Stamford, Connecticut. Piamakin, sagamore of Roaton, sold the territory "beyond Noroton Bay as far as Rowalton or Five-mile river" in 1631. See Reginald P. Bolton, *New York in Indian Possession*, (New York: Museum of the American Indian, 1975).

220   David De Vries, "Korte Historiael," *Narratives of New Netherland*, 208.

221   Berthold Fernow (ed.), *Documents Relating to the Colonial History of the State of New York, Vol. XIII*, "Documents Relating to the History and Settlements of the Towns along the Hudson and Mohawk Rivers from 1630 to 1684," (Albany: Weed, Parsons and Company, 1881), 25. On July 14, 1649, Megtegickhama, Oteyockque and Wegtakachkey, lawful owners of Wisquaskeck, lying on the east side of the Hudson River, divided a tract of land between two streams, the Seweyruc and the Kechkawes, on a line running through the middle of the woods between the Hudson and East Rivers, so that they retained the west half and conveyed the east half to Director-General Peter Stuyvesant.

222   According to two deeds, one dated September 12, 1758 and the other October 23, 1758, the boundary between the Minisinks and the Delaware Indians ran from Mount Tammany at the Delaware Water Gap on a straight course to the Alamatunck Falls, down the North Branch of the Raritan to the fork with the South Branch, thence down along the middle of Raritan River to its mouth. The Minisink or Munsee and the Oping (Wapinger) or Pompton Indians ceded their claims to the lands lying north of this boundary and the Delaware Indians ceded their claims to lands lying south. Regarding differences in dialect, it is interesting to note that the deed with the Minisinks refers to the falls of Alamatunck, whereas the deed with Delawares refers to the falls of Laomoting (Lamington). *Allamawunke* means "under the hill."

223   Adriæn van der Donck, *A Description of the New Netherlands*, 92.

224   Ibid., 92. These Sawanoos are not to be confused with the Sawennoes or Shawnee who later inhabited the neighborhood of Pahaquarry, Warren County, New Jersey, and Shawnee, Pennsylvania, between 1690 and 1728.

225   Johan De Laet, "New World," *Narratives of New Netherland,* 52n.

226   William Nelson, *The New Jersey Coast in Three Centuries*, Vol. I., (New York: The Lewis Publishing Company, 1902), 12-13.

227   Alanson Skinner and Max Schrabisch (compilers), *Bulletin 9, A Preliminary Report of the Archaeological Survey of the State of New Jersey*, 1913, 60.

228   Johan De Laet, "New World," *Narratives of New Netherland*, 58.

229   Peter Force (ed.), *Tracts and Other Papers relating principally to the Origin, Settlement, and Progress of the Colonies in North America from the Discovery of the Country to the Year 1776, Vol. II*, "Master Evelins Letter," from A Description of the Province of New Albion, (Washington, D. C.: Peter Force, 1838), 21-24; "Relation of Captain Thomas Young, 1634," Albert Cook Myers

(Ed.), *Narratives of Early Pennsylvania, West New Jersey and Delaware 1630-1707*, (New York: Barnes & Noble, Inc., 1912), 31-40.

230 Peter Force (ed.), *Tracts and Other Papers relating principally to the Origin, Settlement, and Progress of the Colonies in North America from the Discovery of the Country to the Year 1776, Vol. II*, "Master Evelins Letter," from A Description of the Province of New Albion, 21.

231 Ibid., 22.

232 Ibid., 22.

233 Peter Lindeström, *Geographia Americæ*, 165.

234 Ibid., 166.

235 Ibid., 167.

236 Peter Force (ed.), *Tracts and Other Papers relating principally to the Origin, Settlement, and Progress of the Colonies in North America from the Discovery of the Country to the Year 1776, Vol. II*, "Master Evelins Letter," from A Description of the Province of New Albion, 22.

237 The Indians called Boompjes Hook, *Canaresse*.

238 Peter Force (ed.), *Tracts and Other Papers relating principally to the Origin, Settlement, and Progress of the Colonies in North America from the Discovery of the Country to the Year 1776, Vol. II*, "Master Evelins Letter," from A Description of the Province of New Albion, 22.

239 Ibid., 22.

240 Ibid., 22.

241 Ibid., 22.

242 Wirantapeck Kill is possibly a corruption of *Welemukquek*, meaning, "round hill."

243 Peter Force (ed.), *Tracts and Other Papers relating principally to the Origin, Settlement, and Progress of the Colonies in North America from the Discovery of the Country to the Year 1776, Vol. II*, "Master Evelins Letter," from A Description of the Province of New Albion, 22.

244 Ibid., 22.

245 Lindeström referred to Crosswicks Creek as the Packquimensi Sippo, from *Pachganuntschi*, meaning, "white walnut, butternut" and *sipo*, "creek." He calls Doctor's Creek the Mechansio, from *Mechen*, meaning, "big" and *sipo*, meaning "creek", combining to form *Mechensipo*, "big creek." Mosilian possibly derives from *Mos*, meaning, "deer, or elk", and *allauwin*, meaning, "to hunt," combining to form *Mosallauwin*, "to hunt deer."

246 Peter Force (ed.), *Tracts and Other Papers relating principally to the Origin, Settlement, and Progress of the Colonies in North America from the Discovery of the Country to the Year 1776, Vol. II*, "Master Evelins Letter," from A Description of the Province of New Albion, 22.

247 Ibid., 22.

248 Cadwallader Colden, *The History of the Five Indian Nations Depending on the Province of New York in America*, (Ithaca, NY: Cornell University Press, 1958), 4.

249 Edna Kenton, (ed.), *The Jesuit Relations and Allied Documents*, 303-304.

250 Ibid., 303-304.

251 Reuben Gold Thwaites, (ed.), "Letter from François du Peron," *The Jesuit and Allied Documents, Vol. XV, Hurons and: 1638-1639*, (Cleveland: The Burrows Brothers Company, 1898), 157.

252 "Relation of what occurred among the Hurons in the year 1635, Sent to Quebec to Father le Jeune by Father Brebeuf," The Jesuit and Allied Documents, 113.

253 Edna Kenton, (ed.), *The Jesuit Relations and Allied Documents*, 111; Agnierrhonons is probably based upon *Ongwe-houwe*, meaning "men surpassing all others, superior to the rest of mankind," from which Mengwe or Minquaas is probably derived; these people were also known as the Aniez, Maquaas or Mohawks.

254 John Heckewelder, *History, Manners and Customs of the Indian Nations*, 54-55.

255 Possibly a habitation of the *Ochquoha* or *Oknaho*, the Wolf clan.

256 "Narrative of a Journey into the Mohawk and Oncida Country, 1634-1635," *Narratives of New*, 141.

257 Ibid., 142. Kanagiro, habitation of the *Ochquari* or *Ochkari*, the Bear clan.

258 Ibid., 142.

259 Also called Asserué, the habitation of the *Anaware* or *Schawariwane*, the Tortoise clan.

260 Thenondiogo was the castle of the *Ochquoha* or *Oknaho*, the Wolf clan.

261 "Narrative of a Journey into the Mohawk and Oneida Country, 1634-1635," *Narratives of New Netherland*, 155.

262 Ibid., 156.

263 The Mohawks manufactured canoes and barrels of bark. "Narrative of a Journey into the Mohawk and Oneida Country, 1634-1635," J. Franklin Jameson (ed.) *Narratives of New Netherland*, 140-141.

264 Ibid., 148.

265 Ibid., 149.

266 John Heckewelder, *History, Manners and Customs of the Indian Nations*, xlii.

267 Reuben Gold Thwaites, (ed.), *The Jesuit and Allied Documents, Vol. XV*, 151.

268 Ibid., 151.

269   Adolph B. Benson (translator and editor), *Peter Kalm's Travels in North America*, 463.

270   Edna Kenton, (ed.), *The Jesuit Relations and Allied Documents*, 139.

271   Teandeouiata, also called Toanche, on the shores of Lake Huron, burned twice and was moved three-quarters of a league inland in 1635

272   Edna Kenton, (ed.), *The Jesuit Relations and Allied Documents*, 99; 99n; 100.

273   Ibid., 85, 99.

274   Ibid., 91.

275   Lyon G. Tyler (ed.), *Original Narratives of Early American History, Narratives of Early Virginia, 1606-1625*, (New York: Charles Scribner's Sons, 1907), 88.

276   Ibid., 105.

277   Ibid., 87-89; 105-106.

278   William Wallace Tooker, *The Indian Place-Names On Long Island and Islands Adjacent*, (New York: G. P. Putnam's Sons, 1911), 107-108.

279   Benjamin B. Thatcher, *Indian Biography: Manners, Customs, and Wars*, (New York: D. M. MacLellan Book Company, 1910), 1-2.

280   Francis Parkman, *France and England in North America, Vol. I*, 176n.

281   Berthold Fernow (ed.), *Documents Relating to the Colonial History of the State of New York, Vol. XIII, Documents Relating to the History and Settlements of the Towns along the Hudson and Mohawk Rivers from 1630 to 1684*, 95.

282   Peter Lindeström, *Geographia Americæ*, 229.

283   Ibid., 241.

284   Ibid., 242-243.

285   Adriæn van der Donck, *A Description of the New Netherlands*, 97.

286   Adolph B. Benson (translator and editor), *Peter Kalm's Travels in North America*, 472.

287   Adriæn van der Donck, *A Description of the New Netherlands*, 97.

288   Amandus Johnson, *The Swedish Settlements on the Delaware 1638-1664, Vol. I*, 387.

289   Daniel Van Winkle, *Reference Pamphlet 1609-1632*, 20.

290   Gacheos may derive from Garios, meaning "deer." The Konetotays may be a form of Canaderage, referring to the Conestoga River.

291   Charles A. Hanna, *The Wilderness Trail, Vol. I*, 28.

292   J. Franklin Jameson, (ed.), *Original Narratives of Early American History, The Voyages of Samuel Champlain 1604-1618*, (New York, Charles Scribner's Sons, 1907), 335.

293   Carl Carmer, *The Susquehanna*, (New York: Rinehart & Co., Inc., 1955), 16-26.

294   J. Franklin Jameson, (ed.), *Original Narratives of Early American History, The Voyages of Samuel Champlain 1604-1618*, 335.

295   W. L. Grant (ed.), *Voyages of Samuel de Champlain 1604-1618*, (New York: Barnes & Noble, Inc., 1946), 285-296; 354-357.

296   Reuben G. Thwaites (ed.), *The Jesuit Relations and Allied Documents, Vol. XLV*, (Cleveland: The Burrows Brothers, 1898), 203.

297   Ibid., 203-205.

298   Ibid., 205; Edna Kenton, (ed.), *The Jesuit Relations and Allied Documents*, 304.

299   "The Representation of New Netherland, 1650," *Narratives of New Netherland*, 300.

300   Peter Lindeström, *Geographia Americæ*, 191-192.

301   Ibid., 191-192.

302   Ibid., 191-192; 235.

303   Adriæn van der Donck, *A Description of the New Netherlands*, 94.

304   Gabriel Thomas, "An Historical and Geographical Account of Pensilvania and West New-Jersey," (1698), Albert Cook Myers (ed.), *Narratives of Early Pennsylvania, West New Jersey and Delaware 1630-1707*, (New York: Charles Scribner's Sons, 1912), 340.

305   Adriæn van der Donck, *A Description of the New Netherlands*, 93-94.

306   Francis D. Pastorius, "Circumstantial Geographical Description of Pennsylvania," *Narratives of Early Pennsylvania, West New and Delaware 1630-1707*, 384.

307   Gabriel Thomas, "An Historical Description of the Province and Country of West New Jersey in America," (1698), Ibid., 341.

308   Peter Lindeström, *Geographia Americæ*, 235.

309   Ibid., 191.

310   "Journal of New Netherland," *Narratives of New Netherland*, 270; "The Representation of New Netherland, 1650," *Narratives of New Netherland*, 300.

311   "The Representation of New Netherland, 1650," *Narratives of New Netherland*, 301.

312   Adolph B. Benson (translator and editor), *Peter Kalm's Travels in North America*, 195.

313   Ibid., 190.

314   Arthur James Weise, *The Discoveries of America to the Year 1525*, 307-08

315   Peter Lindeström, *Geographia Americæ*, 198.

316   Adriæn van der Donck, *A Description of the New Netherlands*, 66-67.

317   Arthur James Weise, *The Discoveries of America to the Year 1525*, 307-08

318   Ibid., 307-308.

319   Adriæn van der Donck, *A Description of the New Netherlands*, 72-74.

320   Peter Lindeström, *Geographia Americæ*, 191.

321   "The Representation of New Netherland, 1650," *Narratives of New Netherland*, 301.

322   Francis D. Pastorius, "Circumstantial Geographical Description of Pennsylvania," *Narratives of Early Pennsylvania, West New Jersey and Delaware 1630-1707*, 384.

323   Gabriel Thomas, "An Historical and Geographical Account" Albert Cook Myers (ed.), *Narratives of Early Pennsylvania, West New and Delaware 1630-1707*, 333.

324   Adriæn van der Donck, *A Description of the New Netherlands*, 79.

325   Journal of Jasper Danckaerts 1679-1680, 35.

326   "A Short Account of the Mohawk Indians, by Reverend Johannes Megapolensis, Jr., 1644," *Narratives of New Netherland*, 173-174.

327   Adolph B. Benson (translator and editor), *Peter Kalm's Travels in North America*, 379.

328   Adriæn van der Donck, *A Description of the New Netherlands*, 94.

329   Ibid., 38.

330   Ibid., 38.

331   Ibid., 38.

332   Peter Lindeström, *Geographia Americæ*, 221.

333   David De Vries, "Korte Historiael," *Narratives of New Netherland*, 217.

334   Adolph B. Benson (translator and editor), *Peter Kalm's Travels in North America*, 472.

335   Gabriel Thomas, "An Historical and Geographical Account" *Narratives of Early Pennsylvania, West New Jersey and Delaware 1630-1707*, 341.

336   "The Representation of New Netherland, 1650," *Narratives of New Netherland*, 300-301.

337   Adriæn van der Donck, *A Description of the New Netherlands*, 78.

338   Edna Kenton, (ed.), *The Jesuit Relations and Allied Documents*, 19.

339   Peter Lindeström, *Geographia Americæ*, 244-245.

340   Adolph B. Benson (translator and editor), *Peter Kalm's Travels in North America*, 472.

341   Ibid., 577-578.

342   David De Vries, "Korte Historiael," *Narratives of New Netherland*, 217.

343   "The Representation of New Netherland, 1650," *Narratives of New Netherland*, 301.

344   Adolph B. Benson (translator and editor), *Peter Kalm's Travels in North America*, 180.

345   Adriæn van der Donck, *A Description of the New Netherlands*, 79.

346   *Journal of New Netherland*, 270; "The Representation of New Netherland, 1650," *Narratives of New Netherland*, 301.

347   David De Vries, "Korte Historiael," *Narratives of New Netherland*, 217.

348   "Letter of Isaack De Rasieres to Samuel Blommaert, 1628 (?)," *Narratives of New Netherland*, 106.

349   Peter Lindeström, *Geographia Americæ*, 221-222.

350   *The American Magazine of Entertaining and Useful Knowledge, Vol. I*, (Boston: The Boston Bewick Company, 1835), 172.

351   Edna Kenton, (ed.), *The Jesuit Relations and Allied Documents*, 19.

352   David De Vries, "Korte Historiael," *Narratives of New Netherland*, 217.

353   Adriæn van der Donck, *A Description of the New Netherlands*, 78. The Dutch ell became the meter.

354   David De Vries, "Korte Historiael," *Narratives of New Netherland*, 221; "Journal of Jasper Danckaerts 1679-1680, 56.

355   "The Representation of New Netherland, 1650," *Narratives of New Netherland*, 301; Adriæn van der Donck, *A Description of the New Netherlands*, 78.

356   Adriæn van der Donck, *A Description of the New Netherlands*, 56. Sewan derives from the Algonquian word *seahwhóun*, meaning "scattered" or "loose."

357   Adriæn van der Donck, *A Description of the New Netherlands*, 93.

358   Peter Lindeström, *Geographia Americæ*, 229-230.

359   Ibid., 230.

360   Ibid., 231.

361   Francis D. Pastorius, "Circumstantial Geographical Description of Pennsylvania," *Narratives of Early Pennsylvania, West New Jersey and Delaware 1630-1707*, 382.

362   *Venus mercenaria* is the quahog or hard-shell clam. Adolph B. Benson (translator and editor), *Peter Kalm's Travels in North America*, 472.

363   Peter Lindeström, *Geographia Americæ*, 229.

364   Ibid., 229.

365   Adriæn van der Donck, *A Description of the New Netherlands*, 93.

366   "The Representation of New Netherland, 1650," *Narratives of New Netherland*, 298; 301.

367   *Documents Relating to the Colonial History of the State of New York Vol. XII*, 47.

368   Peter Lindeström, *Geographia Americæ*, 231.

369   Adriæn van der Donck, *A Description of the New Netherlands*, 93.

370   Peter Lindeström, *Geographia Americæ*, 230.

371   Francis D. Pastorius, "Circumstantial Geographical Description of Pennsylvania," *Narratives of Early Pennsylvania, West New Jersey and Delaware 1630-1707,* 382.

372   Peter Lindeström, *Geographia Americæ*, 230.

373   "The Representation of New Netherland, 1650," *Narratives of New Netherland,* 301.

374   Francis D. Pastorius, "Circumstantial Geographical Description of Pennsylvania," *Narratives of Early Pennsylvania, West New Jersey and Delaware 1630-1707,* 382.

375   "The Representation of New Netherland, 1650," *Narratives of New Netherland,* 301.

376   Adriæn van der Donck, *A Description of the New Netherlands*, 79.

377   Ibid., 39; 79; 94.

378   Francis D. Pastorius, "Circumstantial Geographical Description of Pennsylvania," *Narratives of Early Pennsylvania, West New and Delaware 1630-1707,* 385.

379   Adriæn van der Donck, *A Description of the New Netherlands*, 94.

380   Adolph B. Benson (translator and editor), *Peter Kalm's Travels in North America,* 147.

381   Peter Lindeström, *Geographia Americæ*, 221; 250.

382   *New York State Local History Source Leaflets*, "Verrazano's Voyage Along The Atlantic Coast of North America, 1524," (Albany, NY: The University of the State of New York, 1916), 9.

383   Nelson, William, *The New Jersey Coast in Three Centuries, Vol. I.,* 5.

384   Adolph B. Benson (translator and editor), *Peter Kalm's Travels in North America,* 259.

385   Ibid., 307-308; 533.

386   Adriæn van der Donck *A Description of the New Netherlands*, 92

387   Ibid., 75-76.

388   Arthur James Weise, *The Discoveries of America to the Year 1525*, 313.

389   Ibid., 325.

390   Johan De Laet, "New World," *Narratives of New Netherland,* 48.

391   "The Representation of New Netherland, 1650," *Narratives of New Netherland,* 302.

392   Peter Lindeström, *Geographia Americæ*, 211.

393   Adriæn van der Donck, *A Description of the New Netherlands*, 80.

394   Adolph B. Benson (translator and editor), *Peter Kalm's Travels in North America,* 307-308; 533; Adriæn van der Donck, *A Description of the New Netherlands,* 81; "The Representation of New Netherland, 1650," 96; "Letter of Isaac De Rasieres to Samuel Blommært, 1628," *Narratives of New Netherland,* 108.

395   "Journal of Jasper Danckaerts 1679-1680," 55.

396   Captain David De Vries estimated that maize was "sown three or four feet apart, in order to have room to weed it thoroughly." See David De Vries, "Korte Historiael," *Narratives of New,* 219.

397   Peter Lindeström, *Geographia Americæ,* 179.

398   Edna Kenton, (ed.), *The Jesuit Relations and Allied Documents,* 68-69; Adolph B. Benson (translator and editor), *Peter Kalm's Travels in North America,* 423-424.

399   David De Vries, "Korte Historiael," *Narratives of New Netherland,* 222.

400   Peter Lindeström, *Geographia Americæ,* 219-220.

401   M. S. Henry, *History of the Lehigh Valley,* (Easton: Bixler & Corwin, 1859), p. 264

402   "Letter of Isaack De Rasieres to Samuel Blommaert, 1628 (?)," *Narratives of New Netherland,* 105.

403   Edna Kenton, (ed.), *The Jesuit Relations and Allied Documents,* 69.

404   While camped along the Delaware River near Cochecton, New York, on the night of July 9, 1719, West Jersey Boundary Commissioner John Reading watched as "the Indians advanced from an Indian wigwam on the Pennsylvania side with lighted torches in their hand, made of split pine, in No. 5, on fishing for eels, which they struck with sticks shaped on purpose for it. [They] employ a light at dead of night, very dreadful, yet pleasant to behold." "Journal of John Reading,"103-104.

405   Peter Lindeström, *Geographia Americæ,* 219-220.

406   Isaac Jogues, "Novum Belgium, 1646," *Narratives of New Netherland,* 261; Adolph B. Benson (translator and editor), *Peter Kalm's Travels in North America,* 53; 127.

407   Adolph B. Benson (translator and editor), *Peter Kalm's Travels in North America,* 126-127.

408   Peter Lindeström, *Geographia Americæ,* 213

409   Adriæn van der Donck, *A Description of the New Netherlands,* 20-21.

410   Fernow, B., *Documents Relating to the History and Settlements of the Towns along the Hudson and Mohawk Rivers from 1630 to 1684,* (Albany: Weed, Parsons and Company, 1881), 100.

411   John Gifford, *Annual Report of the State Geologist for the Year 1899, Report on Forests,* Part IV, "The Forestal Conditions and Silvicultural Prospects of the Coastal Plain of New Jersey," (Trenton: MacCrellish & Quigley, 1900), 259.

412   Adriæn van der Donck, *A Description of the New Netherlands*, 20-21

413   Ibid., 21

414   Peter Lindeström, *Geographia Americæ*, 213-214.

415   Adriæn van der Donck, *A Description of the New Netherlands*, 47.

416   David De Vries, "Korte Historiael," *Narratives of New Netherland*, 220.

417   Ibid., 220

418   Adriæn van der Donck, *A Description of the New Netherlands*, 43.

419   "Letter of Isaack De Rasieres to Samuel Blommaert, 1628 (?)," *Narratives of New Netherland,* 114

420   Adriæn van der Donck, *A Description of the New Netherlands*, 44-45; Edna Kenton, (ed.), *The Jesuit Relations and Allied Documents*, 68.

421   Adriæn van der Donck, *A Description of the New Netherlands*, 43.

422   "Letter of Isaack De Rasieres to Samuel Blommaert, 1628 (?)," *Narratives of New Netherland,* 114; Adriæn van der Donck, *A Description of the New Netherlands*, 48; Edna Kenton, (ed.), *The Jesuit Relations and Allied Documents*, 68.

423   Early Swedish settlers in the Delaware Valley claimed, "that the Indians formerly used to eat all kinds of flesh, except that of the mink." See Adolph B. Benson (translator and editor), *Peter Kalm's Travels in North*, 241-242

424   The Minisinks and their affiliate communities called raccoons, *espan* or *hespan*, whereas some Southern Lenape along the Lower Delaware Basin called them *nahanum*.

425   Adolph B. Benson (translator and editor), *Peter Kalm's Travels in North America*, 534

426   Ibid., 239-240

427   Ibid., 241-242

428   Edna Kenton, (ed.), *The Jesuit Relations and Allied Documents*, 67- 68.

429   Adolph B. Benson (translator and editor), *Peter Kalm's Travels in North America*, 146-147.

430   Adriæn van der Donck, *A Description of the New Netherlands*, 46-47.

431   Peter Lindeström noted that natives called the mountain lions, *Manunckees mochijrick Singwaes*, literally "the evil large cat or lion." See "Letter of Isaack De Rasieres to Samuel Blommaert, 1628 (?)," *Narratives of New Netherland,* 114; Adriæn van der Donck, *A Description of the New Netherlands*, 47; Peter Lindeström, *Geographia Americæ*, 185.

432   "A Short Account of the Mohawk Indians, by Reverend Johannes Megapolensis, Jr., 1644," *Narratives of New Netherland,* 169; Adriæn van der Donck, *A Description of the New Netherlands*, 53.

433   "A Short Account of the Mohawk Indians, by Reverend Johannes Megapolensis, Jr., 1644," *Narratives of New Netherland,* 169; Nicolaes Wassenaer, "Historisch Verhæl, 1624-1630," *Narratives of New Netherland,* 71; "The Representation of New Netherland, 1650," *Narratives of New Netherland,* 297.

434   Nicolaes Wassenaer, "Historisch Verhæl, 1624-1630," *Narratives of New Netherland,* 72.

435   Edna Kenton, (ed.), *The Jesuit Relations and Allied Documents,* 68

436   Adriæn van der Donck, *A Description of the New Netherlands,* 50; Other observers confirmed that wild turkeys weighed between thirty and forty pounds and lived in flocks of up to forty individuals.

437   David De Vries, "Korte Historiael," *Narratives of New Netherland,* 221.

438   "Letter of Isaack De Rasieres to Samuel Blommaert, 1628 (?)," *Narratives of New Netherland,* 115.

439   Adriæn van der Donck, *A Description of the New Netherlands,* 50.

440   Adolph B. Benson (translator and editor), *Peter Kalm's Travels in North America,* 111.

441   Ibid., 237.

442   George C. Warren and H. J. Burlington (compilers), *The Outdoor Heritage of New Jersey,* (Camden: The Haddon Craftsmen, Inc., 1937), 65-67.

443   *A Book of Ornithology for Youth,* (Boston: William Hyde & Co., 1832), 110.

444   Warren, George C. and Burlington, H. J. (compilers), *The Outdoor Heritage of New Jersey,* 33.

445   *The American Magazine of Entertaining and Useful Knowledge,* Vol. III, (Boston: The Boston Bewick Company, 1835), 470.

446   Adolph B. Benson (translator and editor), *Peter Kalm's Travels in North America,* 288.

447   Adriæn van der Donck, *A Description of the New Netherlands,* 51; David De Vries, "Korte Historiael," *Narratives of New Netherland,* 221.

448   Adolph B. Benson (translator and editor), *Peter Kalm's Travels in North America,* 252; 369; *A Book of Ornithology for Youth,* 1832, 138-144.

449   Adriæn van der Donck, *A Description of the New Netherlands,* 51.

450   A Dutchman at Fort Amsterdam reportedly killed "eighty-four of these birds at one shot" in Governor Kieft's orchard. Not to be outdone, Jacob Van Curler felled 170 blackbirds in a single shot, not counting crippled birds that escaped. See David De Vries, "Korte Historiael," *Narratives of New Netherland,* 222; Adriæn van der Donck, *A Description of the New Netherlands,* 52.

451   Adolph B. Benson (translator and editor), *Peter Kalm's Travels in North America,* 79.

452   Adriæn van der Donck, *A Description of the New Netherlands*, 71; David De
       Vries, "Korte Historiael," *Narratives of New Netherland*, 219.

453   At Nyack, on the western end of Long Island, Jasper Danckærts observed an
       eighty-year-old woman "busily employed beating Turkish beans out of the
       pods by means of a stick, which she did with astonishing force and dexterity."
       See *Journal of Jasper Danckaerts 1679-1680*, 54-55.

454   On December 30, 1679, Jasper Danckærts ate at a sachem's hut, located
       southwest of Rocky Hill, several miles from the Millstone River. He and his
       companions were offered "some boiled beans in a calabash [or gourd bowl],
       cooked without salt or grease, though they brought us our own kind of spoons
       to take them out with." He also received "a piece of their bread, that is, pounded
       maize kneaded into a cake and baked under the ashes." See "Journal of Jasper
       Danckaerts 1679-1680," 159.

455   Peter Lindeström, *Geographia Americæ*, 179-180.

456   To manufacture a wooden mortar, the natives "cut a thick and large tree, one
       and a half ells from the root, in the stump of which they dig out a round hole
       and thus make a mortar which is suited for the purpose." When they traveled,
       they carried "a flat stone" upon which they pounded the corn "with another
       stone placed upon the first..." See Adriæn van der Donck, *A Description of the
       New Netherlands*, 218.

457   "Letter of Isaack De Rasieres to Samuel Blommaert, 1628 (?)," *Narratives of
       New Netherland*, 108; Peter Lindeström, *Geographia Americæ*, 254; David De
       Vries, "Korte Historiael," *Narratives of New Netherland*, 219; "Journal of Jasper
       Danckaerts 1679-1680, 56.

458   "The Representation of New Netherland, 1650," *Narratives of New Netherland*,
       303; Adriæn van der Donck, *A Description of the New Netherlands*, 75-76.

459   Adolph B. Benson (translator and editor), *Peter Kalm's Travels in North America*,
       183; 516-517.

460   Adriæn van der Donck, *A Description of the New Netherlands*, 68.

461   Adolph B. Benson (translator and editor), *Peter Kalm's Travels in North America*,
       641; 74.

462   Peter Lindeström, *Geographia Americæ*, 178-179; 255.

463   "Letter of Isaack De Rasieres to Samuel Blommaert, 1628 (?)," *Narratives of
       New*, 108; David De Vries, "Korte Historiael," *Narratives of New Netherland*,
       219-220.

464   Adolph B. Benson (translator and editor), *Peter Kalm's Travels in North America*,
       269.

465   Peter Lindeström, *Geographia Americæ*, 253.

466   Adolph B. Benson (translator and editor), *Peter Kalm's Travels in North America*,
       394.

467　Since the medlar (*Mespilus germanica*) is native to Europe and Asia, it is possible that the Common American Persimmon (*Diospyros virginiana*) was misidentified or described as a "medlar.

468　Peter Lindeström, *Geographia Americæ*, 177-178.

469　Adolph B. Benson (translator and editor), *Peter Kalm's Travels in North America*, 181.

470　Thomas Paschall, "Letter of Thomas Paschall, 1683," *Narratives of Early Pennsylvania, West New and Delaware 1630-1707*, 253.

471　Adolph B. Benson (translator and editor), *Peter Kalm's Travels in North America*, 336.

472　Peter Lindeström, *Geographia Americæ*, 178.

473　Adriæn van der Donck, *A Description of the New Netherlands*, 26.

474　Nicolaes Wassenaer, "Historisch Verhæl, 1624-1630," *Narratives of New Netherland*, 71; "A Short Account of the Mohawk Indians, by Reverend Johannes Megapolensis, Jr., 1644," *Narratives of New Netherland*, 169; "The Representation of New Netherland, 1650," *Narratives of New Netherland*, 295; Gabriel Thomas, "An Historical and Geographical Account" *Narratives of Early Pennsylvania, West New Jersey and Delaware 1630-1707*, 322.

475　F. Schuyler Mathews, *Field Book of American Wild Flowers*, (Boston: 1902), 260.

476　Adolph B. Benson (translator and editor), *Peter Kalm's Travels in North America*, 336.

477　Gabriel Thomas, "An Historical and Geographical Account" *Narratives of Early Pennsylvania, West New Jersey and Delaware 1630-1707*, 322; 348.

478　Adolph B. Benson (translator and editor), *Peter Kalm's Travels in North America*, 251.

479　Adriæn van der Donck, *A Description of the New Netherlands*, 23; 61.

480　Adolph B. Benson (translator and editor), *Peter Kalm's Travels in North America*, 286.

481　Thomas Paschall, "Letter of Thomas Paschall, 1683," *Narratives of Early Pennsylvania, West New Jersey and Delaware 1630-1707*, 253.

482　Adolph B. Benson (translator and editor), *Peter Kalm's Travels in North America*, 262.

483　Ibid., 164.

484　Adriæn van der Donck, *A Description of the New Netherlands*, 22.

485　Ibid., 23.

486　Adolph B. Benson (translator and editor), *Peter Kalm's Travels in North America*, 165.

487　Adriæn van der Donck, *A Description of the New Netherlands*, 28.

488   Adolph B. Benson (translator and editor), *Peter Kalm's Travels in North America*, 533; 642.

489   Ibid., 269.

490   Ibid., 259-260.

491   Ibid., 53; 151; 261.

492   Peter Lindeström, *Geographia Americæ*, 158-159.

493   Gabriel Thomas, "An Historical and Geographical Account" *Narratives of Early Pennsylvania, West New Jersey and Delaware 1630-1707*, 348.

494   Johan De Laet, "New World," *Narratives of New Netherland,* 57.

495   Johan De Laet, "New World," *Narratives of New Netherland,* 49.

496   Ibid., 49.

497   Adriæn van der Donck, *A Description of the New Netherlands*, 79-80.

498   Ibid., 22.

499   Ibid., 39.

500   Peter Lindeström, *Geographia Americæ*, 211-212.

501   Ibid., 255.

502   William Penn, "Some Account of the Province of Pennsilvania by William Penn, 1681," *Narratives of Early Pennsylvania, West New Jersey and Delaware 1630-1707*, 232.

503   Gabriel Thomas, "An Historical and Geographical Account" *Narratives of Early Pennsylvania, West New Jersey and Delaware 1630-1707*, 341.

504   Francis D. Pastorius, "Circumstantial Geographical Description of Pennsylvania," *Narratives of Early Pennsylvania, West New Jersey and Delaware 1630-1707*, 385.

505   Francis D. Pastorius, "Circumstantial Geographical Description of Pennsylvania," *Narratives of Early Pennsylvania, West New Jersey and Delaware 1630-1707*, 435.

506   "Journal of Jasper Danckaerts 1679-1680," 55.

507   Kenton, Edna (ed.), *The Jesuit Relations and Allied Documents*, 108.

508   David De Vries, "Korte Historiael," *Narratives of New Netherland*, 217-218.

509   Peter Lindeström, *Geographia Americæ*, 257-258.

510   David De Vries, "Korte Historiael," *Narratives of New Netherland*, 217-218.

511   Adriæn van der Donck, *A Description of the New Netherlands*, 95.

512   The Algonquian word for villages is *uteneyik*. The Teaneck Path, now Teaneck Road, ran to the New Hackensack villages near Fyke Lane in Teaneck, New Jersey.

513   Adriæn van der Donck, *A Description of the New Netherlands*, 81.

514   Peter Lindeström, *Geographia Americæ*, 170-171.

515   Petuguepaen may be a corruption of *Petaquiechen*, which means, "The stream is rising," a possible reference to Five Mile River. Some sources place the village in Pound Ridge, New York, while other suggest Cos Cob, Connecticut.

516   "Journal of New Netherland 1647," *Narratives of New Netherland*, 283.

517   Nicolaes Wassenaer, "Historisch Verhæl, 1624-1630," *Narratives of New Netherland*, 80.

518   Adriæn van der Donck, *A Description of the New Netherlands*, 80-81.

519   Ibid., 81.

520   Ibid., 80-81.

521   Johan De Laet, "New World," *Narratives of New Netherland*, 43.

522   "Journal of New Netherland 1647," *Narratives of New Netherland*, 281.

523   Peter Lindeström, *Geographia Americæ*, 206; 241.

524   "The Indians of Bergen County," Frances A. Westervelt, (ed.), *History of Bergen County, New Jersey 1630-1923, Vol. I*, (New York: Lewis Historical Publishing Company, Inc., 1923), 38.

525   Peter Lindeström, *Geographia Americæ*, 193.

526   Adriæn van der Donck, *A Description of the New Netherlands*, 99.

527   Ibid., 99.

528   "The Representation of New Netherland, 1650," *Narratives of New Netherland*, 300-301; Adriæn van der Donck, *A Description of the New Netherlands*, 99.

529   Peter Lindeström, *Geographia Americæ*, 203-204.

530   Adriæn van der Donck, *A Description of the New Netherlands*, 99.

531   Peter Lindeström, *Geographia Americæ*, 206.

532   Adriæn van der Donck, *A Description of the New Netherlands*, 100.

533   Ibid., 100.

534   Peter Lindeström, *Geographia Americæ*, 239.

535   Arthur James Weise, *The Discoveries of America to the Year 1525*, 325.

536   Adriæn van der Donck, *A Description of the New Netherlands*, 95.

537   William Penn, "Some Account of the Province of Pennsilvania by William Penn, 1681," *Narratives of Early Pennsylvania, West New Jersey and Delaware 1630-1707*, 233.

538   Nicolaes Wassenaer, "Historisch Verhæl, 1624-1630," *Narratives of New Netherland*, 72.

539   Johan De Laet, "New World," *Narratives of New Netherland*, 55; Nicolaes Wassenaer, "Historisch Verhæl, 1624-1630," *Narratives of New Netherland*, 72; "The Representation of New Netherland, 1650," *Narratives of New Netherland*,

292; 295; 301; Adriæn van der Donck, *A Description of the New Netherlands,* 28; 95.

540   Gabriel Thomas, "An Historical and Geographical Account" *Narratives of Early Pennsylvania, West New Jersey and Delaware 1630-1707,* 348; American white hellebore (*Veratrum viride*), a perennial herb with very poisonous roots, commonly found in wet meadows and low ground, is known as Indian poke. Pokeberry (*Phytolacca americana*), perhaps best known for the staining juice of its red dish-purple berries, also has poisonous roots and berries.

541   Adolph B. Benson (translator and editor), *Peter Kalm's Travels in North America,* 438.

542   Ibid., 611.

543   Peter Lindeström, *Geographia Americæ,* 239-240.

544   Adolph B. Benson (translator and editor), *Peter Kalm's Travels in North America,* 437-438; 606; 611.

545   Peter Lindeström, *Geographia Americæ,* 239.

546   Adolph B. Benson (translator and editor), *Peter Kalm's Travels in North America,* 110.

547   Rattlesnake root (*Prenanthes altissima*), also known as white lettuce, is a common member of the composite family found in thin woods. *Cimicifuga racemosa* (or black cohosh), a tall woodland plant with feathery white flowers in June-July, and *Sanicula Marylandica,* a member of the parsley family with tiny greenish-yellow flowers in May-July, are both known as black snakeroot. *Eupatorium ageratoides,* a member of the composite family with white flowers in July-September, is known as white snakeroot. *Polygala senega,* a milkwort found in rocky woodlands, is Seneca snakeroot; *Aristolochia serpentaria,* a woolly-stemmed birthwort, is Virginia snakeroot.

548   "The Representation of New Netherland, 1650," *Narratives of New Netherland,* 298; Adriæn van der Donck, *A Description of the New Netherlands,* 58.

549   Arthur James Weise, *The Discoveries of America to the Year 1525,* 313.

550   Adolph B. Benson (translator and editor), *Peter Kalm's Travels in North America,* 230.

551   Ibid., 230.

552   Adolph B. Benson (translator and editor), *Peter Kalm's Travels in North America,* 229.

553   Johan De Laet, "New World," *Narratives of New Netherland,* 57.

554   Adolph B. Benson (translator and editor), *Peter Kalm's Travels in North America,* 229.

555   Ibid., 230.

556   "The Representation of New Netherland, 1650," *Narratives of New Netherland,* 301.

557   Arthur James Weise, *The Discoveries of America to the Year 1525*, 312.

558   Adolph B. Benson (translator and editor), *Peter Kalm's Travels in North America*, 230-231; 333.

559   Ibid., 85; 333.

560   Peter Lindeström, *Geographia Americæ*, 237-238.

561   Adolph B. Benson (translator and editor), *Peter Kalm's Travels in North America*, 551.

562   Ibid., 551.

563   Ibid., 551.

564   Ibid., 551.

565   "Journal of John Reading," 104.

566   Ibid., 90.

567   Johan De Laet, "New World," *Narratives of New Netherland*, 57.

568   Adolph B. Benson (translator and editor), *Peter Kalm's Travels in North America*, 231-232.

569   Peter Lindeström, *Geographia Americæ*, 249.

570   Johan De Laet, "New World," *Narratives of New Netherland*, 49.

571   Belleville was called Second River.

572   Adolph B. Benson (translator and editor), *Peter Kalm's Travels in North America*, 202

573   Ibid., 524

574   Gabriel Thomas, "An Historical and Geographical Account" *Narratives of Early Pennsylvania, West New Jersey and Delaware 1630-1707*, 341.

575   Adolph B. Benson (translator and editor), *Peter Kalm's Travels in North America*, 71; 278.

576   Ibid., 278.

577   Ibid., 277-278.

578   Ibid., 284; 564.

579   Adolph B. Benson (translator and editor), *Peter Kalm's Travels in North America*, 564.

580   Peter Lindeström, *Geographia Americæ*, 222.

581   Ibid., 221.

582   Adolph B. Benson (translator and editor), *Peter Kalm's Travels in North America*, 35.

583   Ibid., 176; 179.

584   Ibid., 185.

585   Adriæn van der Donck, *A Description of the New Netherlands*, 70.

586   Adolph B. Benson (translator and editor), *Peter Kalm's Travels in North America*, 173.

587   Ibid., 231.

588   Ibid., 231.

589   Ibid.,172.

590   Ibid., 172.

591   Ibid., 172-173.

592   Ibid., 439.

593   Ibid., 270.

594   Peter Williamson, "A Short Account of the Indians of North America," *Bulletin of the Archeological Society of New Jersey*, No. 31 Fall/Winter 1974, 16.

595   Bartlett Burleigh James and J. Franklin Jameson, (Eds.), "Journal of Jasper Danckaerts 1679-1680," 77-78.

596   David De Vries, "Korte Historiael," *Narratives of New Netherland*, 230.

597   Adolph B. Benson (translator and editor), *Peter Kalm's Travels in North America*, 53.

598   Francis Parkman, *France and England in North America, Vol. I*, 379.

599   Charles T. Gehring, and Robert S. Grumer, "Observations of the Indians from Jasper Dackaerts's Journal, 1679-1680," *The William and Mary Quarterly*, 3rd Series, Vol. XLIV, January 1987, 110-111.

600   Ibid., 110-111.

601   Nicolaes Wassenaer, "Historisch Verhæl, 1624-1630," *Narratives of New Netherland*, 71.

602   David De Vries, "Korte Historiael Ende Journaels Aenteyckeninge," *Narratives of Early Pennsylvania, West New Jersey and Delaware 1630-1707*, 17.

603   Peter Lindeström, *Geographia Americæ*, 223.

604   Ibid., 224-225.

605   *Documents Relating to the Colonial History of the State of New York Vol. VII*, 135-136.

606   *Documents Relating to the Colonial History of the State of New York Vol. XII*, 156-158.

607   Peter Lindeström, *Geographia Americæ*, 225.

608   *Documents Relating to the Colonial History of the State of New York Vol. XII*, 187.

609   Ibid., 228.

610 Nicolaes Wassenaer, "Historisch Verhæl, 1624-1630," *Narratives of New Netherland*, 73.

611 Nicolaes Wassenaer, "Historisch Verhæl, 1624-1630," *Narratives of New Netherland*, 73.

612 Adolph B. Benson (translator and editor), *Peter Kalm's Travels in North America*, 269.

613 Ibid., 269.

614 Peter Lindeström, *Geographia Americæ*, 198-199.

615 Ibid., 198-199.

616 The years covered: 1677 (4 deeds), 1679, 1684, 1686, 1687 (2 deeds), 1688 (4 deeds), 1689, 1693, 1694, 1699, 1701, 1702 (2 deeds), 1708, and 1714 (2 deeds).

617 Frieze is a heavy, coarse woolen overcoat used for winter outerwear.

618 Kersey is a finished, woolen fabric with a lustrous nap used for uniforms.

619 Adolph B. Benson (translator and editor), *Peter Kalm's Travels in North America*, 519-521.

620 Nicolaes Wassenaer, "Historisch Verhæl, 1624-1630," *Narratives of New Netherland*, 77.

621 "Letter of Isaack De Rasieres to Samuel Blommaert, 1628 (?)," *Narratives of New Netherland*, 105.

622 Adriæn van der Donck, *A Description of the New Netherlands*, 72.

623 "Letter of Isaack De Rasieres to Samuel Blommaert, 1628 (?)," *Letter, Narratives of New Netherland*, 107.

624 "The Representation of New Netherland, 1650," *Narratives of New Netherland*, 302.

625 Ibid., 303.

626 "Letter of Isaack De Rasieres to Samuel Blommaert, 1628 (?)," *Narratives of New Netherland*, 105; Nicolaes Wassenaer, "Historisch Verhæl, 1624-1630," *Narratives of New Netherland*, 85; David De Vries, "Korte Historiael," *Narratives of New Netherland*, 217.

627 Peter Lindeström, *Geographia Americæ*, 195.

628 Ibid., 196.

629 Adriæn van der Donck, *A Description of the New Netherlands*, 4.

630 Peter Lindeström, *Geographia Americæ*, 196-200.

631 Ibid., 196-200.

632 "Letter of Isaack De Rasieres to Samuel Blommaert, 1628 (?)," *Narratives of New Netherland*, 106.

633 "The Representation of New Netherland, 1650," *Narratives of New Netherland*, 302; Gabriel Thomas, "An Historical and Geographical Account" *Narratives of*

Early Pennsylvania, West New Jersey and Delaware 1630-1707, 341; Adriæn van der Donck, *A Description of the New Netherlands*, 96.

634   Nicolaes Wassenaer, "Historisch Verhæl, 1624-1630," *Narratives of New Netherland*, 69.

635   Ibid., 69.

636   Gabriel Thomas, "An Historical and Geographical Account," *Narratives of Early Pennsylvania, West New Jersey and Delaware 1630-1707*, 341.

637   Arthur James Weise, *The Discoveries of America to the Year 1525*, 325.

638   Nicolaes Wassenaer, "Historisch Verhæl, 1624-1630," *Narratives of New Netherland*, 85.

639   Ibid., 85.

640   Adriæn van der Donck, *A Description of the New Netherlands*, 86.

641   Thomas Clarkson, *Memoirs of the Private and Public Life of William*, (Dover, New Hampshire: Samuel C. Stevens, 1827), 147.

642   Gabriel Thomas, "An Historical and Geographical Account," *Narratives of Early Pennsylvania, West New Jersey and Delaware 1630-1707*, 341.

643   Nicolaes Wassenaer, "Historisch Verhæl, 1624-1630," *Narratives of New Netherland*, 85; David De Vries, "Korte Historiael," *Narratives of New Netherland*, 217.

644   Peter Lindeström, *Geographia Americæ*, 199-200.

645   Adriæn van der Donck, *A Description of the New Netherlands*, 78.

646   "Letter of Isaack De Rasieres to Samuel Blommaert, 1628 (?)," *Narratives of New Netherland*, 106; Adriæn van der Donck, *A Description of the New Netherlands*, 78.

647   Peter Lindeström, *Geographia Americæ*, 199-200.

648   Adriæn van der Donck, *A Description of the New Netherlands*, 78.

649   David De Vries, "Korte Historiael," *Narratives of New Netherland*, 217.

650   Adriæn van der Donck, *A Description of the New Netherlands*, 77.

651   Ibid., 77-78.

652   Sereno Edwards Dwight, *Memoirs of the Rev. David Brainerd*, (New Haven: S. Converse, 1822), 177.

653   William Penn, "Some Account of the Province of Pennsilvania by William Penn, 1681," *Narratives of Early Pennsylvania, West New Jersey and Delaware 1630-1707*, 231.

654   Adriæn van der Donck, *A Description of the New Netherlands*, 83.

655   Nicolaes Wassenaer, "Historisch Verhæl, 1624-1630," *Narratives of New Netherland*, 70.

656   "Letter of Isaack De Rasieres to Samuel Blommaert, 1628 (?)," *Narratives of New Netherland*, 109.

657   Adriæn van der Donck, *A Description of the New Netherlands*, 84.

658   "Letter of Isaack De Rasieres to Samuel Blommaert, 1628 (?)," *Narratives of New Netherland*, 106-107.

659   Adriæn van der Donck, *A Description of the New Netherlands*, 84.

660   Letter of Isaack De Rasieres to Samuel Blommaert, 1628 (?)," *Narratives of New Netherland*, 107.

661   William Penn, "Some Account of the Province of Pennsilvania by William Penn, 1681," *Narratives of Early Pennsylvania, West New Jersey and Delaware 1630-1707*, 231.

662   "Letter of Isaack De Rasieres to Samuel Blommaert, 1628 (?)," *Narratives of New*, 106-107; William Penn, "Some Account of the Province of Pensilvania by William Penn, 1681," *Narratives of Early Pennsylvania, West New Jersey and Delaware 1630-1707*, 231.

663   Nicolaes Wassenaer, "Historisch Verhæl, 1624-1630," *Narratives of New Netherland*, 70.

664   Peter Lindeström, *Geographia Americæ*, 193-194,

665   Ibid., 193.

666   "Journal of New Netherland," *Narratives of New Netherland*, 270; "The Representation of New Netherland, 1650," *Narratives of New Netherland*, 302; Adriæn van der Donck, *A Description of the New Netherlands*, 83.

667   Adriæn van der Donck, *A Description of the New Netherlands*, 83.

668   Ibid., 83.

669   William Penn, "Some Account of the Province of Pensilvania by William Penn, 1681," *Narratives of Early Pennsylvania, West New Jersey and Delaware 1630-1707*, 232.

670   Adriæn van der Donck, *A Description of the New Netherlands*, 84-85.

671   Peter Lindeström, *Geographia Americæ*, 186.

672   Adriæn van der Donck, *A Description of the New Netherlands*, 84-85.

673   Ibid., 85.

674   William Penn, "Some Account of the Province of Pennsilvania by William Penn, 1681," *Narratives of Early Pennsylvania, West New Jersey and Delaware 1630-1707*, 231; Francis D. Pastorius, "Circumstantial Geographical Description of Pennsylvania," *Narratives of Early Pennsylvania, West New Jersey and Delaware 1630-1707*, 434.

675   Adriæn van der Donck, *A Description of the New Netherlands*, 85.

676   William Penn, "Some Account of the Province of Pennsilvania by William Penn, 1681," *Narratives of Early Pennsylvania, West New Jersey and Delaware*

1630-1707, 231; Francis D. Pastorius, "Circumstantial Geographical Description of Pennsylvania," *Narratives of Early Pennsylvania, West New Jersey and Delaware 1630-1707,* 434.

677   Peter Lindeström, *Geographia Americæ,* 201.

678   Ibid., 201.

679   William Penn, "Some Account of the Province of Pennsilvania by William Penn, 1681," *Narratives of Early Pennsylvania, West New Jersey and Delaware 1630-1707,* 231.

680   Peter Lindeström, *Geographia Americæ,* 210.

681   "Journal of Jasper Danckaerts 1679-1680," 56.

682   Adriæn van der Donck, *A Description of the New Netherlands,* 86.

683   Michaelius, "Letter," *Narratives of New Netherland,* 128.

684   Nicolaes Wassenaer, "Historisch Verhæl, 1624-1630," *Narratives of New Netherland,* 73.

685   Francis D. Pastorius, "Circumstantial Geographical Description of Pennsylvania," *Narratives of Early Pennsylvania, West New Jersey and Delaware 1630-1707,* 434.

686   Nicolaes Wassenaer, "Historisch Verhæl, 1624-1630," *Narratives of New Netherland,* 71; 73; 85.

687   Francis D. Pastorius, "Circumstantial Geographical Description of Pennsylvania," *Narratives of Early Pennsylvania, West New and Delaware 1630-1707,* 385.

688   Peter Lindeström, *Geographia Americæ,* 210.

689   William Penn, "Some Account of the Province of Pennsilvania by William Penn, 1681," *Narratives of Early Pennsylvania, West New Jersey and Delaware 1630-1707,* 231; Francis D. Pastorius, "Circumstantial Geographical Description of Pennsylvania," *Narratives of Early Pennsylvania, West New Jersey and Delaware 1630-1707,* 434.

690   William Penn, "Some Account of the Province of Pennsilvania by William Penn, 1681," *Narratives of Early Pennsylvania, West New Jersey and Delaware 1630-1707,* 231.

691   Adriæn van der Donck, *A Description of the New Netherlands,* 94.

692   Peter Lindeström, *Geographia Americæ,* 207-208.

693   Adriæn van der Donck, *A Description of the New Netherlands,* 82.

694   Arthur James Weise, *The Discoveries of America to the Year 1525,* 325.

695   "Journal of New Netherland," *Narratives of New Netherland,* 271; Johan De Laet, "New World," *Narratives of New Netherland,* 57-58.

696   "The Representation of New Netherland, 1650," *Narratives of New Netherland,* 302.

697   Peter Lindeström, *Geographia Americæ*, 170-171.

698   Nicolaes Wassenaer, "Historisch Verhæl, 1624-1630," *Narratives of New Netherland,* 69.

699   Peter Lindeström, *Geographia Americæ*, 206.

700   "Letter of Isaack De Rasieres to Samuel Blommaert, 1628 (?)," *Narratives of New Netherland,* 109.

701   Adriæn van der Donck, *A Description of the New Netherlands*, 94.

702   Ibid., 98.

703   Ibid., 98.

704   Peter Lindeström, *Geographia Americæ*, 193.

705   Peter Lindeström, *Geographia Americæ*, 205.

706   Adriæn van der Donck, *A Description of the New Netherlands*, 98.

707   Ibid., 98.

708   Nicolaes Wassenaer, "Historisch Verhæl, 1624-1630," *Narratives of New Netherland,* 77.

709   "Journal of Jasper Danckaerts 1679-1680," 56.

710   Peter Lindeström, *Geographia Americæ*, 193.

711   Ibid., 255.

712   Adriæn van der Donck, *A Description of the New Netherlands*, 98.

713   Francis D. Pastorius, "Circumstantial Geographical Description of Pennsylvania," *Narratives of Early Pennsylvania, West New Jersey and Delaware 1630-1707,* 425.

714   William Penn, "Some Account of the Province of Pennsilvania by William Penn, 1681," *Narratives of Early Pennsylvania, West New Jersey and Delaware 1630-1707,* 233.

715   Peter Lindeström, *Geographia Americæ*, 132.

716   Thomas Young, *Narratives of Early Pennsylvania, West New Jersey and Delaware 1630-1707,* 37-49.

717   William Penn, "Some Account of the Province of Pennsilvania by William Penn, 1681," *Narratives of Early Pennsylvania, West New Jersey and Delaware 1630-1707,* 234-235.

718   Ibid., 235.

719   Adriæn van der Donck, *A Description of the New Netherlands*, 88.

720   Ibid., 88.

721   William Penn, "Some Account of the Province of Pennsilvania by William Penn, 1681," *Narratives of Early Pennsylvania, West New Jersey and Delaware 1630-1707,* 235.

722   "Letter of Isaack De Rasieres to Samuel Blommaert, 1628 (?)," *Narratives of New Netherland,* 109.

723   William Penn, "Some Account of the Province of Pennsilvania by William Penn, 1681," *Narratives of Early Pennsylvania, West New and Delaware 1630-1707,* 235-236.

724   "Letter of Isaack De Rasieres to Samuel Blommaert, 1628 (?)," *Narratives of New Netherland,* 108.

725   Ibid., 109.

726   Johan De Laet, "New World," *Narratives of New Netherland,* 50.

727   Nicolaes Wassenaer, "Historisch Verhæl, 1624-1630," *Narratives of New Netherland,* 69-70.

728   Adriæn van der Donck, *A Description of the New Netherlands,* 99.

729   Ibid., 98.

730   Ibid., 98.

731   David De Vries, "Korte Historiael Ende Journaels Aenteyckeninge," *Narratives of Early Pennsylvania, West New Jersey and Delaware 1630-1707,* 20-21.

732   Ibid., 21.

733   Frances A. Westervelt (ed.), *History of Bergen County, New Jersey 1630-1923,* Vol. I, 37.

734   "The Indians of Bergen County," Frances A. Westervelt, (ed.), *History of Bergen County, New Jersey 1630-1923,* Vol. I, (New York: Lewis Historical Publishing Company, Inc., 1923), 31.

735   Ibid., 32.

736   Sereno Edwards Dwight, *Memoirs of the Rev. David Brainerd,* 178.

737   William Penn, "Some Account of the Province of Pennsilvania by William Penn, 1681," *Narratives of Early Pennsylvania, West New and Delaware 1630-1707,* 233.

738   "Journal of New Netherland, 1647," *Narratives of New Netherland,* 271; "The Representation of New Netherland, 1650," *Narratives of New Netherland,* 303.

739   Adriæn van der Donck, *A Description of the New Netherlands,* 100.

740   Nicolaes Wassenaer, "Historisch Verhæl, 1624-1630," *Narratives of New Netherland,* 80.

741   Peter Lindeström, *Geographia Americæ,* 205.

742   William Penn, "Some Account of the Province of Pennsilvania by William Penn, 1681," *Narratives of Early Pennsylvania, West New and Delaware 1630-1707,* 232.

743   Nicolaes Wassenaer, "Historisch Verhæl, 1624-1630," *Narratives of New Netherland,* 85.

744 "The Representation of New Netherland, 1650," *Narratives of New Netherland*, 303; Adriæn van der Donck, *A Description of the New Netherlands*, 101.

745 "Letter of Isaack De Rasieres to Samuel Blommaert, 1628 (?)," *Narratives of New Netherland*, 108.

746 "Letter of Isaack De Rasieres to Samuel Blommaert, 1628 (?)," *Narratives of New Netherland*, 109; Adriæn van der Donck, *A Description of the New Netherlands*, 101.

747 William Penn, "Some Account of the Province of Pennsilvania by William Penn, 1681," *Narratives of Early Pennsylvania, West New and Delaware 1630-1707*, 236.

748 Adriæn van der Donck, *A Description of the New Netherlands*, 101.

749 Ibid., 101.

750 David De Vries, "Korte Historiael Ende Journaels Aenteyckeninge," *Narratives of Early Pennsylvania, West New Jersey and Delaware 1630-1707*, 15-16.

751 Ibid., 16-17.

752 Ibid., 17.

753 Ibid., 17.

754 "Journal of New Netherland," *Narratives of New Netherland*, 275.

755 David De Vries, "Korte Historiael," *Narratives of New Netherland*, 213.

756 Ibid., 215-216.

757 William Penn, "Some Account of the Province of Pennsilvania by William Penn, 1681," *Narratives of Early Pennsylvania, West New Jersey and Delaware 1630-1707*, 232.

758 Nicolaes Wassenaer, "Historisch Verhæl, 1624-1630," *Narratives of New Netherland*, 68.

759 Johan De Laet, "New World," *Narratives of New Netherland*, 49.

760 Arthur James Weise, *The Discoveries of America to the Year 1525*, 299.

761 Nicolaes Wassenaer, "Historisch Verhæl, 1624-1630," *Narratives of New Netherland*, 68.

762 "The Representation of New Netherland, 1650," *Narratives of New Netherland*, 302.

763 Adriæn van der Donck, *A Description of the New Netherlands*, 102.

764 Ibid., 102.

765 William Penn, "Some Account of the Province of Pennsilvania by William Penn, 1681," *Narratives of Early Pennsylvania, West New Jersey and Delaware 1630-1707*, 234.

766 Adriæn van der Donck, *A Description of the New Netherlands*, 102, 106.

767   Sereno Edwards Dwight, *Memoirs of the Rev. David Brainerd; Missionary to the Indians on the Borders of New-York, New-Jersey and Pennsylvania*, 345.

768   David De Vries, "Korte Historiael," *Narratives of New Netherland*, 225.

769   Nicolaes Wassenaer, "Historisch Verhæl, 1624-1630," *Narratives of New Netherland*, 68.

770   Johan De Laet, "New World," *Narratives of New Netherland*, 49; 57.

771   Peter Lindeström, *Geographia Americæ*, 247.

772   Daniel G. Brinton and Rev. Albert Seqaqkind Anthony, *A Lenâpé-English Dictionary*, (Philadelphia: The Historical Society of Pennsylvania, 1888), 74.

773   Edna Kenton, (ed.), *The Jesuit Relations and Allied Documents*, 321.

774   Jonas Michælius, "Letter of Reverend Jonas Michaelius, 1628," *Narratives of New Netherland,* 127.

775   Johan De Laet, "New World," *Narratives of New Netherland*, 57.

776   "The Representation of New Netherland, 1650," *Narratives of New Netherland,* 303.

777   Ibid., 302.

778   Adriæn van der Donck, *A Description of the New Netherlands*, 102.

779   Peter Lindeström, *Geographia Americæ*, 214-215.

780   "Journal of Jasper Danckaerts 1679-1680," 76-77.

781   Ibid., 76-77.

782   Adriæn van der Donck, *A Description of the New Netherlands*, 106.

783   Ibid., 107.

784   Ibid., 108.

785   Edna Kenton, (ed.), *The Jesuit Relations and Allied Documents*, 112.

786   Ibid., 112.

787   Ibid., 112.

788   "A Short Account of the Mohawk Indians, by Reverend Johannes Megapolensis, Jr., 1644," *Narratives of New Netherland,* 173-174.

789   Edna Kenton, (ed.), *The Jesuit Relations and Allied Documents*, 56.

790   Ibid., 56.

791   Adriæn van der Donck, *A Description of the New Netherlands*, 106.

792   Ibid., 106.

793   The name is given as Tantaqué.

794   Adolph B. Benson (translator and editor), *Peter Kalm's Travels in North America,* 686-687.

795   Ibid., 686-687.

796   "Journal of Jasper Danckaerts 1679-1680," 175.

797   Peter Lindeström, *Geographia Americæ*, 207-208.

798   Sereno Edwards Dwight, *Memoirs of the Rev. David Brainerd*, 344.

799   Adolph B. Benson (translator and editor), *Peter Kalm's Travels in North America*, 270.

800   Edna Kenton, (ed.), *The Jesuit Relations and Allied Documents*, 113; 141- 142.

801   Ibid., 113; 141- 142.

802   Sereno Edwards Dwight, *Memoirs of the Rev. David Brainerd*, 347.

803   Ibid., 347-348.

804   Adriæn van der Donck, *A Description of the New Netherlands*, 104-105.

805   Ibid., 105.

806   Ibid., 105.

807   "The Representation of New Netherland," *Narratives of New Netherland,* 302.

808   Michælius, "Letter," *Narratives of New Netherland,* 127.

809   Ibid., 127.

810   Ibid., 128.

811   Sereno Edwards Dwight, *Memoirs of the Rev. David Brainerd*, 178.

812   Ibid., 178.

813   Adriæn van der Donck, *A Description of the New Netherlands*, 104-105.

814   Ibid., 104-105.

815   Edna Kenton, (ed.), *The Jesuit Relations and Allied Documents*, 53-56.

816   Adolph B. Benson (translator and editor), *Peter Kalm's Travels in North America*, 378.

817   Edna Kenton, (ed.), *The Jesuit Relations and Allied Documents*, 53-54.

818   Ibid., 53-56.

819   Ibid., 56-57; 112-113.

820   Sereno Edwards Dwight, *Memoirs of the Rev. David Brainerd*, 237-238

821   William Penn, "Some Account of the Province of Pennsilvania by William Penn, 1681," *Narratives of Early Pennsylvania, West New Jersey and Delaware 1630-1707*, 234.

822   Francis D. Pastorius, "Circumstantial Geographical Description of Pennsylvania," *Narratives of Early Pennsylvania, West New Jersey and Delaware 1630-1707,* 434.

823   Nicolaes Wassenaer, "Historisch Verhæl, 1624-1630," *Narratives of New Netherland,* 86.

824   Edna Kenton, (ed.), *The Jesuit Relations and Allied Documents*, 56.

825   Adriæn van der Donck, *A Description of the New Netherlands*, 86-87.

826   Peter Lindeström, *Geographia Americæ*, 248.

827   Adriæn van der Donck, *A Description of the New Netherlands*, 86-87.

828   Peter Lindeström, *Geographia Americæ*, 249.

829   Adriæn van der Donck, *A Description of the New Netherlands*, 87

830   Ibid., 87.

831   David De Vries, "Korte Historiael," *Narratives of New Netherland*, 223.

832   "A Short Account of the Mohawk Indians, by Reverend Johannes Megapolensis, Jr., 1644," *Narratives of New Netherland*, 176-177.

833   Adriæn van der Donck, *A Description of the New Netherlands*, 87.

834   Adriæn van der Donck, *A Description of the New Netherlands*, 87.

835   Peter Lindeström, *Geographia Americæ*, 249-250.

836   David De Vries, "Korte Historiael," *Narratives of New Netherland*, 223.

837   Adriæn van der Donck, *A Description of the New Netherlands*, 87.

838   Ibid., 87.

839   Ibid., 88.

840   Ibid., 87-88.

841   William Penn, "Some Account of the Province of Pennsilvania by William Penn, 1681," *Narratives of Early Pennsylvania, West New Jersey and Delaware 1630-1707*, 234.

842   Gabriel Thomas, "An Historical and Geographical Account," *Narratives of Early Pennsylvania, West New Jersey and Delaware 1630-1707*, 340-341

843   Ibid., 340-341.

844   Francis D. Pastorius, "Circumstantial Geographical Description of Pennsylvania," *Narratives of Early Pennsylvania, West New and Delaware 1630-1707*, 384.

845   Ibid., 434.

846   David De Vries, "Korte Historiael," *Narratives of New Netherland*, 223-224; De Vries may have borrowed this account from another source, claiming it for his own.

847   Francis Parkman, *France and England in North America, Vol. I*, 395.

848   David De Vries, "Korte Historiael," *Narratives of New Netherland*, 223-224.

849   Gabriel Thomas, "An Historical and Geographical Account," *Narratives of Early Pennsylvania, West New Jersey and Delaware 1630-1707*, 340.

850   It is possible that Reading saw a small ceremonial earthen mound erected by a people who had relocated from the Upper Mississippi Valley? "Journal of John Reading,"95.

851   Max Schrabisch, *Geological Survey of New Jersey, Bulletin 13. Indian Habitations in Sussex County, New Jersey*, (Union Hill, NJ: Dispatch Printing Company, 1915), 19-30.

852   C. A. Weslager, *Delaware's Buried Past*, (New Brunswick: Rutgers University Press, 1968), 183.

853   *Sussex Register*, December 16, 1909; this account is repeated from Ronald J. Dupont and Kevin Wright, *High Point of the Blue Mountains*, Newton: Sussex County Historical Society, 1990, 3-4.

854   Clayton Colman Hall (ed.), *Narratives of Early Maryland 1633-1684*, (New York: Barnes & Noble, Inc., 1910), "Father White's Brief Relation, 45; 87.

855   Ibid., 45; 87.

856   "Indian Cemetery," *The Sussex Register*, May 5, 1842.

857   Adolph B. Benson (translator and editor), *Peter Kalm's Travels in North America*, 74.

858   Ibid., 74.

859   *Bergen Democrat*, May 17, 1872; August 9, 1872

860   See "Were They Indians?" *The Bergen Democrat*, May 18, 1900.

861   Nicolaes Wassenaer, "Historisch Verhæl, 1624-1630," *Narratives of New Netherland*, 69.

862   Adriæn van der Donck, *A Description of the New Netherlands*, 102.

863   Edna Kenton, (ed.), *The Jesuit Relations and Allied Documents*, 139.

864   Sereno Edwards Dwight, *Memoirs of the Rev. David Brainerd*, 346-349.

865   Nicolaes Wassenaer, "Historisch Verhæl, 1624-1630," *Narratives of New Netherland*, 69.

866   Edna Kenton, (ed.), *The Jesuit Relations and Allied Documents*, 60.

867   Nicolaes Wassenaer, "Historisch Verhæl, 1624-1630," *Narratives of New Netherland*, 85-86.

868   Editors, Time-Life Books, *Realm of the Iroquois*, (Alexandria, Va.: Time-Life Books, 1993), 43.

869   William Penn, "Some Account of the Province of Pennsilvania by William Penn, 1681," *Narratives of Early Pennsylvania, West New Jersey and Delaware 1630-1707*, 234.

870   William Penn, "Some Account of the Province of Pennsilvania by William Penn, 1681," *Narratives of Early Pennsylvania, West New Jersey and Delaware 1630-1707*, 234.

871   Francis D. Pastorius, "Circumstantial Geographical Description of Pennsylvania," *Narratives of Early Pennsylvania, West New Jersey and Delaware 1630-1707*, 384.

872   Juniata translates as "standing stone." The island, which Brainerd visited, is now called Haldemans Island.

873   Sereno Edwards Dwight, *Memoirs of the Rev. David Brainerd*, 182.

874   Edna Kenton, (ed.), *The Jesuit Relations and Allied Documents*, 412-413.

875   Adriæn van der Donck, *A Description of the New Netherlands*, 88.

876   William Penn, "Some Account of the Province of Pennsilvania by William Penn, 1681," *Narratives of Early Pennsylvania, West New Jersey and Delaware 1630-1707*, 237.

877   Ibid, 237.

878   Gabriel Thomas, "An Historical and Geographical Account," *Narratives of Early Pennsylvania, West New Jersey and Delaware 1630-1707*, 315-316.

879   Ibid., 340.

880   Nicolaes Wassenaer, "Historisch Verhæl, 1624-1630," *Narratives of New Netherland*, 68.

881   Ibid., 68.

882   Edna Kenton, (ed.), *The Jesuit Relations and Allied Documents*, 142.

883   Sereno Edwards Dwight, *Memoirs of the Rev. David Brainerd*, 348-349.

884   Daniel G. Brinton, *A Lenâpé-English Dictionary*, 52.

885   William Wallace Tooker, *The Indian Place-Names On Long Island and Islands Adjacent*, 44.

886   Edna Kenton, (ed.), *The Jesuit Relations and Allied Documents*, 54-55.

887   Ibid., 54-55.

888   Ibid., 54-55.

889   Sereno Edwards Dwight, *Memoirs of the Rev. David Brainerd*, 349-350.

890   Ibid., 349-350.

891   Ibid., 348.

892   Edna Kenton, (ed.), *The Jesuit Relations and Allied Documents*, 142.

893   Peter Lindeström, *Geographia Americæ*, 247-248.

894   Ibid., 247-248.

895   Nicolaes Wassenaer, "Historisch Verhæl, 1624-1630," *Narratives of New Netherland*, 87.

896   Adriæn van der Donck, *A Description of the New Netherlands*, 88-89.

897   Ibid., 88.

898   Ibid., 88-89.

899   Ibid., 89.

900   Ibid., 89.

901   Sereno Edwards Dwight, *Memoirs of the Rev. David Brainerd*, 235.

902   Ibid., 235.

903   "Narrative of a Journey into the Mohawk and Oneida Country, 1634-1635," *Narratives of New Netherland,* 146.

904   Ibid., 152-153.

905   Sereno Edwards Dwight, *Memoirs of the Rev. David Brainerd*, 237-238.

906   Ibid., 237-238.

907   Adriæn van der Donck, *A Description of the New Netherlands*, 102.

908   Ibid., 89.

909   David De Vries, "Korte Historiael," *Narratives of New Netherland*, 225.

910   William Penn, "Some Account of the Province of Pennsilvania by William Penn, 1681," *Narratives of Early Pennsylvania, West New Jersey and Delaware 1630-1707,* 234.

911   Francis D. Pastorius, "Circumstantial Geographical Description of Pennsylvania," *Narratives of Early Pennsylvania, West New Jersey and Delaware 1630-1707,* 434.

912   Adolph B. Benson (translator and editor), *Peter Kalm's Travels in North America,* 270.

913   Francis D. Pastorius, "Circumstantial Geographical Description of Pennsylvania," *Narratives of Early Pennsylvania, West New Jersey and Delaware 1630-1707,* 384.

914   Sereno Edwards Dwight, *Memoirs of the Rev. David Brainerd*, 174.

915   Adriæn van der Donck, *A Description of the New Netherlands*, 64.

916   Peter Lindeström, *Geographia Americæ*, 239.

917   Gabriel Thomas, "An Historical Description of the Province and Country of West New Jersey in America," 344.

918   Adolph B. Benson (translator and editor), *Peter Kalm's Travels in North America,* 258.

919   Ibid., 150.

920   Ibid., 258-259.

921   Adolph B. Benson (translator and editor), *Peter Kalm's Travels in North America,* 195.

922   Peter Lindeström, *Geographia Americæ*, 234.

923   *Documents Relating to the Colonial History of the State of New York, Vol. VII,* 156-157

924   *Documents Relating to the Colonial History of the State of New York* Vol. XII, 290-291.

925   *Documents Relating to the Colonial History of the State of New York, Vol. XII*, 318.

926   Berthold Fernow, *Documents Relating to the History and Settlements of the Towns along the Hudson and Rivers from 1630 to 1684*, 551.

927   Adolph B. Benson (translator and editor), *Peter Kalm's Travels in North America*, 152-153; 187; 534.

928   Ibid., 166.

929   Francis D. Pastorius, "Circumstantial Geographical Description of Pennsylvania," *Narratives of Early Pennsylvania, West New Jersey and Delaware 1630-1707*, 437-438.

930   Adolph B. Benson (translator and editor), *Peter Kalm's Travels in North America*, 119.

931   William W. Campbell, *Annals of Tryon County; or, the Border Warfare of New-York during the Revolution*, (New York: J. & J. Harper, 1831), 23n.

INDEX

huckleberries 94, 95
Hudson Anchorage 29
Hudson Bay 16
Hudson County Court House 5
Hudson, Henry 13, 18, 19, 20, 21, 22, 23,
24, 25, 26, 27, 28, 29, 31, 32, 33, 34,
35, 39, 82, 95, 98, 110, 111, 114, 169,
179, 180, 181, 182, 183
Hudson Highlands 22
Hudson River 5, 9, 10, 14, 17, 31, 34, 37,
38, 39, 40, 42, 43, 44, 46, 52, 57, 59,
63, 85, 94, 177, 182, 183, 185, 186,
190, 191
Hudson Valley 85, 155
Huguenot 17, 49
human interference 85
humankind 3, 145
human origins 145
humans 2, 140, 146
hummingbirds 88
hundred weight 119
hungry 100
hunt 50, 51, 64, 65, 86, 121, 128, 132,
142, 161, 163, 180, 192. *See* hunting
hunted 51, 88, 89
hunter 89, 150, 162, 163
hunter-gatherers 14, 51, 102
hunters 9, 51, 60, 63, 73, 86, 87, 88, 121,
126, 132, 172
hunters-and-gatherers 63, 82
hunter's path 86
hunting 48, 51, 56, 63, 66, 81, 82, 83, 86,
89, 91, 93, 96, 100, 102, 105, 122, 124,
125, 135, 141, 142, 148, 150, 158, 160,
171, 180, 188
hunting-and-gathering lifestyle 121
hunting camps 83
hunting deer 86
hunting ground(s) 83
hunting season 91
hunting territories 51
Huron 66, 67, 101, 148
Huron dwellings 101
Hurons 12, 37, 63, 64, 66, 67, 69, 70, 75,
76, 79, 143, 155, 158, 159, 161, 163

husband 133, 138, 159
husbands 93, 123, 125, 128, 153
husk(s) 84, 90
hut(s) 85, 89, 99, 100, 101, 125, 170, 172,
202
huts 85, 89, 100, 170, 172, 202

I

ice 17
Iceland 19
idol(s) 101, 122, 128, 139, 146, 168
Ihonatiria 67
illiniou 6
Illinois 6, 8, 67
Illinois Country 51
Illinois River 150
illness 144, 166
illnesses 101
images 66, 99, 167
immortal 150
immortality 140
incantations 165
incanting 163
incense 148
India 18
Indian 3, 8, 13, 15, 17, 20, 21, 24, 29, 33,
37, 40, 41, 47, 49, 50, 53, 54, 58, 59,
63, 76, 81, 83, 89, 93, 94, 95, 96, 97,
100, 103, 104, 106, 107, 108, 109, 110,
111, 112, 114, 121, 124, 128, 130, 131,
134, 136, 137, 138, 141, 147, 148, 149,
155, 157, 159, 187
basketry and weaving 111
birchbark canoes 108
brush burning 85
character 71
childrearing 128
clothing 73
dancing 166
death and burial customs 152
divorce 125, 133
dugout canoes 107
females 122
fishing methods 84

About the Author

Born in Newton, New Jersey to John Ivan and Teresa (Mullen) Wright, Kevin Wright was attracted, even as a child, to the history and legends of Sussex County. After graduating from Rutgers College, he engaged in historical interpretation at the restored village of Waterloo in 1977, eventually becoming tour director in 1979. As curator of the Steuben House, a Revolutionary War landmark in River Edge, he built up a large interest and attendance, working with the Bergen County Historical Society. In 1982, he and Alex Everitt successfully led the fight to preserve the 1848 Sussex Courthouse and Newton's oldest streetscape. Kevin prepared the National Register nomination for the Newton Town Plot Historic District. In 1985, his research brought worldwide media attention to New Jersey's claim of sovereignty over Ellis and Liberty Islands. He became the first Resource Interpretive Specialist for the northern region of New Jersey in 2000 and was central to the visioning process for Historic New Bridge Landing, Lusscroft Farm, and the State History Fair.

Kevin Wright is a past President of the Sussex County Historical Society and of the Bergen County Historical Society. He has been a member of the Newton Historic Preservation Advisory Commission since 1987. Married to art director and graphic designer Deborah Powell, they have three children.

Breinigsville, PA USA
04 December 2009
228667BV00004B/88/P